Exploring
the Religious Life

Exploring
the Religious Life

※ Rodney Stark ※

THE JOHNS HOPKINS UNIVERSITY PRESS
Baltimore & London

© 2004 The Johns Hopkins University Press
All rights reserved. Published 2004
Printed in the United States of America on acid-free paper
2 4 6 8 9 7 5 3 1

The Johns Hopkins University Press
2715 North Charles Street
Baltimore, Maryland 21218-4363
www.press.jhu.edu

Library of Congress Cataloging-in-Publication Data

Stark, Rodney.
Exploring the religious life / Rodney Stark.
p. cm.
Includes bibliographical references and index.
ISBN 0-8018-7844-6 (alk. paper)
1. Religion and sociology. 2. Religious life. I. Title.
BL60.S677 2004
306.6—dc21
2003010641

A catalog record for this book is available from the British Library.

Contents

Preface

Although this book began as a collection of my recent studies, each of which was published as a separate paper, all have been rewritten, some of them very extensively. The revisions were done to create greater unity and sometimes to merge several papers into a single, integrated chapter.

The late Alan Miller is the coauthor of chapters 4 and 6. He was my student, then my colleague, and my friend. Eva Hamburg is the coauthor of chapter 6. I thank her for many years of friendship and stimulation.

Exploring
the Religious Life

Religion, Magic & Science

It is often said that social scientists don't know what they're talking about. And too often it's true, at least to the extent that they are using terms they have not bothered to define or seem unaware that a given disagreement is definitional, not substantive. Nowhere has this been more obvious than in discussions of religion, but the problem is nearly as severe vis-à-vis the concepts of magic and science. There are, of course, no "true" definitions of these terms hovering in hyperspace and awaiting discovery; all definitions are intellectual conventions. But it is entirely feasible to formulate mutually exclusive and theoretically efficient definitions of each, while retaining substantial linguistic continuity.

Ambiguities in Current Usage

For thousands of years the term *religion* usually meant the worship of supernatural beings. Even a century ago, social scientists thought this definition was adequate, Edward Burnett Tylor, the founder of British anthropology, being content to define religion as "belief in spiritual beings" ([1871] 1958, 2:8). Then came Emile Durkheim, and all such clarity was lost.

Durkheim not only denied that supernatural beings were essential to religion, but he regarded them as "no more than a minor accident" and admonished that the wise "sociologist will pay scant attention to the different ways in which" people conceive of the divine and "will see in religion only a social discipline" ([1886] 1994, 19, 21). Hence, Durkheim

An earlier version of this chapter appeared as "Reconceptualizing Religion, Magic, and Science," *Review of Religious Research* 43 (2001): 101–20.

defined religion as "a unified system of beliefs and practices relative to sacred things" ([1912] 1995, 44). The trouble is, nowhere in any of his work did he even attempt to define *sacred,* except to say it is the opposite of *profane* (which he also failed to define) and that sacred things are "set apart and forbidden." Nor was this merely a neglected formality. When Durkheim applied the terms *sacred* and *profane* to specific examples, they proved to be "so closely intermingled as to be inseparable" (Evans-Pritchard 1965, 65).

There is nothing inappropriate about equating religion and the sacred, but doing so sheds no light on what either term means; Durkheim's classic statement therefore defined nothing, merely offering one undefined term as a synonym for another. Unfortunately, several generations of sociologists have embraced Durkheim's "definition" without noticing its inadequacy. Worse yet, having equated religion with the sacred, too many scholars have proceeded to discover the sacred (therefore religion) virtually everywhere, thus depriving the term of analytical power (see Demerath 2000; Demerath et al. 1998).

Many other sociologists have attempted to save Durkheim's definition by specifying what the term *sacred* means, hence the popularity of definitions that focus on the provision of *"ultimate meaning."* In this tradition, religion is any system of beliefs and practices involving answers to questions about the meaning and purpose of life (see Bellah 1964, 1970; Berger 1967; Beyer 1994; Geertz 1973; Luckmann 1967; Yinger 1957). But as the proponents of this definition frankly admit, "[r]eligion, of course, is not alone in attempting to deal with the ultimate problems of human life" (Yinger 1957, 10). Indeed, explicitly irreligious and even antireligious philosophies and political creeds often address the meaning of life, including some that claim life has no meaning. If all of these are religions, then the immediate need is to distinguish between those that are and are not predicated on the existence of the supernatural, in which case the definitional task remains to be achieved and all that has been accomplished has been to waste the term *religion.*

Other current definitions of religion put the stress on *faith,* thus classifying as religions all systems of thought able to generate a substantial degree of conviction (Bailey 1998). However, invincible convictions are as frequently an aspect of nonreligious or antireligious viewpoints— most village atheists epitomize the True Believer in this sense.

Obviously, both ultimate meaning and a high level of conviction are aspects of the phenomenon to be identified as religion. However, definitions based primarily on one or the other (or both) have diverted a great deal of intellectual effort to analyses assuming that Communism is some kind of religion, or to assertions that groups such as Greenpeace or Amway are "implicit religions," "quasi-religions," or "para-religions" (Bailey 1998; Beckford 1984; Greil and Robbins 1994).

In similar fashion, the term *magic* has been a conceptual mess. An amazing number of scholars have been content to write about magic at length while leaving it undefined. For example, although Max Weber's books "are saturated with the subject" of magic, he never defines it (O'Keefe 1982, 10). Bryan Wilson published a very long and dense volume with the title *Magic and the Millennium* (1975) but seems to have assumed that his readers needed no coaching as to the meaning of either term.

Some scholars have equated magic and religion and refer to "magico-religious acts and beliefs" (Goody 1961, 160). Many others have followed Durkheim ([1912] 1995) in distinguishing religion from magic on the basis their goals, identifying religion as mainly concerned with general, long-range goals and magic as concerned with immediate and concrete goals (Malinowski [1948] 1992; Roberts 1995; Yinger 1957). That criterion proves useful, but it is insufficient. How do we distinguish a parent's prayers for the recovery of a sick infant (an immediate and concrete goal) from the recitation of an occult formula directed toward the same result or, indeed, from a medical prescription? Is each an instance of magic? If not, why not? As for Durkheim's nephew Marcel Mauss, in his famous *General Theory of Magic,* he felt that it was sufficient to define magic as "any rite that does not play a part in organized cults" (1950, 24). Given that by "organized cults" Mauss meant religions, his often cited definition says simply that those rites that are not religious are magical, neither term being defined; he did not even define *rites.*

Some recent European scholars define magic as "esoteric knowledge" revealed only "to a select few," as in the Hermetic and Gnostic traditions (Eleta 1997, 52). This unrealistically limits magic to its most "professionalized" and sophisticated forms, while failing to provide a basis for distinguishing it from secular secrets such as classified scientific research. Indeed, social scientists have often identified magic as a primitive or incorrect form of science (Hegel [1840] 1996; Horton 1962, 1964; Lévi-Strauss 1966; Tylor [1871] 1958). Sir James G. Frazer noted that science and magic both assume the "order and uniformity of nature," that the "same causes will always produce the same effects," and that both believe in the existence of "immutable laws, the operation of which can be fore-seen and calculated precisely" ([1922] 1950, 56). But the "fatal flaw of magic lies . . . in its total misconception" of the fundamental principles of causation. When these principles are "legitimately applied they yield science; illegitimately applied they yield magic, the bastard sister of science." This led Frazer to his famous conclusion that "all magic is neces-sarily false and barren; were it ever to become true and fruitful, it would no longer be magic but science" (57).

These views are, of course, inherently evolutionary. If magic is failed science, then it is doomed to be replaced by the rise of real science. Thus, Keith Roberts (1995, 23) asserted that "[m]agic . . . will be replaced in large part by science, technology, and the modern secular world view." But having left *science* undefined (as did Frazer and most others who have contrasted magic and science), Roberts offered no criteria by which we can discover when this replacement has taken place. Such omissions may have encouraged some social scientists who claim there is *no difference* between magic and science, agreeing with Patrick Curry (1999, 403) as to "the tendentiousness of the magic/science opposition." And so it has gone.

Of course, postmodernist scholars deny the worth or even the pos-sibility of general definitions or of cross-cultural comparisons (Derrida 1972). In the most extreme version of postmodernism, abstractions are condemned as acts of attempted political domination; cross-cultural comparisons are said to be intrinsically imperialistic and destructive (Lyo-tard 1993). Even the more moderate proponents condemn the notion of objectivity—Stephen Tyler (1986, 139) dismissed all attempts even to de-scribe a single culture (let alone compare two or more) as merely "a fan-tasy reality of a reality of fantasy." Jonathan Z. Smith (1978, 240–41) has summed up these views as an "ethic of particularity" wherein "any at-tempt at generalization" violates "the personhood of those studied." But, as Smith went on to note, the "process of comparison is a fundamental characteristic of human intelligence . . . comparison, the bringing to-gether of two or more objects for the purpose of noting similarity or dis-similarity, is the omnipresent substructure of human thought. Without it we could not speak, perceive, learn or reason." In point of fact, the post-modernists cannot even attack comparative studies except by making constant comparisons (Eagleton 1996; Holdrege 2000). My position was expressed well by Rosalie and Murray Wax: "If the first sin of the social scientist is the belief that the practices of his own people are superior to

Exploring the Religious Life

all, the second sin is the failure to distinguish genuine differences among peoples" (1962, 180).

Finally, an aversion to definitions, especially to cross-cultural conceptualizations, has a long history in social science (long predating postmodernism) and has been especially frequent in the area of religion (cf. Needham 1985). Thus, Martin Southwold (1978, 362) argued that religion is such "a compound of diverse elements" that it cannot usefully be defined and that we should instead concentrate on understanding "why religions are compounded as they are." But had he truly left religion undefined, Southwold could never have known whether he was studying the cultural compounds of religions rather than of, say, military tactics. In similar fashion, many social scientists have approvingly quoted Jane Harrison's advice (1912, 29) that rather than to define religion, one should "collect the facts that are admittedly religious and see from what human activities they appear to have sprung." However, as Jack Goody (1961, 142) explained, Harrison "was merely taking refuge in an implicit rather than an explicit judgment of what constitutes the 'admittedly religious.'" Had Southwold and Harrison truly been unable to "define" religious phenomena, their work would have been incoherent.

In fact, even most of those who fear to define their terms seem willing to identify some general categories of social and cultural phenomena across cultures, *colonialism* and *hegemony* being common examples. Moreover, meaningful conversation, as well as the exigencies of social science, requires us to classify phenomena in mutually exclusive ways. To propose that Judaism and socialism or physics and voodoo are the same results in intellectual fruit salad. Therefore, in this chapter I offer clear criteria for distinguishing among *religion, magic,* and *science.*

In pursuit of useful definitions, I begin with a feature so basic that religion, magic, and science have it in common.

Control

From the dawn of human existence, our efforts to control nature and events have been constant and unrelenting. For example, when early humans confronted the dangers and uncertainties involved in hunting large mammals, sometimes they sought to maximize results and minimize dangers by attempting to stampede a herd over a cliff. When this was impossible, they sometimes recited spells over their spear and arrow points to make them more deadly, and in most instances they prayed to a supernatural being to protect them and deliver the game into their hands. In each example the goal was control. It is the desire for control that motivates humans to develop skills, crafts, technologies, and, ultimately, science. People do magic for the same reason, and the desire to control one's fate is an essential element of religion.

I am not yet prepared to define religion or magic, because it will be more effective to let these definitions emerge. However, it is necessary at the start to limit what I mean by science.

DEFINITION 1: *Science* is *a method utilized in organized efforts to explain nature, always subject to modifications and corrections through systematic observations.*

Put another way, science consists of two components: *theory* and *research*. Theorizing is the explanatory part of science. Scientific theories are abstract statements about *why* and *how* some portion of nature (including human social life) fits together and works. However, not all abstract statements, even those offering explanations, qualify as scientific theories; otherwise, theology would be a science. Abstract statements are scientific only if it is possible to deduce from them some definite predictions and prohibitions about what will be observed. And that's where research comes in. It consists of making those observations that are relevant to the empirical predictions and prohibitions. Clearly, then, science is limited to statements about natural and material reality—about things that are in principle observable. Hence, there are entire realms of discourse that science does not address.

By *organized,* I mean to note that science is not random discovery, nor is it achieved in solitude. Granted, some scientists have worked alone, but not in isolation. From earliest days, scientists have constituted networks and have been very communicative. Not even Nicolaus Copernicus is an exception to this rule. He was anything but an obscure Catholic canon in far-off Poland. Copernicus was educated at Cracow, one of the greatest universities of that time, and then spent another three and a half years at the University of Bologna, possibly the best university in Europe. Next, he spent about four years at the university in Padua, interrupted by a brief visit to the University of Farrara, where he received the degree of Doctor of Canon Law. Returning to Cracow, Copernicus attracted students, one of whom, Georg Joachim Rhäticus, linked him to scholars in newly Protestant German universities. Had Copernicus actually been only an obscure Polish canon, it seems safe to suppose that he would not have constructed a heliocentric model of the solar system. First of all, it is unlikely that he would have learned of the sophisticated discussions of how the sun's apparent motion was the result of the rotation of the earth, first proposed by the then well-known scholastic natural philosophers Jean Buridan (1300–1358) and Nicole Oresme (1325–82). Their discussions of planetary motion were so well-informed that "Copernicus could not improve upon them" (Grant 1996, 169). Nor did Copernicus need to explain why buildings and other things on the earth were not toppled by a rotating earth, since Buridan and Oresme had solved that problem, too, with their work on impetus and motion. Copernicus's actual achievement lay in working out the geometry of a heliocentric system and showing that planetary positions could be predicted from it, albeit with some loss of accuracy. Second, without the reassurance and urging of his large network of scholarly friends, Copernicus never would have published his work (as it was, he almost didn't).

Consistent with the views of most contemporary historians as well as philosophers of science, the definition of science presented above excludes all efforts through most of human history to explain and control the material world, even those not involving supernatural means. Most of these efforts can be excluded from the category of science because until recent times "technical progress—sometimes considerable—was mere empiricism," as Marc Bloch (1961, 83) put it. That is, progress was the product of observation and of trial and error but was lacking in explanations—in theorizing. This objection can even be applied to Copernicus, since his heliocentric conception of the solar system was merely a descriptive claim (much of it wrong). He had little to say about *why* planets remain in their orbits around the sun or moons about the planets. Until Newton there was no *scientific theory* of the solar system. I am willing to include Copernicus among the founders of modern science only because of his influence on and participation in a network of astronomers whose work soon qualified as truly scientific. But the earlier technical innovations of Greco-Roman times, of Islam, of Imperial China, and of prehistoric times, do not constitute science and are better described as lore, skills, wisdom, techniques, crafts, technologies, engineering, or simply knowledge. Thus, for example, even without telescopes the ancients excelled in astronomical observations. But until they were linked to testable theories, these observations remained merely facts. Charles Darwin expressed this point vividly: "About thirty years ago there was much talk that geologists ought to observe and not theorize; and I well remember someone saying that at that rate a man might as well go into a gravel-pit and count the pebbles and describe the colours. How odd it is that any-one should not see that all observation must be for or against some view if it is to be of any service!" (1903, 1:195).

As for the intellectual achievements of Greek or Eastern philosophers, their empiricism was quite atheoretical, and their theorizing was non-empirical. Consider Aristotle. Although praised for his empiricism, he didn't let it interfere with his theorizing. For example, he taught that the speed at which objects fall to earth is proportionate to their weight—that a stone twice as heavy as another will fall twice as fast (*On the Heavens*). A trip to any of the nearby cliffs would have allowed him to falsify this proposition. He also explained in his *Physics* that the motion of a projec-tile is due to the push given it from the air closing behind it, paying no heed to the need to open the air in front of it. The superb, and sadly neglected, scholastic scientist-theologian Jean Buridan dispatched this Aristotelian proposition by observing that when a man runs, he "does not feel the air moving him, but rather feels the air in front strongly re-sisting him" (quoted in Clagett 1961, 536).

The same can be said of the rest of the famous Greeks: either their work is entirely empirical or it does not qualify as science for lack of empiricism, being sets of abstract assertions that disregard or do not im-ply observable consequences. Thus, when Democritus proposed the the-sis that all matter is composed of atoms, he did not anticipate scientific atomic theory. His "theory" was mere speculation, having no basis in observation and suggesting no empirical implications. That it turned out to be "correct" (and most of it did not) lends no more significance to his "guess" than to that of his contemporary Empedocles, who asserted that all matter is composed of fire, air, water, and earth, or Aristotle's version a century later that matter consists of heat, cold, dryness, moistness, and quintessence. Indeed, for all his brilliance and analytical power, Euclid was not a scientist either, because, in and of itself, geometry lacks sub-stance. It has only the capacity to describe reality, not to explain any por-tion of it.

Of course, these millennia of technological and intellectual progress were vital to the eventual development of science, but it is the consensus among contemporary historians, philosophers, and sociologists of sci-ence that the "scientific endeavor" that arose "in the West [was] an enter-prise different from its medieval European, Arabic, Chinese, or Indian antecedents" (Ben-David 1990, 258). Real science arose in only one place: Europe (Cohen 1985; Collins 1998; Dorn 1991; Grant 1996; Huff 1993;

Kuhn 1962; Lindberg 1992). In this regard it is instructive that China, the Middle East, and India, as well as ancient Greece and Rome, had a highly developed alchemy. But only in Europe did alchemy develop into in chemistry. Moreover, only this very exceptional instance offers *any* basis for suggesting that magic is primitive science. There are substantial grounds, however, for the claim that science developed out of religion, out of the fundamental axiom of Christian theology that God had created a logical universe based on universal laws that could be discovered though reason and observation (Jaki 2000; Stark 2003; Whitehead [1925] 1967).

I reject the notion that religion evolved from magic, which is why I have avoided the usual word order of "magic, religion, and science." This order was established in the nineteenth century by the leading social evolutionists who did think religion originated in magic—an assumption that goes back at least to Hegel and was embraced by Tyler, Spencer, and Frazer (O'Keefe 1982). Perhaps as part of their antipathy to all things British, Durkheim and his circle disagreed. Durkheim explained:

> Thus magic is not, as Frazer held, a primary datum and religion only its derivative. Quite the contrary, the precepts on which the magician's art rests were formed under the influence of religious ideas . . . Hubert and Mauss . . . have brought to light a whole background of religious conceptions that lie behind the apparently secular mechanisms used by the magician, a whole world of forces the idea of which magic took from religion. We can now see why magic is so full of religious elements: It was born out of religion. ([1912] 1995, 366)

Neither view is persuasive. Both the ethnographic and the historical records suggest that religion and magic developed in tandem and were always recognized as different—that even very early humans were fully aware of the difference between offering a sacrifice to the Rain God or casting a spell (just as modern athletes know the difference between saying a prayer before a game and wearing their lucky underwear).

Worldly Rewards

Religion, magic, and science also share an apparent ability to produce results. Not only do people seek worldly rewards via each of these methods, but each of the three often seems able to deliver. Keep in mind that not only are scientific efforts often stymied (efforts to cure a particular disease, for example), but magical and religious attempts at control are frequently followed by the desired consequence. In the case of magic, for example, it often rains following rain dances, since rain dances are held in the rainy season; and rather than being prompted by a *lack* of rain, usually they are done in *anticipation* of rain. Love potions often work, too, since they typically are only one part of the courting process. As for religion, it produces many worldly satisfactions (including respectability) without recourse to supernatural means (Iannaccone 1994; Stark and Finke 2000). As for calling on the divine, prayers often do seem to be answered—for example, prayers for the sick often are followed by recovery.[1]

Thus far we have seen ways in which religion, science, and magic are alike. Each is an effort to control nature; each offers worldly rewards. Now it is time to begin to differentiate these concepts.

The Supernatural

Only magic and religion depend upon the supernatural.

DEFINITION 2: **Supernatural** *refers to forces or entities beyond or outside nature which can suspend, alter, or ignore physical forces.*

Notice that this definition makes no mention of supernatural *beings*. As will be seen, magic does not assume the existence of such beings, whereas *most* religions do. However, some religions conceive of the supernatural as an omnipresent *essence* or principle governing life, but something that is impersonal, remote, and definitely not a being. The Tao (or Way) is an example. Some Taoists claim that it is merely the philosophical principle governing reality. Others allow it as the origin of the universe, but many of them also say that the Tao does not exist, although it is always existent. The term that best fits such a vague conception of the supernatural is *essence*.

It is unproductive to equate essences and beings, and therefore:

DEFINITION 3: **Gods** *are supernatural "beings" having consciousness and desire.*

This definition leads to the recognition that there exist *Godless religions,* which is, of course, what intellectual devotees of Buddhism, Taoism, and Confucianism have always claimed. It also must be recognized, though, that Godless religions are unable to gather a mass following, always being limited in their appeal to intellectual elites. Thus, in Imperial China, the forms of Taoism, Buddhism, and Confucianism practiced in various monasteries and among court philosophers and the Mandarins of the civil service were (relatively)[2] Godless. But the common people always associated an abundant pantheon of Gods with the Taoist, Confucianist, and Buddhist ideals (Parrinder 1983; Smart 1984). Mistaking the Godless Buddhism of Eastern elites for the Buddhism of the Eastern masses caused Durkheim to exclude the Gods from his definition of religion in order to save the generalization that all societies have religions. Beginning with the first major reviews of *Elementary Forms,* anthropologists have ridiculed Durkheim's knowledge of ethnography (see Goldenweiser 1915), and his error concerning the Godlessness of popular Buddhism has always been seen as an extraordinary blunder (see Spiro 1966a, 1966b). Unfortunately, for several generations sociologists remained unaware of this error (see Goode 1951), and many still haven't heard. Nevertheless, Godless religions are of little interest to social scientists, since they exist primarily as *scriptures,* not as human activities. However, because these scriptures are so abstruse and abundant, they are highly esteemed by scholars.

Given this qualification concerning the lack of mass appeal of Godless religions, it is possible to say that most examples of what qualifies as religion are predicated on conceptions of Gods. But this is not true of magic. Magic is *limited to impersonal conceptions of the supernatural,* what the celebrated Bronislaw Malinowski described as a "mystic, impersonal power." He went on to describe the nearly "universal idea found wherever magic flourishes" that there exists "a supernatural, impersonal force" ([1948] 1992, 19–20).

Summing up more than a century of anthropological studies of magic, John Middleton (1967, ix) pointed out that "the realm of magic is that in which human beings believe that they may directly affect nature and each other, for good or for ill, by their own efforts (even though the precise mechanism may not be understood by them), as distinct from appealing to divine powers by sacrifice or prayer." Of course, Middleton did not mean to place in the magical realm just any or even most human efforts to affect nature or one another. He assumed his readers understood that, just as rain dances differ from irrigation projects, only efforts involving a resort to supernatural means constitute magic. Hence, as a *first step* toward a definition of magic, we may identify it as *efforts to manipulate supernatural forces to gain rewards (or avoid costs)* **without reference to a**

God or Gods. This is consistent with Frazer's position ([1922] 1950) that desired results are inherent in magical acts, whereas religion depends on effects granted by external agents.

When a Catholic wears a Saint Christopher's medal to ensure a safe journey, that is *not* magic because the power of the medal is attributed to the patron saint, whose powers, in turn, are granted by a God. The medal is intrinsic to an exchange with a God. But when devotees of the New Age place "mystic" crystals under their pillows in order to cure a cold, that *is* magic because no appeal has been made to a God. The same applies to astrology. The idea that, for example, tomorrow is not an auspicious day for travel, is not a message from God but is a calculation concerning the location of heavenly bodies relative to one's birth date. Magic deals in impersonal supernatural forces, often in the belief that such forces are *inherent properties* of particular objects or words—especially written or spoken formulas and incantations. Ruth Benedict distinguished religion and magic in this way, proposing that the former involves "personal relations with the supernatural," and the latter deals with "mechanistic manipulation of the impersonal" (1938, 637).

Anthropologists often use the Melanesian word *mana* to identify these impersonal supernatural forces or properties. More than a century ago, R. H. Codrington defined *mana* as "a force altogether distinct from physical power which acts in all kinds of ways for good and evil and which it is of the greatest advantage to possess and control" (1891, 118–19). Paul Radin (1957, 13) quoted an interview with a Maori who "regarded *mana* as . . . something localized in a specific object." Ruth Benedict offered a more precise description of mana: "this supernatural quality [is] an attribute of objects just as color and weight are attributes of objects. There [is] just the same reason that a stone should have supernatural power as one of its qualities as there [is] that it should have hardness. It [does] not imply the personification of the stone" (1938, 631–32).

Admittedly, the most sophisticated form of magic, known as *sorcery,* sometimes may involve supernatural forces a bit more animate than mana. That is, sometimes sorcerers do attempt to compel certain primitive spiritual entities such as imps and demons to perform certain services or, as in the case of necromancy, to communicate with the dead. Even so, it still remains possible to "distinguish between magic and religion on the basis of the criterion of compulsion" (Levack 1995, 6; also see Peters 1978). As Benedict (1938, 637) expressed it, *"[m]agic* is mechanical procedure, the compulsion of the supernatural." Later in her essay, Benedict explained that there are "two techniques for handling the supernatural— at the one extreme compulsion and at the other rapport" (647). Compulsion of spiritual entities remains within the realm of magic, but exchanges with the Gods (which imply rapport) shift the activity into the realm of religion. Although Max Weber failed to define magic, he did notice that magic involved the compulsion of supernatural forces, in contrast to religion, which involved supplications to the Gods: "those beings that are worshipped and entreated religiously may be termed 'gods,' in contrast to the 'demons,' which are magically coerced and charmed" ([1922] 1993, 28).

Explanations & Ultimate Meaning

Just as the notion of mana is vague even among those who believe in it, the underlying explanations utilized in magic are vague almost to the point of nonexistence. Magic asserts causal claims (if you do this, that will happen), but with little or no attempt to say why. Malinowski ([1948] 1992, 70) said that magic is "circumscribed in its beliefs, stunted in its fundamental assumptions."

Richard Kieckhefer (1976, 6) contrasted technology with the use of magic, such as attempting to harm another person by sticking pins in a wax doll, in this way: "For most [technologies] that they employ, people have some vague (and perhaps incorrect) notion of the mechanisms involved, or else they assume that they could ascertain this mechanism if they so endeavored, or they take it on faith that someone understands the link between cause and effect. But the man who mutilates his enemy's representation cannot make any of these claims. He may believe that the magical act works, but he cannot explain how."

Indeed, magical lore displays remarkably little curiosity or speculation.[3] Not only does it not have reference to the Gods, but it does not engage questions of "ultimate meaning," defined by Talcott Parsons (1951, 367) as concerning the fundamental point and purpose of "nature, human nature, society, the vicissitudes of human life, etc." Does life have a purpose? Why are we here? What can we hope? Why do we suffer? Does justice exist? Is death the end? Magic offers no answers. As Durkheim noted ([1912] 1995, 42), magic is not concerned with the meaning of the universe, but with "technical and utilitarian ends," and hence "it does not waste its time in speculation." Or, in Middleton's words (1967, ix), "Magical beliefs and practices are particularly significant in being mainly instrumental, with little expressive content."

DEFINITION 4: *Magic* refers to *all efforts to manipulate supernatural forces to gain rewards (or avoid costs)* **without reference to a God or Gods** *or to general explanations of existence.*

In contrast to magic, the fundamental purpose of both religion and science is to provide *explanations*. Why does this happen? How did things come to be? This sets them very sharply apart from magic, while references to the supernatural distinguish religious from scientific explanations. Having access only to the observable world helps to account for the relative reluctance of science to deal with questions of ultimate meaning. Those who associate their science with atheism, as Bertrand Russell did, tend to deny that such questions are themselves "meaningful." Some others attempt to discover ultimate meaning within the scientific sphere — the late Carl Sagan substituted "Cosmos" for God and, when waxing philosophical, always capitalized Nature (Ross 1985). But many scientists simply defer to theology when such questions come up. In table 1.1 I reflect this variation by "perhaps" vis-à-vis science and questions of ultimate meaning.

Finally, I am able to define religion:

DEFINITION 5: **Religion** consists of **explanations** *of existence based on supernatural assumptions and including statements about the **nature** of the **supernatural** and about **ultimate meaning**.*

Thus, religion tells us the meaning of life (if any) and what the supernatural is like, whether beings or essences, and if the former, about their character and concerns. Because Gods are conscious beings, they are potential exchange partners because all beings are assumed to want something for which they might be induced to give something valuable. Indeed, the core of Godly religious doctrines consists of explanations about what Gods want and what one must do to earn their blessings. Or more formally:

DEFINITION 6: **Theology** consists of *explanations that justify and specify the **terms of exchange** with Gods, based on reasoning about **revelations**.*

DEFINITION 7: **Revelations** are *communications believed to come from Gods.*

Put another way, theology is the result of *applying reason to revelation* in order to expand understanding of divine concerns and desires and to increase the range of applications to which that understanding may be

Table 1.1 Contrasting Religion, Magic, and Science

	Religion	Magic	Science
Attempts to control nature and events	Yes	Yes	Yes
Offers worldly rewards	Yes	Yes	Yes
Depends on the supernatural	Yes	Yes	No
Invokes a God or Gods	Usually	No	No
Offers general explanations of relevant domains	Yes	No	Yes
Addresses questions of "ultimate meaning"	Yes	No	Perhaps
Can offer "otherworldly" rewards	Yes	No	No
Can sanctify the moral order	Yes	No	No
Subject to empirical falsification	No	Yes	Yes
Scope limited to natural or material reality	No	No	Yes

applied. This definition is entirely traditional. In *Summa theologiae* (pt. I, q. 1, a. 1), Thomas Aquinas (c. 1225–74) referred to theology as "doctrine about God according to divine revelation," and Karl Rahner (1975, 1687), stated the authoritative contemporary Catholic view: "Theology is the *science* of faith. It is the conscious and methodical explanation and explication of the divine revelation." A classic example of such reasoning is the evolution of an elaborate theology concerning Mary despite how little actually is said about her in the New Testament (Pelikan 1996).

Because divine essences are incapable of exchanges, they may present mysteries, but they pose no tactical questions and thus prompt no effort to discover terms of exchange. Of course, the sacred books of Godless religions also tell us about the supernatural, but the sacred books of Godly religions claim to report what the divine has to tell us. Eisai, the first Zen master, taught what he had *intuited* about the supernatural realm; Joseph Smith, the first Mormon, taught what had been *revealed* to him. According to Avery Dulles (1992, 3), "Judaism, Christianity, and Islam . . . profess to derive their fundamental vision not from mere human speculation, which would be tentative and uncertain, but from God's own testimony—that is to say, from a historically given divine revelation." Indeed, the authority of the Mishnah rests on the Jewish belief that God continues to reveal himself to scholars through their close study of the Torah.

It is important to see that this definition of theology does not reduce Godly religions to a set of commandments or divine demands. Terms of exchange with the Gods provide the foundation for religious thought, but there will be an extensive collection of ideas, principles, myths, symbols, images, and other elements of religious culture built upon this base. Within the context of clarifying what the Gods want, religious explanations often explain the fundamental meaning of life: how we got here and where we are going. Religion is, first and foremost, an intellectual product, and hence I propose that *ideas* are its truly fundamental aspect. It is this that made religion a necessary antecedent to the emergence of science, whereas indifference to ideas is what separates magic from both.

Many social scientists will condemn this definition of religion as intellectualist, being limited to beliefs; they claim that religion consists primarily of actions and feelings, especially of rites and various forms of awe and ecstasy (Beattie 1966; Douglas 1966; Morris 1987). Robert Bellah (1970, 220) dismissed my approach as the "objectivist fallacy." These criticisms are a form of premature elaboration. Once we know what religion *is,* then (and only then) can we distinguish actions and feelings that are religious from those that are not. A high mass and a Nazi Party rally both qualify as rites, and both can inspire deep emotions in participants. Only by noting which is grounded in supernatural assumptions and which is not, can one effectively distinguish between them. In similar fashion, William James rejected the idea of "religious sentiments" or "emotions" per se. Rather, he said, what can be identified as "religious fear, religious love, religious awe, religious joy, and so forth" are nothing more (or less) than natural emotions "directed to a religious object"—objects being religious because they involve "the divine" ([1902] 1958, 39–42). Hence, when I refer to religious rites, for example, I mean rites that are performed for religious motives or purposes. Using the adjective *religious* makes it possible to incorporate all aspects of religion and the religious life without the use of more complex definitions.

Otherworldly Rewards & Morality

Although magic assumes the supernatural realm, it locates its rewards here and now, whereas religion locates its most valuable rewards (and often its most extreme costs) in another realm. This "other" world is not only a sacred sphere but a "place" that humans may expect to enter, if only after death. By far the most vivid notions of the "other" world and belief in its accessibility—often conceived of as dual worlds of heaven and hell—tend to be limited to the great monotheisms. But all religions posit "other" realms—even Taoist intellectuals anticipate immortality, and Confucian philosophers are concerned about pleasing the spirits of their ancestors.

Religions that posit the availability of the most valuable rewards in a life to come have the capacity to involve humans in *extended* exchange relations with the Gods. That is, in order to qualify for immense rewards in the afterlife and (often) to avoid immense costs, humans must sustain their obligations to the Gods. One may seek magical results on a one-time basis, but otherworldly rewards tend to require lifelong commitment. Indeed, otherworldly rewards enable religions to impose *extensive* requirements for sustaining relationships with the Gods. These usually are sets of specific rules, such as modesty in dress, chastity outside marriage, sobriety, honesty, dietary rules, restrictions on speech, and the like. In this way, Godly religions are enabled to define and sanctify the moral order.

In contrast, the impersonality of the supernatural component of Godless religions and of magic makes human motives and morals irrelevant. Thus, the Gods may require that supplicants be pure in heart, but mana and the Tao ask no questions. Even if, in order to "work," a spell must be recited by someone having special attributes, such as being a virgin or a hunchback, the concern is not with inner feelings or moral virtue, but with the instrumentality alone. Thus, magic cannot inspire morality. The same is true of divine essences, as they do not judge (or do anything) and hence cannot sanctify the moral order. This surely is not to suggest that societies or individuals lacking Gods are necessarily lacking moral codes. It is simply to note that these codes will not make reference to religious justifications.

Nor can science justify morality. Donald N. Levine (1995, 306) has suggested that "social theory" can address "questions that science may not answer but which we feel compelled to pursue nevertheless." Such a suggestion assumes that social theory is a form of unscientific moralizing, which is, in fact, too often the case. Indeed, when Auguste Comte coined the term *sociology,* it was to identify a field that would serve as a scientific substitute for religion as the basis for establishing morality. It has long has been recognized, however, that although one can shift one's concerns between moral questions and scientific questions, the phrase *science of morality* violates the domain assumptions of both terms. Dostoyevsky's character Ivan Karamazov came much closer to the truth when he said, "If God is dead, everything is permitted." Of course, as noted, any number of moral rules can be *asserted* on purely secular grounds. And they can be enforced, given sufficient group solidarity (Miller and Kanazawa 2000; Stark 2001). But a crucial philosophical problem persists: lacking the legitimacy provided by divine will, how is it possible to *justify* moral rules, to prevent them from being seen as arbitrary, provisional, and subject to individual choice? This is a matter of considerable interest in chapters 6 and 7.

Empirical Falsification

Science has been defined in terms of its reliance on observations. Not only do systematic observations yield empirical generalizations that can prompt the construction of theories. Far more important is that any scientific theory is subject to contradiction by observations. As noted, a scientific theory predicts and prohibits certain observable states of affairs. It says that this is what *must* occur and this is what *may not* occur. When these predictions and prohibitions are not consistent with the relevant observations, it is necessary to reject or revise that theory. It is by being able to falsify theories that science makes progress. By ruthlessly weeding out theories that fail, or theories that are less efficient or precise, we gain confidence in those that continue to survive confrontations with the facts.

Just as vulnerability to falsification is the primary scientific virtue, it is a primary weakness of magic. It is assumed that scientific "truths" are provisional, subject to future rejection or revision, but this is not the assumption on which magic rests. When magic fails, as it often does, this seldom inspires magicians to revise. They are much more likely merely to try again, and again. As Malinowski ([1948] 1992, 19) claimed, whereas "[s]cience is guided by reason and corrected by observation, magic [is] impervious to both."

In contrast, because religion is able to confine its major explanations to a realm not subject to empirical inspection, unlike magic it *can be* immune to falsification. I am, of course, entirely aware of religious prophecies and activities that are vulnerable to failure. But these are unnecessary, and often inimical, to the success of religious organizations; and as religions mature, they tend to cease such undertakings—which gives religion immense social and institutional advantages in contrast with magic. Religion may propose to compensate a person for suffering in this life by admitting them to paradise, but magic seeks to provide pleasures here and now. Or while religion reassures the lonely that God loves them, magic offers them charms to attract lovers. These specific and worldly promises are extremely vulnerable to disconfirmation; when they fail, that fact will be obvious to all concerned. Consequently, compared with religion, magic is *very risky goods*. Therefore, over time magic and religion will tend to be differentiated: specialists in providing religion will tend to reduce or eliminate magic from their "product line," leaving it to specialists in magic.

In a classic paper on this topic, David G. Mandelbaum (1966) described how the priests of all of the great Eastern religions maintain an acknowledged symbiosis with local magicians. People seek to ensure their general welfare and gain otherworldly rewards through religion but consult magicians for specific and immediate needs. Thus, he explained (1177), a Brahman priest will not (or only very rarely) attempt "to cure an immediate and specific ailment." For this, people must consult a magician. The Brahman priests need not risk empirical failures, because they have far more valuable commodities to offer without risk. In contrast, the risks of magic are immense, as reflected in the very high turnover of practitioners, at least in a given locale, and by the lower-class origins of magicians (Mandelbaum 1966).

The unreliable character of magic also prevents magicians from establishing extended exchange relationships with a lay following. *"There is no Church of magic.* Between the magician and the individuals who consult him, there are no durable ties that make them members of a single moral body, comparable to the ties that join the faithful of the same god or the adherents of the same cult. The magician has a clientele, not a Church" (Durkheim [1912] 1995, 42). By the same token, magical failures become the basis for intense competition and conflict. This creates a very dangerous situation when religions do not divorce themselves from magic but attempt to provide it in competition with magicians—as demonstrated by the European witch hunts (Stark 2003).

Scope

When people discuss the existence of God, they are not speaking with the authority of science. Nor can anyone confer the authority of science on statements such as "Everyone deserves happiness." These statements have no contingent empirical implications. It is quite impossible to demonstrate either the existence of nonexistence of God, nor can statements about what people "deserve" be put to scientific tests. The point is that the *scope* of science is limited to natural or material reality. It cannot penetrate nonempirical realms any more than it can tell us how we ought to *feel* about the natural or material world. Even a simple statement such as "That's a beautiful sunset" is beyond science. Science can determine what sorts of sunsets most people in a given culture will judge to be beautiful—but that's an entirely different order of question. The limited scope of science explains why it is not fundamentally incompatible with religion.

To sum up: magic differs from religion because it does not posit the existence of Gods, does not either offer explanations of its own domain or address questions of ultimate meaning, does not offer otherworldly rewards, and is unable to sanctify the moral order, whereas religion does all of these. Magic and religion also differ in that the former is subject to empirical falsification, but the latter need not be. Magic differs from science because its primary mechanism is supernatural, because it offers no general explanations even of its own workings, and because, unlike science, its scope is not limited to natural or material reality. Science and religion differ over reliance on the supernatural and on Gods, on the promise of otherworldly rewards, and on the issues of sanctification of the moral order, falsification, and scope.

Table 1.1 compares religion, magic, and science on all of the dimensions discussed above and *could* eliminate confusions.

Conclusion

An anonymous reviewer of the original paper on which this chapter is based asked why the field should accept these definitions, suggesting that it might be better to embrace definitions on the basis of how words have been used rather than to impose arbitrary standards about how they "ought" to be used. A survey of past usage is appropriate for term papers on the history of social thought, but science, even social science, is not served by ancestor worship. No introductory physics book offers Aristotle's definition of matter as one of the respectable alternatives. The same principle applies in the social scientific study of religion. We are not obliged to stick with poorly defined terms simply because some celebrated founders defined them that way. What we must seek are definitions of terms that are coherent, mutually exclusive, and theoretically efficient. If I have not achieved these goals, then this chapter too belongs in the dustbin of intellectual history.

In Praise of "Idealistic Humbug"

Generations of social scientists have embraced a remarkable contradiction: they often blame all manner of social pathologies on religion, while simultaneously denying that religion can have any real social consequences, that whatever appears to be a religious effect is, when properly examined, found to be merely a mask for something more basic, something "material."

In most other areas of social scientific study, it has long been acknowledged that if people *define* something as real, it can have real consequences, but this truism generally has been denied vis-à-vis religion. Instead, it is proposed that the Gods are obviously imaginary and it must therefore follow that, as Karl Marx put it, any attempt to explain "reality" by reference to an "unreality" such as religion is pure "idealistic humbug." One must explain religion itself by reference to "realities" such as the "mode of production," because one "does not explain practice from the idea but explains the formation of ideas from material practice" ([1845] 1998, 61). Or, as Marx's collaborator Friedrich Engels explained, "[a]ll religion . . . is nothing but the fantastic reflection in men's minds of those external forces which control their daily life . . . the economic conditions . . . the means of production" (in Marx and Engels 1964, 147–48).

These views did not originate with Marx. Two centuries earlier, Thomas Hobbes explained that religion is nothing but "credulity," "ignorance," and "lies," and the Gods are but "creatures of [human] fantasy" ([1651] 1956, 1:98), even though Hobbes proposed to seek the ori-

A portion of this chapter appeared as "Religious Effects: In Praise of 'Idealistic' Humbug," *Review of Religious Research* 41 (2000): 289–310.

gins of these fantasies in the human psyche rather than in the economy. Over time, the idea that religion is but a mask for more fundamental factors became increasingly popular among social scientists, so that by the time Marx and Engels wrote, their views were not especially original. For example, their contemporary Ludwig von Feuerbach proposed that religion is nothing but the reflection of society and that "the secret of theology is nothing else than anthropology" ([1841] 1957, 207). Emile Durkheim ([1897] 1951, [1912] 1995) repeated Feuerbach's view (without attribution) and, although it is widely taught that Durkheim traced variations in suicide rates to religious roots, in fact he reduced religion to something "more basic," namely social solidarity, to which he traced both religion and suicide (Stark and Bainbridge 1997). Even Max Weber shied away from religious effects. Having attributed the rise of capitalism to the "Protestant ethic," he then traced the source of the ethic to material conditions (including the rise of the bourgeoisie, population growth, colonialism, etc.), thus limiting Puritan doctrines to being at most a *proximate,* rather than a *fundamental* cause of capitalism. Even so, Weber has often been attacked for affording religion *any* causal role.

When Weber shrank from regarding doctrine as the fundamental basis of the rise of capitalism, he set the stage for H. Richard Niebuhr to proclaim the primacy of the social and material over the doctrinal. In his celebrated *Social Sources of Denominationalism* (1929), wherein appears the first statement of a theory concerning the transformation of sects into churches, Niebuhr attempted to explain the proliferation of disputatious religious groups, each claiming to have the true doctrines. He proposed that doctrinal disputes had little or nothing to do with the splintering of religions and sneered at the ancient Jewish historian Josephus for missing the point when he contrasted the doctrines of the Pharisees and the Sadducees. The primary difference between the two, according to Niebuhr, was not "religious opinions" but was of "a social character," the Sadducees being aristocrats and the Pharisees being commoners. "Differences of opinion were surely present between the Pharisees and the Sadducees, but these differences had their roots in more profound social divergences. So it is with the Christian sects" (13).

Thus did Niebuhr dismiss the claims by religious groups that their differences were about doctrines. He cited the "universal human tendency to find respectable reasons for a practice desired from motives quite independent of the reasons urged" (1929, 13–14), for the fact is, said Niebuhr, that "theological opinions have their roots in the relationship

Exploring the Religious Life

of the religious life to the cultural and political conditions prevailing in any group of Christians" (16).

This long line of dismissals of religious effects eventuated in the received wisdom: *whenever religion appears to be having social effects, look deeper until you discover the material factor that is the true cause.* Rodney Needham (1972) has even proposed that by looking deeper one will discover that there is no such thing as an "interior state" that can be called religion—that the illusion is an illusion!

Only those misled by sociological humbug could fail to notice the immense capacity of religion to motivate and direct human action, as will be seen by inspection of the cases that follow. Perhaps the most vociferously argued instance involves the chorus of denials that the great medieval heretical and sectarian religious movements were based on religious concerns. These voices state, following Marx and Niebuhr, that the movements really were caused by "the desires of the poor to improve the material conditions of their lives," which desires "become transfused with phantasies of a new Paradise" (Cohn 1961, xiii). In chapter 3 I show that the real "phantasy" is to suppose that the poor played *any* significant role in most of these movements. In this chapter I expose the materialist humbug concerning the Crusades, the Great Awakenings in America, Medieval Jewish messianic movements, the "mystical 1960s," and the post–World War II outburst of Japanese religions. Against this background I consider the fact that not all religions are created equal, that some have much greater capacity to generate human commitment and action.

Crusading for Land & Loot

In the aftermath of the attack by Muslim terrorists on New York City, frequent mention was made of the Crusades as a basis for Islamic fury. It was argued that Muslim bitterness over mistreatment by the Christian West can be dated back to 1096, when the First Crusade set out for the Holy Land. Far from being motivated by piety or by concern for the safety of pilgrims and the holy places in Jerusalem, the Crusades (it is alleged) were but the first extremely bloody chapter in a long history of brutal European colonialism—that the knights of Europe marched east not out of idealism but out of greed.

These claims did not originate with the media. They were formulated by well-known twentieth-century Western historians (Duby 1977; France 1997; Mayer 1972). As summed up by the distinguished Hans Eberhard

Mayer, the Crusades alleviated a severe financial squeeze on Europe's "knightly class." According to Mayer and others who share his views, at this time there was a substantial and rapidly growing number of "surplus" sons, members of noble families who would not inherit and whom the heirs found it increasingly difficult to provide with even modest incomes. Hence, as Mayer put it, "the Crusade acted as a kind of safety valve for the knightly class . . . a class which looked upon the Crusade as a way of solving its material problems" (22–25). A group of American economists recently proposed that the crusaders hoped to get rich from the flow of pilgrims (comparing the shrines to modern amusement parks) and that the pope sent the crusaders east in pursuit of "new markets" for the church, presumably to be gained by converting people away from Islam (Ekelund et al. 1999). Since this is the received wisdom on the subject, one should not blame the author of a leading textbook on Western civilization for telling college students, "From the perspective of the pope and European monarchs, the crusades offered a way to rid Europe of contentious young nobles . . . [who] saw an opportunity to gain territory, riches, status, possibly a title, and even salvation" (Spielvogel 2000, 259).

Contrary to all of this "scholarship," the Crusades were precipitated by Islamic provocations and were sustained by Western piety. They were provoked by centuries of attempts by Muslims to colonize the West and by attacks on Christian pilgrims and holy places. The Crusades were not organized and led by surplus sons but by the heads of great families who were fully aware that the costs of crusading would far exceed the very modest material rewards that could be expected. Most individuals went at immense personal cost, some of them knowingly bankrupting themselves in order to go. Moreover, the crusader kingdom in the Holy Land was not sustained by local exactions but instead required immense subsidies from Europe. Thus do the many alleged material causes evaporate, leaving intact the traditional interpretation that the crusaders marched out of faith. I now justify each of these assertions.

Muslims began invading and colonizing Christian areas in the lifetime of Muhammad. Then, during the next four centuries prior to the Crusades, they overwhelmed Roman North Africa (once a flower of Christian civilization) and colonized Spain, Sicily, and portions of southern Italy. Early in the eighth century, major thrusts were made into France before the Franks managed to rout the Muslim forces at Tours (or Poitiers) in 732 (Fregosi 1998; Hodgson 1974; Kennedy 2001). Meanwhile, Muslim forces had turned the Mediterranean into a virtual Islamic lake, destroying

Exploring the Religious Life

the economic life of European cities once dependent on maritime trade. It seems very odd that those who are so vociferous about the misery and injustice imposed by Europeans on their former colonial empires fail to perceive (or to admit) any such consequences of Muslim imperialism.

In any event, it is against this general background of chronic and long-standing Western grievances that the very specific provocations for the Crusades must be considered. These involved the destruction of and the threat to holy places in Jerusalem and the murder, torture, enslavement, robbery, and general harassment of Christian pilgrims.

In 1009, at the direction of Fatimid Caliph al-Hākim, Muslims destroyed the Church of the Holy Sepulcher in Jerusalem—the splendid basilica that Constantine had erected over what was believed to be the site of the tomb where Christ lay before the Resurrection. As word of the desecration of the holiest of all Christian shrines reached Europe, it prompted considerable anger and concern. But the crisis soon passed because Al-Hākim was killed by political opponents, and religious tolerance was restored in Jerusalem, thus permitting resumption of the substantial flow of Christian pilgrims. The value of the pilgrim traffic probably was a major factor in the very liberal policies that had prevailed in Muslim-controlled Jerusalem through the centuries. Despite the great distances involved and the limited means of transportation, pilgrimages to Jerusalem were surprisingly common. In the first of his distinguished three volumes on the Crusades, Sir Steven Runciman reported that "an unending stream of travellers poured eastward, sometimes travelling in parties numbering thousands, men and women of every age and every class, ready . . . to spend a year or more on the [journey]" (1951, 1:49). A major reason for going to the Holy Land was the belief that a pilgrimage would absolve even the most terrible sins. Thus, many pilgrims came all the way from Scandinavia and some even from Iceland. As Runciman explained, the Norse "were violent men, frequently guilty of murder and frequently in need of an act of penance" (1:47).

But then, later in the eleventh century, everything changed. The Seljuk Turks, recent converts to Islam, became the new rulers of Asia Minor, pushing to within one hundred miles of Constantinople. Perhaps because they were new to Islam, or perhaps because they were still seminomadic tribesmen untainted by city-dwelling, the Turks were unflinching particularists. There was only one true God, and his name was Allah, not Yahweh or Jehovah. Tolerance was at an end. Not that the Turks officially prohibited Christian pilgrimages, but they made it clear that Christians were fair game. Hence, every Anatolian village along the route to Jerusalem began to exact a toll on Christian travelers. Far worse, many pilgrims were seized and sold into slavery; others were tortured, seemingly as much for entertainment as for edification. Those who survived these perils "returned to the West weary and impoverished, with a dreadful tale to tell" (Runciman 1951, 1:79).

Thus, anger and anxiety about the Holy Land grew. It is important to understand just how vivid was the image of the Holy Land to sincere medieval Christians. It was where Christ and the disciples had lived and to an almost palpable degree still did. In the words of Robert Payne, in Palestine Christians "expected to find holiness in a concrete form, something that could be seen, touched, kissed, worshipped, and even carried away. Holiness was in the pathways trodden by Christ, in the mountains and valleys seen by Christ, in the streets of Jerusalem where Christ had wandered" (Payne 1984, 18–19). In Jerusalem, a Christian could even climb the hill on which the cross had borne the Son of God. But no longer. Living "enemies of Christ, the spawn of Satan," now barred Christians from walking in Christ's footsteps.

It was in this climate of opinion that Alexius Comnenus, emperor of Byzantium, wrote from his embattled capital to the count of Flanders requesting that he and his fellow Christians in the West come to the rescue. In his letter, the emperor detailed gruesome tortures of Christians and vile desecrations of churches, altars, and baptismal fonts. Should Constantinople fall to the Turks, not only would thousands more Christians be murdered, tortured, and raped, but "the most holy relics of the Saviour," gathered over the centuries, would be lost. "Therefore in the name of God . . . we implore you to bring this city all the faithful soldiers of Christ . . . in your coming you will find your reward in heaven, and if you do not come, God will condemn you" (Payne 1984, 28–29).

When Pope Urban II read this letter, he was determined that it be answered in deeds. He arranged for a great gathering of clergy and laity in the French city of Clermont on November 27, 1095. Standing on a podium in the middle of a field, and surrounded by an immense crowd that included poor peasants as well as nobility and clergy, the pope gave one of the most effective speeches of all time. Blessed with an expressive and unusually powerful voice, he could be heard and understood at a great distance. Subsequently, copies of the speech (written and spoken in French) were circulated all across Europe. Five major versions of the speech exist, each being incomplete, and there are several translations of each into English. I have selected excerpts from several versions (all in Payne 1984, 33–35) in order to reveal the means by which the pope aroused thousands in attendance to commit themselves to sew a cross onto their clothing as an emblem that they would serve. Pope Urban began by reciting a long list of atrocities committed on Christians and destruction and desecration inflicted on Christian holy places:

Christians have been made captive and God's churches have been violated and others have been made to serve their own religious rites. They have ruined the altars with filth and defilement. They have circumcised Christians and smeared the blood on the altars or poured it into baptismal fonts. It amused them to kill Christians by opening up their bellies and drawing out the end of their intestines, which they then tied to a stake. Then they flogged their victims and made them walk around and around the stake until their intestines had spilled out and they fell dead on the ground . . . What shall I say about the abominable rape of women? On this subject it may be worse to speak than to remain silent . . .

Who shall avenge these wrongs . . . if not you? You are the race upon whom God has bestowed glory in arms . . . Rise up, then, and remember the virile deeds of your ancestors, the glory and renown of Charlemagne . . . and all your other kings who destroyed the kingdoms of pagans and planted the holy church in their lands. You should be especially aroused by the knowledge that the Church of the Holy Sepulchre is now in the hands of unclean nations and that holy places are shamelessly misused and sacrilegiously defiled with their filth. Oh, most valiant knights, descendants of unconquerable ancestors, remember the courage of your forefathers and do not dishonor them.

At this point Pope Urban raised a second issue, to which he already had devoted years of effort—the chronic warfare of medieval times. The pope had been attempting to achieve a "Truce of God" among the feudal nobility, many of whom seemed inclined to make war, even on their friends, just for the sake of a good fight. After all, it was what they had trained to do every day since early childhood. Here was their chance! "Christian warriors, who continually and vainly seek pretexts for war, rejoice, for you have today found a true pretext. You, who so often have been the terror of your fellow men, go and fight against the barbarians, go and fight for the deliverance of the holy places . . . If you are conquered, you will have the glory of dying in the very same place as Jesus

Christ, and God will never forget that he found you in the holy battalions." Then he hit them with it: "If you must have blood, bathe in the blood of the infidels . . . Soldiers of Hell, become soldiers of the living God!" Now, shouts of *"Dieu li volt!"* (God wills it!) began to spread through the crowd. Thereupon the pope raised his crucifix and roared: "It is Christ himself who comes from the tomb and presents you with this cross . . . Wear it upon your shoulders and your breasts. Let it shine upon your arms and upon your standards. It will be to you the surety of victory or the palm of martyrdom. It will increasingly remind you that Christ died for you, and that it is your duty to die for him!" At once, the crowd began to cut up cloaks and other pieces of cloth to make crosses and to sew them on their shoulders and chests. Everyone agreed that next spring they would march to Jerusalem. And they did.

It has often been suggested that we should not trust the pope or the emperor on what was taking place in the Holy Land. Perhaps they were misinformed. Perhaps they were lying to arouse a military venture for reasons of their own. And perhaps not. As Runciman pointed out, Europeans, especially the nobility, had trustworthy independent information on the brutalization of the Christian pilgrims—from their own relatives and friends who had managed to survive. But even had the pope and the emperor been cynical propagandists, that would not alter the motivation of the crusaders, for that depends entirely on *what the knights believed*. And they believed they were serving God not Mammon.

It could hardly have been otherwise, for had there actually been a financial squeeze on the knightly class, about the last thing they would have done was to march off on a Crusade to the Holy Land. As Peter Edbury explained, "[c]rusading was expensive, and the costs were borne by the crusaders themselves, their families, their lords and, increasingly from the end of the twelfth century, by taxes levied on the Church in the West" (1999, 95). Even the many crusader castles and the garrisons by which Christians held the Holy Land for two centuries were not built or sustained by local exactions, but by funds sent from Europe. Indeed, the great wealth of the knightly crusading orders—the Hospitalers and the Templars—was not loot but came from donations and legacies in Europe (Edbury 1999; Read 1999). All told, "large quantities of Western silver flowed into the crusader states" (Edbury 1999, 95). The Crusades were possible only because this was not a period of economic decline but one of *growth,* "which put more resources and money into the hands of the ruling elites on Western Europe" (Gillingham 1999, 59).

Moreover, it was not "surplus" sons who went. Because the "cost of crusading was truly enormous" (Madden 1999, 12), only the heads of upper-class households could raise the money to go: it was kings, princes, counts, dukes, barons, and earls who enrolled companies of knights and led the way, as Jonathan Riley-Smith (1997) has demonstrated in his remarkable reconstruction of crusader rosters. Even so, they raised the needed funds at a very great sacrifice. Many sold all or substantial amounts of their holdings, borrowed all they could from relatives, and impoverished themselves and their families in order to participate (Riley-Smith 1997). As for making up their losses by looting and colonizing in the Holy Land, most of them had no such illusions—indeed, most of them had no plans to remain in the East once the fighting was done. Finally, had the crusaders truly gone in pursuit of loot and land, the knights of Europe would have responded earlier, in 1063, when Pope Alexander II proposed a crusade to drive the infidel Muslims out of Spain. Unlike the Holy Land, Moorish Spain was extremely wealthy, possessed an abundance of fertile lands, and was close at hand. But hardly anyone responded to the pope's summons. Yet only twenty years later, thousands of crusaders set out for the dry, impoverished wastes of faraway Palestine. What was different? Spain was not the Holy Land! Christ had not walked the streets of Toledo, nor was he crucified in Seville.

Let me add, however, that although it was faith, not greed, that launched the Crusades, eventually it was greed, envy, and pride that conspired to bring them down.

The Great Awakenings

There was a wave of public religious enthusiasm in various American cities from 1739 through 1741. In each city, "huge crowds of crying, sobbing people [gathered], thousands upon thousands of desperate souls, asking what they must do to be saved" (Wood 1993, 20). Then, at the start of the nineteenth century, came widespread reports of similar activities going on in rural areas along the western frontier as again crowds gathered and people moaned and groaned for divine forgiveness. These events came to be known as the first and second Great Awakenings, and social scientists have devoted a great deal of effort to explaining why each took place when and where it did.

Until recently, all social scientists began their explanations by postulating a sudden, generalized *need* for more intense religion. Thus, William

G. McLoughlin (1978, 2), regarded by many as the leading authority on awakenings, attributed them to sudden periods of "grave personal stress." Such stress, in turn, has been traced to such "underlying causes" as floods, epidemics, crop failures, business failures, financial panics, financial booms, the incursions of a market economy, industrialization, rapid immigration, and so on (Barkun 1986; Gordon-McCutchan 1983; Thomas 1989). Recently, a far more plausible interpretation of these "awakenings" makes no mention of any intensifications of religious needs nor of the impact of social or natural crises (Butler 1982, 1990; Finke and Stark 1992; Lambert 1990, 1999; Smith 1983). Instead, these scholars trace the revivals in question to organized *religious* innovations and actions. Specifically, proponents of this view note that religious organizations led by George Whitefield in the eighteenth century and by Barton Stone and by Charles Finney in the nineteenth used vigorous and effective marketing techniques to sustain revival campaigns, which later historians have classified as "awakenings." In contrast to scholars who explain that because of various crises "the times" were right for huge crowds to "materialize" to hear Whitefield, the new interpretation stresses that "[w]hat was new about Whitefield was [his] skill as an entrepreneur, an impresario" (Lambert 1990, 813). In fact, Whitefield may have been the first exponent of mass marketing techniques — certainly he seems to have been the first to apply them to religion. His revivals were planned several years ahead and climaxed a long campaign to build up local interest. He was a master of the press release and advance publicity, sending out a constant stream of reports on the success of his revivals elsewhere to newspapers in the cities he intended to visit. In addition, Whitefield had thousands of copies of his sermons printed and distributed to stir up interest. Then, as the date of his first revival service neared, he ran newspaper advertisements announcing his impending arrival. All subsequent revivalists — from Charles Finney to Billy Graham — have based their campaigns on Whitefield's original model. It was from these efforts that crowds "materialized" (Finke and Stark 1992).

As I have clarified elsewhere (Stark and Finke 2000), what Whitefield accomplished was not to exploit new religious needs arising from "the times," but to appeal successfully to needs that had long gone essentially unserved by the lax, state-supported churches in the American colonies at this time. This was something that Whitefield fully recognized, remarking during his visit to Boston in 1740, "I am persuaded, the generality of preachers [in New England] talk of an unknown and unfelt

Exploring the Religious Life

Christ. The reason why congregations have been so dead, is because they have had dead men preach to them" (Whitefield [1747] 1969, 471). In other words, the first Great Awakening was a supply-side phenomenon. There was no sudden increase in *demand* (although Whitefield's efforts may have activated and intensified it). Widespread belief in a God of judgment and concerns about salvation had been there all along. What changed was a sudden increase in the *supply* of intense religion. It was Whitefield's dramatic portrayals of hell, not fear of an expanding market economy, that caused people to cry out to God. Religion was not only the obvious but also the underlying cause.

Medieval Jewish Messianic Movements

For Jews, the messiah has yet to come. But again and again over the centuries, groups of Jews have hailed his arrival. An early episode resulted, of course, in Christianity. It would not be an exaggeration, however, to say that scores of other messiahs (perhaps several hundred) have appeared in Jewish communities over the past two millennia; such movements were especially common in the European Diaspora during medieval times (Cohen 1967; Lenowitz 1998; Sharot 1982).

In his sophisticated analysis of these Jewish religious movements, Stephen Sharot (1982, 18) noted the huge literature on messianic movements, which stresses that they are "responses to the disruption of social and cultural patterns . . . [produced by] a disaster such as an epidemic, famine, war, or massacre. Following a disaster, persons feel vulnerable, confused, full of anxiety, and they turn to millennial beliefs in order to account for otherwise meaningless events. They interpret the disaster as a prelude to the millennium; thus their deepest despair gives way to the greatest hope." The trouble is that although some messianic Jewish movements did erupt following a disaster, as he worked his way through all of the better-known cases, Sharot was forced to agree with Gershon D. Cohen's earlier study (1967) that many movements seemed to come out of nowhere, in the sense that they arose during periods of relative quiet, and therefore that "disaster was not a necessary condition of a messianic outburst" (Sharot 1982, 65–66).

Sharot made this concession very reluctantly, and in many passages of his monograph he seems to have forgotten it. Nevertheless, his scrupulous accounts of specific incidents often show that a movement was the direct result of religious rather than secular influences. Frequently, an episode began with an individual or a small group pouring over the *Kabbalah* (a collection of Jewish mystical writings) out of purely personal motives with the result that they "discovered" that the millennium was at hand. Thereupon they shared this knowledge with others, who, in turn, assisted in arousing a mass following. In other instances, someone became convinced that he was the messiah and was able to convince his family and friends (see chapter 5).

One can, of course, argue that Jews living in medieval Europe were always victims and hence always ripe for millenarian solutions. But constants cannot explain variations, and in as many cases as not, nothing special was going on to cause a movement to arise then rather than at some other time—*except* for direct religious influences in the form of people advocating a new religious message or circumstance. Let me acknowledge that humans often *do* turn to religion in times of trouble and crises. My aim is not to deny something so obvious but only to reject it as a necessary condition and to recognize that religious phenomena can be caused by other religious phenomena.

The Mystical 1960s

A huge literature attributes the "explosive growth" of new religious movements in the United States in the late 1960s and early 1970s to profound social causes. Particular attention has been given to uncovering the secular causes of the special appeal of Eastern faiths for Americans during this period. Harvey Cox (1983, 42) blamed "the most deteriorated, decadent phase of consumer capitalism," charging that converts to Eastern faiths had "been maddened by consumer culture" (40). Serious journals published equally hysterical explanations. As Thomas Robbins summarized (1988, 60), each of these identified one or more "acute and distinctively modern dislocation which is said to be producing some mode of alienation, anomie or deprivation to which Americans are responding." With her usual grasp of the essentials, Eileen Barker (1986, 338) commented that "those who have read some of the sociological literature could well be at a loss to understand why *all* young adults are not members [of new religious movements], so all-encompassing are some of the explanations."

In fact, there was *no growth,* explosive or otherwise, of new religious movements in this era (Finke and Stark 1992; Melton 1988). The rate of new movement formation was constant from 1950 through 1990. As for the brief increase in the proportion of Eastern faiths among new American movements, capitalism had nothing to do with it. Rather, in 1965 the elimination of exclusionary rules against Asian immigration made it possible for the first time for authentic Indian and other Eastern religious leaders to directly seek American followers. Consequently, there was an increase in the number of Eastern religious organizations, but the number of actual converts was minuscule. Even so, these movements were the result of *religious* efforts—of face-to-face recruitment activities motivated by religious convictions.

Post–World War II Japanese Religions

Explosive growth by new religions did occur in Japan following World War II; so many new groups appeared that observers spoke of "the rush hour of the gods" (McFarland 1967). It has been assumed that the cause of this religious fervor was the devastation and suffering produced by the war. But no similar religious activity took place in postwar Germany or in the Soviet Union, where devastation and suffering surely equaled that of Japan. There also was a religious "rush hour" in South Korea, which was hardly touched by the war, at the end of which it was liberated from Japanese rule. But the liberation of Taiwan from the Japanese did not result in any outburst of new faiths.

The common element is religious liberty in postwar Japan and Korea and the lack thereof in Germany, the Soviet Union, and Taiwan. State churches suppress religious competition and dampen all religious enthusiasm (Stark and Iannaccone 1994; Stark and Finke 2000), and the German state church apparatus remained intact in the Western Zone of Germany. In the Eastern Zone, of course, the Soviets repressed all religion, as they did in the USSR. Thus, new religious groups could not prosper in either Germany or the Soviet Union. In Japan, though, the "MacArthur" constitution inaugurated complete religious freedom in a nation where the government previously had strictly repressed all but a few traditional religions. In South Korea, too, a policy of religious liberty replaced the prior Japanese religious repression. In both nations the emergence of new religions took place almost at once. The end of Japanese rule brought no similar eruption of new religions in Taiwan because its new Nationalist Chinese rulers did not condone religious freedom.

The notion that the war caused Japan's "rush hour" is further refuted by the fact that nearly all of what became the leading new religious movements in the postwar period originated *prior* to the war—sometimes long before. Konkō-kyō was founded in 1885 and Reiyukai Kyodan in 1925; the immensely successful Sōka Gakkai movement was organized in 1930, as were PL Kyōdan and Seichō no Ie; and Risshō Kōsei-kai began in 1938 (McFarland 1967; Moroto 1976). However, government repression was sufficient to limit them to small groups of followers, often restricted to a single village or neighborhood. Thus, Neill McFarland (1967, 4) described them as "innumerable captive and incipient religious movements" and noted that the new constitution allowed "their voice to be heard." As Aiko Moroto (1976, 1) noted, these groups originated in prewar Japan; what was new after the war was that "these groups came out into the open and flourished." Harry Thomsen (1963, 17) pointed out that what was new about these religions was that their new freedom allowed them to utilize "new methods of evangelism." Hence, the primary "secular" cause of the proliferation of new religions in Japan and Korea was merely the legal right to function, and the rest of the story involves actions by religious organizations based on religious motives. The primary "religious" cause of the proliferation of religious movements in Japan is that where most people's religiousness is not anchored in a religious organization, there is a huge pool available for recruitment to such organizations (see chapter 6).

But we can go further. If we admit that the first Great Awakening was caused by George Whitefield's revival campaign, that many medieval messianic outbursts resulted from "discoveries" found in the *Kabbalah*, that Indian gurus came to America in search of followers, and that small Japanese sects pursued converts when given the right to do so, we then should ask why. Why did George Whitefield embark on his great revival campaign? Why did any number of medieval Jewish scholars pore over the *Kabbalah*? What drove the gurus westward? Why do sect members seek converts? For generations the only answers to such questions that were acceptable to social scientists imputed various psychological conditions or deficiencies as the cause of such "strange" actions (Stark and Finke 2000). It was taken for granted that no rational and normal person would do such things (although it was presumed that perfectly normal people would labor to decode the obscurities of Freudian or Marxist doctrines or would join campaigns to "free" farm livestock).

Today, many people involved in the social scientific study of religion are willing to entertain the notion that George Whitefield's motives, like those of the gurus and of sect members, were mainly religious—that the obligation to proselytize is inherent in some systems of religious doctrines. Moreover, many scholars today will see nothing pathological in efforts by people to study scriptures in the hope of discovering divine plans. To accept these as reasonable actions is, of course, to admit the reality of religious motivation and to credit the claim that doctrines can matter. Once one sets off along this path, however, there is no stopping with the mere admission that doctrines can matter. Unavoidably, the question arises, Do doctrines *differ* in their capacity to direct human actions? And of course the answer is yes. Therefore, it will be useful here to contrast the responses of early Christians and their pagan neighbors when deadly plagues broke out and to trace the role of doctrine in prompting these differences.

Plagues & Doctrines

In the year 165, during the reign of Marcus Aurelius, a devastating epidemic swept through the Roman Empire. Some medical historians suspect that it was the first appearance of smallpox in the West (Zinsser [1934] 1960). Whatever the actual disease was, it was lethal. During the fifteen-year duration of the epidemic, from a quarter to a third of the population of the empire died from it (Gilliam 1961; McNeill 1976; Russell 1958). At the height of the epidemic, mortality was so great in many cities that Marcus Aurelius spoke of caravans of carts and wagons hauling out the dead. Then, a century later it all happened again. This time it may have been measles. No matter. Both smallpox and measles can result in huge mortality rates when they strike a previously unexposed population. So once again the entire Greco-Roman world trembled as, on all sides, family, friends, and neighbors died horribly.

In a world in which even soap had yet to be invented, no one knew how to treat the stricken. Nor did most of the people try. During the first of the plagues, Galen, the most famous physician of classical times, fled Rome for his country estate, where he stayed for several years until the danger passed. But for those who had nowhere else to go, the typical response was to try to avoid all contact with those afflicted—it was understood that the disease was contagious. Hence, when their first symptom appeared, victims were thrown out into the streets, where the dead and dying lay in piles. In a pastoral letter written during the second epidemic (c. 251), Bishop Dionysius (in Eusebius, *Ecclesiastical History*, 7.22) described events in Alexandria: "At the first onset of the disease, they [pagans] pushed the sufferers away and fled from their dearest, throwing them into the roads before they were dead and treated unburied corpses as dirt, hoping thereby to avert the spread and contagion of the fatal disease; but do what they might, they found it difficult to escape." It must have caused most people considerable pain and grief to abandon loved ones in this manner. But what else were they to do? What about prayer? Writing during an earlier plague that struck Athens, Thucydides (*History of the Peloponnesian War*, 2.47–55) noted that people soon discovered that "prayers made in the temples" were "useless" and "in the end people were so overcome by their sufferings that they paid no further attention to such things . . . As for the Gods, it seemed to be the same thing whether one worshipped them or not, when one saw the good and the bad dying indiscriminately." This was the consensus throughout the empire, based in part on experience, as Thucydides noted. Indeed, if people did go to the temples in search of divine help, usually there were no priests there to conduct rites, having themselves fled.

But that was not true of Christian priests, and the Christians did not abandon their afflicted. In the same letter quoted above, Bishop Dionysius offered a lengthy tribute to the heroic nursing efforts of local Christians, many of whom lost their lives while caring for others.

> Most of our brother Christians showed unbounded love and loyalty, never sparing themselves and thinking only of one another. Heedless of danger, they took charge of the sick, attending to their every need and ministering to them in Christ, and with them departed this life serenely happy; for they were infected by others with the disease, drawing on themselves the sickness of their neighbors and cheerfully accepting their pains. Many, in nursing and curing others, transferred their death to themselves and died in their stead . . . The best of our brothers lost their lives in this manner, a number of presbyters, deacons, and laymen winning high commendation so that death in this form, the result of great piety and strong faith, seems in every way the equal of martyrdom.

Lest it be thought that this was mere bragging, it seems highly unlikely that a bishop would write a pastoral letter to his members containing falsehoods about things they would have known from direct observation. Moreover, such behavior was central to the entire Christian message. First, because death is not the end. Second, because the responsibility to care for one another is subordinate only to faith as the duty of

Exploring the Religious Life

all Christians. As William H. McNeill summed up in his classic work *Plagues and Peoples* (1976, 108),

[a]nother advantage Christians enjoyed over pagans was that the teaching of their faith made life meaningful even amid sudden and surprising death . . . even a shattered remnant of survivors who had somehow made it through war or pestilence or both could find warm, immediate and healing consolation in the vision of a heavenly existence for those missing relatives and friends . . . Christianity was, therefore, a system of thought and feeling thoroughly adapted to a time of troubles in which hardship, disease, and violent death commonly prevailed.

This is how Cyprian, bishop of Carthage, explained to his people that the virtuous had nothing to fear from the plague:

How suitable, how necessary it is that this plague and pestilence, which seems horrible and deadly, searches out the justice of each and every one and examines the minds of the human race; whether the well care for the sick, whether relatives dutifully love their kinsmen as they should, whether masters show compassion for their ailing slaves, whether physicians do not desert the afflicted . . . Although this mortality has contributed nothing else, it has especially accomplished this for Christians and servants of God, that we have begun gladly to seek martyrdom while we are learning not to fear death. These are trying exercises for us, not deaths; they give to the mind the glory of fortitude; by contempt of death they prepare for the crown . . . our brethren who have been freed from the world by the summons of the Lord should not be mourned, since we know that they are not lost but sent before; that in departing they lead the way; that as travellers, as voyagers are wont to be, they should be longed for, not lamented . . . and that no occasion should be given to pagans to censure us deservedly and justly, on the ground that we grieve for those who we say are living. (*Mortality*, 15–20)

What happened, then? Christians did nurse the sick, not only their own but many pagans as well, and the result was greatly reduced mortality. As McNeill (1976, 108) pointed out, under the circumstances that prevailed back then, even "quite elementary nursing will greatly reduce mortality. Simple provision of food and water, for instance, will allow persons who are temporarily too weak to cope for themselves to recover instead of perishing miserably." The best estimate is that Christian mortality would have been reduced by as much as two-thirds. The fact that large numbers of Christians survived did not go unnoticed, lending immense credibility to Christian "miracle-working."

The basis for both the Christian and the pagan responses was doctrine. Christians nursed the sick because Christ had commanded that they do so: "Truly, I say to you, as you did it to one of the least of these my brethren, you did it to me" (Matt. 25:40).[1] Christians did not limit their good works to times of crisis—this was a central aspect of their everyday life, attested by Christian and pagan sources alike. As Tertullian claimed (*Apologetics,* 39): "It is our care of the helpless, our practice of loving kindness that brands us in the eyes of many of our opponents. 'Only look,' they say, 'look how they love one another!'"

Among the opponents who "looked" was the Emperor Julian, who, late in the fourth century, tried to restore pagan power. Among his efforts was a campaign to institute pagan charities in order to offset the Christians. Julian complained in a letter to the high priest of Galatia in 362 that the pagans needed to equal the virtues of Christians, for recent Christian growth was caused by their "moral character, even if pretended," and by their "benevolence toward strangers and care for the graves of the dead." In a letter to another priest, Julian wrote, "I think that when the poor happened to be neglected and overlooked by the priests, the impious Galileans observed this and devoted themselves to benevolence" (Johnson 1976, 75). And he also wrote, "[T]he impious Galileans support not only their poor, but ours as well, everyone can see that our people lack aid from us" (Ayerst and Fisher 1971, 179–81).

Clearly, Julian loathed "the Galileans." He even suspected that their benevolence had ulterior motives. But he recognized that his charities and those of organized paganism paled in comparison with Christian efforts, which had created "a miniature welfare state in an empire which for the most part lacked social services" (Johnson 1976, 75). By Julian's day in the fourth century, it was too late to overtake this colossal result, the seeds for which had been planted in such teachings as "I am my brother's keeper," "Do unto others as you would have them do onto you," and "It is more blessed to give than to receive" (Grant 1977). In contrast, for all Julian's urging that pagan priests match these Christian practices, there was little or no response, because *there were no doctrinal bases or traditional practices* for them to build upon. It was not that Romans knew nothing of charity, but that it was not based on service to the Gods. Pagan Gods did not punish ethical violations because they imposed no ethical demands—humans offended the Gods only through neglect or by violation of ritual standards (MacMullen 1981, 58). Since pagan Gods only required propitiation and beyond that left human affairs in human hands, a pagan priest could not preach that those lacking in the spirit of charity risked their salvation. Indeed, the pagan Gods offered no salvation. They might be bribed to perform various services, but the Gods did not provide an escape from mortality. We must keep that in sight as we compare the reactions of Christians and pagans to the shadow of sudden death. Galen lacked belief in life beyond death.[2] The Christians were certain that this life was but a prelude. For Galen to have remained in Rome to treat the afflicted would have required bravery far beyond that needed by Christians to do likewise.

So there it is. Only trained social scientists ever could have doubted that what people believe influences what they do. Moreover, doctrines differ greatly in the kinds of behavior they can sustain. Christian doctrines fostered a massive effort to act out the injunction to love one another. Pagan doctrines included no such injunction. Let us now explore some basic principles about what makes doctrines effective, at least in the sociological sense.

Effective Religious Doctrines

A few years ago I pointed out that eventually social scientists would be unable to hide behind cultural relativism vis-à-vis religious doctrines. Given the admission that doctrine matters, eventually we would "need to confront the possibility that some theologies are inherently more plausible; some are more easily and effectively communicated; some are more able to satisfy deeply felt needs of large numbers of people; indeed, some probably are inherently more interesting, even more exciting, than others" (Stark 1987, 26). Nevertheless, more than a decade later, social scientists still seem reluctant to pursue these matters. It's not as if my suggestions were unprecedented. Surely *The Protestant Ethic and the Spirit of Capitalism* was precisely an attempt to identify aspects of doctrine that were effective for purposes of underwriting the rise of capitalism. Indeed, Max Weber stressed the importance of doctrine in much of his work. I happen to think he was wrong about the link between Calvinism and commerce. However, my disagreement with Weber is not about whether religious doctrines influenced the rise of the West, but about *which* doctrines had such an influence. I think that the industrial and scientific revolutions were rooted in the general commitment of Christian theology to rationality, rather than in Protestantism alone (Stark 2003). In any event, it is not too difficult to notice a number of generic variations in religious doctrines which seem likely to have behavioral consequences.

Before pursuing these matters, though, let me emphasize that I am not attempting to do theology: I am not trying to construct a sound body of doctrine, nor am I trying to discover divine law. Instead, I am trying to discover what makes a doctrine socially effective. What makes it persuasive, credible, forceful, and productive of social results? I suspect that "good" theology maximizes these sociological features too, but my interest is not in theological merit, only in social influence.

Perhaps the first important aspect of effective doctrine is *clarity*. Layers of metaphor and obscure symbolism may stimulate scholarly reflection or meditation, but it takes clear statements to direct human behavior. Generations of Jewish mystics may have pored over the *Kabbalah,* but it was not from this that they discovered how to be good Jews. The essentials of the Law need not be decoded from poetry; the commandments are quite specific, which is why they can be kept. In addition, of course, there must be sufficient *motivation* built into the doctrine. *Why* should one do as directed? Thus, as with good parenting, the expectations should be clear and the consequences equally clear: thou shalt, thou shalt not, *or else*. And, of course, it was the "or else" part of Christianity that underlay the moans and groans for forgiveness voiced by the crowds gathered to hear George Whitefield.

In many religions, what is required is clear enough and the consequences of conformity and nonconformity are equally clear, but the system has very little impact on social life because the *scope* of the demands is very limited. The Greco-Roman Gods required propitiation but little more. One might go to them in pursuit of specific favors (better health, good crops, romance) in exchange for an appropriate sacrifice as specified by the doctrines, but standards of long-term "worthiness" were not applied. Indeed, the concept of sin is not universal, and the extension of sin to include actions done toward other humans is rarer still. All cultures teach that it is wrong to steal (at least from members of the group), and all impose worldly punishments on those caught doing so. But it adds a potent deterrent to also teach that God knows when you sin and keeps a balance sheet that must be settled in eternity (chapter 7). One cannot expect religious doctrines to cause or to prevent behavior that they do not address.

                                                                      Exploring the Religious Life

In addition to the scope of the moral and behavioral demands made by a religion, the *value* of the *rewards* and the *severity* of the *punishments* also are important. Here Islam and traditional versions of Christianity head the list. Each offers its followers an eternal life of unending bliss or unrelenting pain. In tandem with the liberal views of child-rearing, many liberal Christian bodies these days limit eternal sanctions to those of positive reinforcement—hell has been abandoned or transformed into a symbol in many denominations. But even the promise of heaven alone would seem to invest divine commandments with far greater force than do notions of a shadowy, uneventful existence in a netherworld, as presented by Greco-Roman religions.

Probably all faiths offer some level of *worldly rewards* in return for compliance, whether compliance merely involves propitiation or extensive behavioral demands. But here, too, some faiths deliver far more than others. And by the very fact of demanding more, a faith is able to return more (Finke and Stark 1992; Iannaccone 1992, 1994; Kelley 1972; Stark 1996a; Stark and Finke 2000). Consider the contrast between the early Christians and their pagan neighbors. Because Christians were expected to do unto others, they had the security of knowing they would be done unto. Widows, orphans, the disabled, and the elderly were looked after; the stricken were nursed; the hungry were fed. Indeed, data taken from monuments and gravestones (Burn 1953) indicate that Christians lived longer than their pagan neighbors—which is the best single summary measure of a superior quality of life. The benefits of Christianity were *tangible.* They also were regarded as *exclusive* to the community of the faithful and as *contingent.* God did not bless unbelievers or reprobates. One must *earn* one's blessings, including salvation.

I have mentioned that doctrines also differ in terms of *plausibility:* some simply are more believable than others. Of importance here is that doctrines will be better able to retain their plausibility to the extent that they are *nonempirical* and thereby impervious to empirical falsification. The chronic weakness of magic lies in its need to produce results here and now, and when they do not appear, that can be seen. Religion need not commit itself to such risks and is more durable when it does not.

Finally, doctrines can only be effective to the extent that they can claim to be *authoritative.* Where did they come from? On what grounds are they to be regarded as true? What distinguishes religious doctrines from nonreligious doctrines? The core of any system of religious doctrine is *a general account of existence predicated on a description of the supernatural.* Hence, the authority of a religious doctrinal system is a function of the *characteristics* attributed to the supernatural. As noted in chapter 1, chief among these is whether the supernatural is conceived of as an *unconscious essence* such as the Tao or Paul Tillich's "Ground of Being," or as a *conscious being*, a God. This distinction is the basis for distinguishing religions as to whether they are *revealed* or *natural*. That is, some religions derive from truths "discerned within the natural order," whereas revealed religion "comes from a source other than that of the human recipient, usually God (Bowker 1997, 814). Consequently, there is an immense difference in the *authority* attributed to various systems of religious doctrines—a matter central to chapters 6 and 7.

Conclusion

Not content to "discover" that material interests and factors always underlie everything that would appear to be caused by religion, social scientists also have tried to define the Gods as creatures of economic or social forces. Emile Durkheim, of course, taught that "god . . . can be nothing else than [society] itself, personified and represented to the imagination" ([1912] 1995, 206). Guy Swanson (1960, 16) interpreted Durkheim as proposing that humans "develop a concept of personified supernatural beings directly from the model which their society provides." And Ralph Underhill (1975, 860) concluded: "God, I suggest, is a 'representative of the forces of history.' He is a reflection of existing economic and social relationships."

But it was Ebenezer Scrooge who finally got it right: "Bah humbug."

3

Upper-Class Asceticism

In 1073 Everard II, viscount of Breteuil, deeded all of his lands to relatives, gave all of his gold and silver to the poor, and then went on a pilgrimage to the Holy Land—as did thousands of Europeans every year. Upon his return he entered the abbey of Marmoutier, where he spent the rest of his life (Riley-Smith 1997, 47). Everard's peers and family did not see anything particularly odd about his choices: many members of the medieval upper classes, including kings and queens, opted for the ascetic life, often within the framework of the Catholic Church, but often, too, by joining the ranks of an austere sectarian movement.

The usual basis for these actions was to ensure salvation. Some became ascetics as penance for what they believed to have been their mortal sins—many who journeyed to the Holy Land had committed murders or other heinous crimes and had been advised by their confessors that only by praying in the holiest sites could they escape endless centuries in purgatory (Payne 1984; Riley-Smith 1997; Runciman 1951). But most embraced austerity and "holy poverty" because they believed that wealth and worldly pleasures were intrinsically sinful. The New Testament says as much when it suggests that it would be easier for a camel to pass through the eye of a needle than for a rich man to squeeze into heaven.

Unfortunately, the prevalence of upper-class asceticism has been ignored by social scientists. When Karl Marx ([1844] 1964, 42) wrote that "religion is the sigh of the oppressed creature . . . the opium of the people," he merely gave poetic expression to the sociological axiom that faith

A version of this chapter appeared as "Upper Class Asceticism: Social Origins of Ascetic Movements and Medieval Saints," *Review of Religious Research* 45 (2003) 5–19.

is rooted in want and misery and therefore that piety is most prevalent among the poor. Until recently, this view has enjoyed virtually unanimous assent among social scientists. Georg Simmel ([1905] 1959, 32) pronounced religion "a sedative," and Kingsley Davis (1949, 532) explained that the "greater his disappointment in this life, the greater [a person's] faith in the next." This view came to be known as the "deprivation thesis" when Charles Y. Glock (1964) constructed a typology of deprivations and connected a modal religious response to each type.

The fundamental mechanism said to account for the piety of the poor is referred to as the *transvaluation of values*—the capacity of religion to turn "worldly" values upside down. Hence, the have-nots redefine poverty as a virtue and wealth as sinful, concluding that what they cannot have they should not have, and that through these means "the last shall be first, and the first last."

The claim that religiousness is rooted in deprivation dominates the textbooks, even though in recent decades it has suffered from an acute lack of consistent empirical support. With the advent of survey research, a long series of investigators have reported the lower classes to be conspicuously absent from the pews on Sunday mornings and from church membership rolls (Bultina 1949; Burchinal 1959; Cantril 1943; Demerath 1965; Dynes 1955; Lenski 1953; Stark 1964, 1971). This is true even among "evangelical" and "fundamentalist" Protestants—members of these groups are as likely to have gone to college and to earn high incomes as are members of more liberal Protestant denominations or Roman Catholics, whereas the unchurched are the least educated and have the lowest incomes (Smith 1998; Roof and McKinney 1987). Even very strict sects such as the Jehovah's Witnesses include many people of privilege and enroll far fewer low-status people than their percentage in the population (Stark and Iannaccone 1997). This led me to suggest in an early paper that "if the poor are drawing compensation from religion, they are obviously doing so without benefit of clergy" (1971, 484).

In a celebrated attempt to repair this shortcoming of the deprivation thesis, N. J. Demerath III (1965) found that *within* denominations (among those who are official church members), lower-status persons were a bit more likely to hold a "sectlike orientation," that is, to hold more literal beliefs and to be more expressive in their religious actions. I subsequently confirmed and extended these results (Stark 1964, 1971). Even so, the demonstrated class effects on religiousness are very small within the churches and quite unreliable in general populations (Stark and Finke 2000). The most that can be said is that the empirical basis for the deprivation thesis is meager and amounts to little more than a very modest tendency for less educated people to be less "sophisticated" in their religious outlook.

Of course, it can be argued that surveys are blunt instruments that fail to reveal the religious intensity that is fundamental to the deprivation thesis. What are mere attitudes and verbal agreement with conventional statements of faith, compared with the stuff of *real* religious life? Hence, to discover the effects of deprivation it may be necessary to examine the eruption of sect movements and the appeal of asceticism.

As to the eruption of sects, Friedrich Engels claimed that Christianity began as "the religion of slaves, of poor people . . . of peoples subjugated or dispersed by Rome" (1894–95, 4), and Ernst Troeltsch ([1912] 1931) expanded that claim to assert that *all sect movements* are the product of the lower classes. Subsequently, H. Richard Niebuhr (1929) made the proletarian origins of sects the primary pivot in his famous "church-sect" theory. Nevertheless, it's not so. For example, early Christianity was based primarily on the privileged, not the poor (Grant 1977; Judge 1960; Stark 1996a). And early Christianity was not unusual in this respect. With the exception of some Anabaptist groups (that were led by the privileged but which appear to have been sustained mainly by the urban middle and lower classes), over the course of European history, the major sect movements were very obviously based on persons of considerable wealth and power: the nobility, the clergy, and well-to-do urbanites (Costen 1997; Lambert 1992, 1998; Russell 1965; Stark 2003). For example, at the outbreak of the first French War of Religion in 1562, it is estimated that 50 percent of the French nobility had embraced Calvinism (Tracy 1999), but very few peasants or urban poor rallied to the Huguenots (Ladurie 1974). And as demonstrated in chapter 2, it was not, as has been claimed, landless second sons and knights without property who sustained the early Crusades, but it was the heads of great households—kings, counts, earls, and barons—who led the way, at enormous personal cost.

Thus, the case that religiousness is rooted in deprivation is not supported by statistics on church attendance or membership and is not confirmed by participation in major sect movements or the Crusades. But what about *asceticism?* What about those who embrace lives of pious sacrifice and privation? Surely ascetics are not overrecruited from among the privileged. But I mean to demonstrate in this chapter precisely that they are. I draw on an array of historical materials and conclude with an analysis of a data set consisting of medieval Catholic saints.

Asceticism: Choice or Necessity

Although social scientists have sneered at asceticism as a transparent effort to make a virtue of necessity, historians often discus asceticism in terms of choice (Costen 1997; Lambert 1992, 1998; Russell 1965). This may reflect the tendency of historians to be very attuned to actual cases; and, as will be seen, these tend to reveal that the emphasis placed on poverty by ascetics is not a rationalization for being poor but a call to actively embrace "holy poverty" and to reject worldly comforts. Indeed, it is the opportunity to *choose* poverty—a choice not given to the poor—that seems central to the appeal of asceticism. Fasting seems not to appeal to people who have often been hungry, and privation in general fails to attract the poor. In contrast, it is frequently observed that wealth fails to satisfy many of those born into privilege, and therefore they turn to various religious or even radical political alternatives. I shall leave it to others to probe more deeply into the psychology involved in this phenomenon, restricting my efforts to demonstrating that it is such a common response to privilege that asceticism may well be primarily an upper-class involvement.

Historical Examples

In this section I examine historical cases of ascetic movements for which reasonably reliable class data are available.

BUDDHISM

The oldest reliable data available on recruitment to the ascetic life come from the founding of Buddhism in the fifth century B.C.E. Buddha himself was, of course, a prince prior to his "enlightenment," whereupon he embraced the life of a wandering ascetic. Of far greater importance is that of his first sixty devotees, fifty-five were "of prominent families," and the other five may well have been from privileged backgrounds too. Moreover, the primary appeal of early Buddhism was to Brahman priests (*brahmanas*), who were necessarily of upper-caste origins (Lester 1993, 867). As Buddhism spread to China, there was a similar pattern of upper-class recruitment to the ascetic life. Eric Zürcher (1972, 4–6) referred to this as "gentry Buddhism," because it involved "the formation of a wholly new type of Chinese intellectual *élite,* consisting of cultured monks."

ORPHICS AND PYTHAGOREANS

Even within the permissive Greek religious culture, asceticism found a substantial following. Two of the better-known Greek ascetic movements were the followers of Orpheus and of Pythagoras. Both groups appeared in the sixth century B.C.E., and both taught that one must observe stringent ascetic demands in this life in order to avoid terrible punishments in the life to come (Burkert 1985; James 1960). Thus, "as one rises or goes to bed, puts on shoes or cuts one's nails, rakes the fire, puts on a pot or eats, there is always a rule to be observed, something wrong to be avoided" (Burkert 1985, 303). Orphics ate no meat, eggs, or beans and drank no wine. Suicide was prohibited, and so were various forms of sexual expression—most embraced celibacy. Some even became wandering beggars. Pythagorean asceticism was quite similar. Pythagoreans too observed extensive dietary laws, and they wore only white garments, obeyed elaborate rules concerning ordinary daily activities (including an absolute prohibition on speaking in the dark), and accepted many restrictions on sexual activities.

As with the early Buddhists, the Orphics and the Pythagoreans were not poor folks making a virtue of necessity but rich folks choosing to be virtuous. Thus, Plato wrote in the *Republic* that priests of these religions "come to the doors of the rich and . . . offer them a bundle of books" that persuade them to sacrifice in order to escape "from evil in the afterlife" (Burkert 1985, 296). Euripides also linked Orphics and books. As Burkert noted, this "characteristic appeal to books" (297) reveals these to have been movements of the literate in an era when only a very small number of the most privileged Greeks could read (Harris 1989).

ESSENES

The Essenes were an ascetic Jewish group, active during the period of the Second Temple. Members lived communally in accord with a very strict interpretation of Jewish law. It may have been Essenes who lived at Qumran and whose hidden library became the Dead Sea Scrolls.

Many scholars have assumed that the Essenes embodied proletarian

Upper-Class Asceticism   47

protest and alienation (Cohen 1987; Niebuhr 1929; Saldarini 1988). Not so! As Albert Baumgarten (1997, 51) has convincingly demonstrated, the Essenes "were not lower class dissidents, shunned by the ruling powers" but were recruited from among the privileged. For one thing, the terms of admission to the group "make it clear that new members were expected to have some property which they would commingle with that of the community." For another, the Essenes produced unusually sophisticated and complex scriptures and commentaries, obviously written by and for an intellectual elite. Thus, Baumgarten concluded that the Essenes were firmly rooted in the "economic, social and educational elite . . . who could afford the 'luxury' of indulgence in affairs of the spirit" (47).

CATHARS

The Cathars were the first mass heretical movement of the Middle Ages. They appeared in various places in Europe but were concentrated in the Languedoc area of southern France, where they came to be known as Albigensians because they were headquartered in Albi. The Cathars embraced a nearly symmetrical dualism, dividing the universe into realms of Good and Evil. Since the world is tragic, brutal, and wicked, it could not have been created by the Good God. Having been created by the Evil God, it is entirely evil. Hence the world is to be rejected. Although rank-and-file Cathars were not ascetics, the movement sustained an advanced degree of membership called the *perfecti* (perfects). The *perfecti* attempted heroic levels of asceticism. They lived in cloisters; abstained from sex; refused to fight or kill (even animals); ate no meat, eggs, or dairy products; swore no oaths; and devoted most of their day to prayer.

Who were the *perfecti*? A complete list has survived of all 1,190 persons who advanced to become *perfecti* in the Languedoc during a sixty-year period ending in 1250. Of these, 15 percent were members of the nobility (Costen 1997), at least six times the percentage of nobles in the population (Lenski 1966). Most of the others probably were from affluent families, since it was often noted at the time that there was "widespread support for Catharism . . . among people in authority" (Costen 1997, 70).

WALDENSIANS

The Waldensians began as a heretical ascetic movement and also had their center in southern France (Brooke 1971; Cameron 1984; Lambert

Exploring the Religious Life

1992; Moore 1994; Russell 1965; Tourn 1989). They were named for their founder, a very rich merchant named Waldo (or Valdes), who lived in Lyons, a city just north of the Languedoc. In 1176, inspired by hearing the life story of Saint Alexius (an heir to riches who chose poverty), Waldo gave away all his property—he actually threw substantial sums of money away in the streets—and began to preach a message of apostolic poverty. Waldo rapidly attracted followers who called themselves the Poor Men of Lyons and adopted his ascetic lifestyle. Those who joined "are described as giving up their goods and bestowing them on the poor, a fact which shows they were of some substance" (Lambert 1992, 69). Indeed, as the movement spread north, a significant number of members of the lesser nobility were among the Waldensians in Metz, and "Waldensians in Germany gained the support of the comparatively wealthy" (149; also see 170).

Many scholars, perhaps possessed of excessive sociological imaginations, have claimed that the Cathars and the Waldensians were not really about doctrines or moral concerns. Instead, they argue, the religious aspects of these movements masked their real basis, which was "class conflict." Friedrich Engels set the example followed by many others when he dismissed the religious aspects of these clashes as "the illusions of that epoch" and claimed that the "interests, requirements, and demands of the various classes were concealed behind a religious screen" (in Marx and Engels 1964, 98). Getting down to cases, Engels classified the Cathars (Albigensians) as representing the interests of the town bourgeoisie against the feudal elites of Church and state, while dismissing the Waldensians as a purely "reactionary . . . attempt at stemming the tide of history" by "patriarchal Alpine shepherds against the feudalism advancing upon them" (99–100).

Only the uninformed could conceive of Catharism as being a reaction by townspeople against the feudal elites of Church and state, for it was these elites who made up the backbone of the movement. It is equally absurd to reduce the Waldensians to Alpine shepherds, patriarchal or otherwise. They began as an urban movement, very obviously overrecruited from among people of rank and privilege, and so they continued.

Attributing the major medieval religious movements to poor peasants or proletarian townsfolk flies in the face of clear evidence of the substantial overinvolvement of the wealthy and privileged in most, if not all, of them. Moreover, even if it could be shown that the majority of followers in these movements were poor peasants, that carries little force when we recognize that *nearly everyone* in medieval Europe was a poor peasant. It also is essential to see that the emphasis placed on the virtues of poverty by so many of these groups was not a rationalization for *being* poor but was a call to *become* poor as the means of overcoming worldliness (Russell 1965).

Of course, many who chose poverty did not do so by joining the Cathars, the Waldensians, or any other sect movement. Large numbers found their ascetic opportunity within the Church. In fact, this was so common that the result was the existence of what amounted to two Catholic Churches.

Two Churches

From early times, there were two major religious elements or "churches" in Christendom (Stark 2001). The first of these, which I have designated as the *Church of Power*, was by far the largest and consisted of most of the official Roman Catholic hierarchy, from parish clergy through popes, and the masses of nominal Catholics. The hierarchy of the Church of Power was dominated by the rich and powerful, because throughout the medieval era men often became cardinals, bishops, or even popes by paying huge sums for the offices. Church offices were so highly valued because of the power and income that came from these positions. The result was a church dominated by worldly, ambitious, and sometimes flagrantly immoral incumbents (Duffy 1992, 1997; Fletcher 1997; Murray, 1972). As for the laity, in many areas they were at best "slightly" Christianized. Most would have professed their belief in Jesus, but as part of a supernatural pantheon including all manner of spirits and godlings. Even in areas where Christianization had taken firmer root, the laity seldom attended Mass and treated religion primarily as a kind of magic (Duffy 1992; Murray 1972; Stark 1999; Thomas 1971).

Of course, there also were devout Christians in medieval times, and they constituted a second, if far smaller, element that I designate as the *Church of Piety* (Stark 2001). The power base of the Church of Piety lay in the religious orders—the tens of thousands of monks and nuns whose monasteries and convents dotted the landscape of medieval Europe. Of course, many of those in religious orders failed to measure up to their vows, just as many of the "secular" hierarchy were quite devout. But the relative sacrifices involved tended to sort people into these two camps. Many historians believe that the Church of Piety also was recruited mainly from the upper classes (Hickey 1987; Johnson 1976; King 1999; Knowles 1969; Mayr-Harting 1993). The available evidence offered in support of this generalization is largely impressionistic. Therefore, it seems useful to have hard data on the social origins of members of the Church of Piety based on a large number of cases.

Social Origins of Ascetic Saints, 500–1500

It would be ideal to possess biographical rosters for the medieval religious orders, but nothing of the sort exists or can be reconstructed. However, the "lives" of the many Roman Catholic saints would seem to be a satisfactory substitute, with certain restrictions.

As far as I could determine, there have been two previous quantitative studies based on selections of Catholic saints. In 1950 Pitirim A. Sorokin analyzed a few variables based on all 3,090 cases included in Butler's *Lives of the Saints,* as edited by Herbert Thurston (1926). The earliest of these saints lived in the first century, and the data set ended with one saint from the twentieth century.[1] As will be seen, when comparisons are possible, my results correspond closely to Sorokin's. However, for reasons that I will explain, I have greatly reduced the time span to be examined and have limited the cases to ascetics.

The second data set of saints was created by Donald Weinstein and Rudolph Bell (1986). They selected 864 saints from the period 1000 through 1700 by taking a 50 percent sample from a list assembled by Pierre Delooz (1962). This list has some very odd properties, the most unusual being that groups of martyrs, such as the 7 founders of the Servite order or the 205 martyrs of Japan, were grouped to constitute one case—how one meaningfully codes the gender, age, or family background of 205 individuals to form a single case escapes me. But here, too, the possible comparisons support my results.

Whatever criteria one chooses to impose, it is a formidable task to assemble even a reliable roster of the saints. Since the practice of official canonization began in 1234, there have been fewer than three hundred persons confirmed as saints. That list can be found in many places, including each year's *Catholic Almanac.* However, there are about ten thousand saints whose names and cults have been identified by Church historians (Woodward 1996) and thousands more, most of whose names are lost, who died as members of groups sainted for their martyrdom. The published sources are quite incomplete, which means that assembling a roster is a lengthy and tedious task of comparing entries in many sources. In addition, some saints are remembered under five or six different names, whereas many others have the same name. Worse yet, many saints are merely names—virtually nothing is known of their lives or even why they were thought to be saints. Some long-venerated saints probably never existed. Moreover, as noted, many are recognized as saints merely for having been among those martyred in various persecutions, some of them young children. "[T]he Roman Martyrology contains some 4,500 names, and it is far from exhaustive" (Attwater and John 1995, 5). Consequently, I excluded from the data set many of those included on various lists of saints, based on the following criteria.

First, I excluded all whose existence is doubtful or whose identity is so obscure that virtually nothing is known about them. Some are remembered merely for having been a bishop, an abbot, or an abbess, with no biographical information whatsoever having survived. Often they were made into saints because of the discovery centuries after their deaths that their remains were well preserved, or because their bones were discovered and utilized as "relics," whereupon several miracles were attributed to them. In many such cases, only their names are known.

Second, I did not include persons merely for having been martyred, which often amounted to nothing more than having been murdered, sometimes for being a Christian but often for being in the wrong place, as when Viking raiders struck a convent. Third, I excluded all children (most of whom would also have been excluded for merely having been martyrs). Fourth, for arbitrary reasons of taste, I excluded all persons whose claim to sainthood rested entirely on scholarly achievements—a bias shared by the Church in recent centuries (Woodward 1996). Fifth, I excluded all popes.

After spending several months assembling materials, I decided to restrict the roster to those who lived between 500 and 1500. Earlier than 500 one is confronted with too much mythology and missing data. After 1500 there are few saints, and besides, the medieval era was clearly over. Finally, I included only *ascetic* saints—those who expressed their piety through denial and sacrifice. Even among the saints there are many members of the Church of Power, especially bishops, and their sainthood sometimes seems to have been due to nothing more than the desire to assign a patron saint to a locality or a cathedral; others appear to have been honored solely for their contributions to Church politics and their roles as advisers to kings—their biographies make no mention of unusual piety. I excluded all who appear to have been members of the Church of Power (whether or not they were in orders) and selected only those who made serious lifestyle sacrifices, nearly all of them (including bishops) having belonged to religious orders. After these exclusions, the data set includes 483 individuals.

I did all of the coding myself.[2] As will be clear, the variables I coded do not require subtle judgments. Nevertheless, to minimize error I coded all of the cases and entered the data into a computer file and then repeated the entire process after a lapse of three months. Using a re-key verification function during the reentry of the data, I was able to note any discrepancy and then check to see whether it was due to a coding or an entry error. I found only eleven coding discrepancies out of 4,347 entries. However, many readers will be more concerned about the reliability of the sources than about the accuracy of my coding. With the exception of Alvan Butler's extraordinary twelve-volume classic, published from 1756 to 1759, I have used modern sources (Attwater and Cumming 1994; Attwater and John 1995; Baring-Gould 1914; Bunson, Bunson, and Bunson 1998; Charles 1887; Coulson 1958; Cross and Livingston 1974; Delehaye 1998; Farmer 1997; Herbermann et al. 1913; McBrien 2001). I also made use of the *Saints Index,* maintained by *Catholic Online.* Each of these, though, is largely dependent on biographical accounts written many centuries ago, often immediately following the saint's death. These hagiographies are sometimes dismissed as fiction because they include "implausible" claims as to miracles or endurance. Although some similar claims concerning quite recent saints have stood the test of careful enquiry, it is not necessary for me to enter into such a debate. The variables I coded are relatively mundane matters of fact:

Sex
Century: In what century did the saint live the majority of her or his adult life?
Family background: Royalty, nobility, wealthy, lower, unknown.
Saintly kin: Was an immediate family member (first cousin or closer) also reported to be a saint?
Church office: Cardinal/bishop, abbot/abbess, monk/nun, priest, lay person.
Order: Member of a religious order.
Extreme ascetic: Displayed an unusually high level of asceticism.
Hermit or recluse: Spent some period of time as a hermit or recluse.

Mystic: Was reported to have visions, revelations, stigmata, and so forth, or to make prophecies.

These are nine characteristics that seem likely to have been reported quite accurately (Kieckhefer 1984). Further evidence of the reliability of the data can be found in the stability and credibility of the statistical results.

Table 3.1 shows the frequency of four aspects of asceticism. First of all, nearly nine out of ten of these saints were members of religious orders, including 71.1 percent of the bishops (not shown). Second, although everyone included in the data set was a legitimate ascetic, more than a third (37.9%) of these saints were coded as *extremely* ascetic. These were people who made heroic efforts to overcome temptation and mortify their flesh (Kieckhefer 1984). Some wore hair shirts. Others lived on bread and water. Still others devoted most of their waking hours to prayer. One of the most common forms of extreme asceticism was to limit human contact by becoming hermits or recluses. To gain solitude, hermits typically withdrew into the forest or the desert. Recluses achieved solitude by confining themselves in huts or cells (usually in or near a monastery or convent). In many instances, recluses actually had their cells walled off, and they received food through a small opening.

As can be seen, one of four of these ascetic saints spent a considerable period as a hermit or a recluse. Lest it be thought that hermits and recluses were drawn mainly from among the ranks of socially maladjusted misanthropes or even the mentally ill, as is often claimed (see James [1902] 1958), note that nearly 20 percent of those coded as hermits or recluses subsequently were called from their forests and cells to serve quite successfully as bishops, abbots, and abbesses. For example, Saint Aigulf lived for many years as a hermit near Bourges, France, before being called upon to serve as bishop of that city. He subsequently played a leading part in several Church councils. Many other hermits and recluses were asked to take such administrative posts but managed to beg off. Still others wrote lucid works of scholarship or fine poetry. Clearly, then, in this era choosing solitude mainly reflected religious motives, not maladjustment: solitude not only was regarded as a way to avoid worldly distractions but was adopted as a *sacrifice.*

Finally, and perhaps surprisingly given that these are ascetic medieval saints, they were not often given to mysticism: this figure is only 11.4 percent. Indeed, from my reading I gained the impression that mysticism

Table 3.1 Aspects of Saintly Asceticism (in Percent)

In a religious order	87.8
Extremely ascetic	37.9
Hermit or recluse	25.1
Mystic	11.4
N = 483	

Table 3.2 Gender and Aspects of Asceticism

	Males (337) (%)	Females (146) (%)
In a religious order	84.9	94.5*
Extremely ascetic	39.8	33.6
Hermit or recluse	28.2	17.8*
Mystic	8.3	18.5*

*$p < .01$.

became more common among saints in more recent times, even though the Church always was, and still is, ambivalent about mystics in general (Woodward 1996).

These aspects of asceticism are related to gender in rather interesting ways, as can be seen in table 3.2. Nearly a third (30.2%) of these saints were women. The fact that nearly all of the women belonged to orders merely reflects that there was no other religious role available to them within the Church (those female saints not in orders remained lay persons), whereas many bishops and most priests did not belong to an order. This explains why Sorokin found that only 17 percent of saints were women.[3] He included nonascetic saints, and they were overwhelmingly members of the clergy and thus male. The same applies to Weinstein and Bell's finding that only 18 percent of their list of saints were women.

Overall, men and women were about equally likely to have been classified as extreme ascetics—the modest difference is not statistically significant. However, men were quite significantly more likely to have been hermits or recluses, whereas women were more than twice as likely as men to have been mystics.

Table 3.3 demonstrates that ascetic medieval saints were overwhelmingly from the upper classes. Overall, one in five (two of five among women)[4] came from a royal family: they were kings, queens, princes, and princesses. An additional half (53.0%) were of the nobility: dukes, counts,

Table 3.3 Gender and Family Background

Family Background	Males (%)	Females (%)	Total (%)
Royalty	13.1	42.5	21.9
Nobility	55.2	47.9	53.0
Wealthy	17.2	5.5	13.7
Lower	5.3	3.4	4.8
Unknown	9.2	0.7	6.6
	100.0	100.0	100.0

$p < .000$.

Table 3.4 Family Background and Asceticism

	Royal (106) (%)	Nobility (256) (%)	Wealthy (66) (%)	Lower (23) (%)
In a religious order	96.2	85.2	87.9	78.3*
Extremely ascetic	35.8	34.0	53.0	34.8
Hermit or recluse	20.8	23.0	33.3	21.7
Mystic	6.6	10.2	10.6	39.1*
Another saint in the immediate family	30.2	18.0	4.5	0.0**

$*p < .01$. $**p < .001$.

barons, and earls, or their spouses or children. Hence, three-fourths of these ascetics were from the ranks of the extremely privileged. Of the remainder, the majority were from untitled families of wealth. Only one of twenty came from the lower classes, about the same number as those whose family background is unknown. These findings correspond rather closely to those reported by Sorokin, if one omits the 1,280 cases in his set whose family background was unknown. He reported that 62 percent were from royal or noble backgrounds and most of the rest were from well-to-do families. Weinstein and Bell reported that 51 percent of their saints were from the nobility, 37 percent from well-to-do families, and 12 percent from peasant backgrounds. The modest difference between their findings and mine can be attributed to the fact that their saints are from a later era (1000–1700), wherein the nobility (especially royalty) made up a smaller percentage of the population of Europe while the proportion of untitled, wealthy families had expanded substantially.

Table 3.4 shows that family background is significantly related to being

Exploring the Religious Life

a member of a religious order: 96.2 percent of the royalty compared with 78.3 percent of those from the lower classes. However, family background is not significantly related to being either an extreme ascetic or a hermit. The nobility were as likely to be so classified as those of lower origins—the slightly higher percentages for the wealthy are statistically meaningless. However, mysticism is significantly correlated with family background, saints from lower-class homes being more likely to be mystics. This held for both males and females. I suspect that this correlation was the result of differential selection factors rather than reflecting a greater affinity for mysticism among the poor. That is, people of lower-class origins probably had a somewhat lower probability of being noticed simply for their asceticism—it took something as dramatic as visions and prophecies to gain them sufficient notice to become a saint. This interpretation is encouraged by the fact that saints of lower-class backgrounds were less than half as likely as those born into privilege to have held higher religious office—52 percent of lower-class saints were simple monks or nuns, and nearly one of five was a lay person (not shown).

The last line in table 3.4 shows that sainthood tended to run in families. Nearly one in five (18.0%) had an immediate family member who also was a saint—sibling saints were especially common. However, saintly kinship was highly concentrated among the privileged; no one from the lower classes had another saint in the family.

In summary, medieval ascetic saints were overwhelmingly of upper-class origins. This does not mean, of course, that the lower classes did not produce ascetics too, nor does it even demonstrate that the upper classes were more given to asceticism—although I think they were. What is fully demonstrated by these data on saints is that asceticism had a substantial appeal to the medieval upper classes.

Conclusion

The list of recent saints includes none of royal origins and few from the nobility. That probably reflects nothing more than the virtual disappearance of monarchies and the rapid decline in the number of titled families in Christendom. However, the fact that many recent saints have come from the lower classes is only partly due to more open stratification systems in Christian nations. It is mainly the result of special efforts by the Church to canonize persons who rose from poverty, particularly if they remained among the laity, and especially if they lived in less developed nations (Woodward 1996). During this same period, there also has been a marked decline in asceticism, not only among saints, but in Western religious circles more generally. Whether these shifts are related is uncertain. What is certain is that despite these shifts, a substantial number of nineteenth- and twentieth-century saints (all of them women) still came from privileged backgrounds, including Jane-Elizabeth Bichier des Ages, Katherine Drexel, Juaquina de Vedruna de Mas, Elizabeth Ann Seton, Emily de Vialar, Vicenta Maria Lopez y Vicuna, and "saint-in-the-making" Mother Teresa.

As noted, to refute the deprivation thesis it is not necessary to show that asceticism, or other forms of religiousness, are especially upper-class phenomena. It is sufficient to show that class is of little or no significance. However, I incline to the view that the ascetic impulse *is* more prevalent among persons of privilege, sometimes reflecting guilt about having wealth, but more often stemming from the discovery that wealth is not fulfilling. Andrew Greeley pointed out to me that "it was only the nobility who had the time and opportunity to become saints," because the peasants were too busy trying to scratch out a living. Exactly! Hungry peasants are starving, not fasting. Deprivation is asceticism only when it is voluntary, and that does tend to limit it to those with the privilege, even the burden, of choice. As Robert William Fogel (2000, 2) explained, "throughout history . . . freed of the need to work in order to satisfy their material needs, [the rich] have sought self-realization."

Today, of course, upper-class self-realization rarely takes the form of true asceticism, since organized asceticism has largely disappeared, as has, indeed, a true upper class—wealth and celebrity being only pale analogues of aristocracy. Nevertheless, the search for self-realization remains. One current analogue to upper-class medieval asceticism can be found in leftist politics; hence the extreme overrepresentation of the sons and daughters of wealth in the ranks of American radical activists, especially during the 1960s (McAdam 1988; Sherkat and Blocker 1994). This interpretation is supported by the remarkable proportion of these same activists who subsequently joined high-intensity religious movements (Kent 2001). In similar fashion, the membership of the British Fabian Society during the late nineteenth century was made up of privileged intellectuals who in an earlier era might well have taken holy vows and many of whom eventually became deeply involved in Spiritualism (Barrow 1980; MacKenzie and MacKenzie 1977; Nelson 1969). Another analogue is participation in what might be called therapeutic spirituality centers such as Esalen and

Naropa, which have been funded and patronized by the rich (by Laurance Rockefeller, for one) and by their sons and daughters (Fuller 2001; Roof 1999; Taylor 1999). The "monks" at San Francisco's celebrated Zen Center, which flourished during the 1960s and 1970s, were overwhelmingly from wealthy families who supported them with regular checks or trust funds. As one of the leaders explained, "[n]aturally, the link [by which Zen came] into America was through the aristocracy and the nouveau riche" (Downing 2001, 108).

Thus, Marx might better have said that "religion often is the opium of the dissatisfied upper classes, the sigh of wealthy creatures depressed by materialism." But of course, given his preoccupation with money, Marx couldn't conceive of such a thing.

❋4❋

Faith & Gender

With ALAN S. MILLER

So far as is known, throughout recorded history religious movements have recruited women far more successfully than men, except for those that excluded women from membership. For example, Greek and Roman writers routinely "portrayed women as particularly liable to succumb to the charms of [new religions]" (Beard, North, and Price 1998, 297). Thus, as the cult of Isis spread west from Egypt, it attracted a mainly female following, as did the cult of Dionysus (ibid.; Burkert 1987). Early Christianity was far more appealing to women than to men (Stark 1996a). The same gender difference marked the heretical movements of medieval times. The eighth-century self-styled saint Aldebert gathered huge throngs in northern France and founded many new congregations as "great numbers of women flocked to him and formed the nucleus of his cult" (Russell 1965, 103). Although men dominated the positions of leadership, women dominated the rank and file among the Cathars and the Waldensians, and among "free spirit" groups, the female Beguines greatly outnumbered their Beghard male counterparts (Anderson and Zinsser 1989; Crawford 1993; Lambert 1998, 1992; Russell 1965).

In more recent times the data are far more trustworthy, and the same

A portion of this chapter appeared as "Physiology and Faith: Addressing the 'Universal' Gender Difference in Religiousness," *Journal for the Scientific Study of Religion* 41 (2002): 495–507. Another portion appeared as Alan S. Miller and Rodney Stark," Gender and Religiousness: Can Socialization Explanations Be Saved?" *American Journal of Sociology* 107 (2002): 1399–423.

pattern holds. According to American census reports from the late nineteenth and early twentieth centuries, women far outnumbered men among the Shakers, the Swedenborgians, and the Spiritualists and in Christian Science, Theosophy, and the Vedanta Society (Stark and Bainbridge 1985, 1997). Even so, just as Shannon McSheffrey (1995) argued, it is incorrect to think that women are especially prone to join new or deviant religious movements. Women substantially outnumber men in *conventional* religious groups, too! That folklore has long classified religion as "women's work" is well supported by denominational yearbooks and available religious census data: in every sizable religious group in the Western world, women outnumber men, usually by a considerable margin. This is not due to the greater longevity of women; it is true from adolescence on.

These membership differences are supported by survey research findings. From very early days, American surveys conducted by the Gallup Poll often included items on religion and invariably found that women were more likely than men to belong to and attend church, to pray, to say religion was a very important part of their lives, to read the Bible, and to believe in life after death (see the many publications of the Princeton Religion Research Center, Inc.). Other studies revealed similar gender effects. Shortly after World War II, Roman Catholic women in Louisiana were found to be almost twice as likely as men to go to confession (Fichter 1952). Women also were found to be far more likely than men to go forward at Billy Graham's revivals (Colquhoun 1955). As the use of surveys spread to Europe and Latin America, these same substantial gender differences persisted (Argyle 1959; Beit-Hallahmi and Argyle 1997). By now it is so taken for granted that women are more religious than men that every competent quantitative study of religiousness routinely includes sex as a control variable.

Nevertheless, as Tony Walter and Grace Davie (1998, 640) recently pointed out, despite the huge and rapidly expanding social scientific literature on gender and religion, the most significant of all questions about this connection has been almost completely ignored: *Why* are women more religious than men? For example, in their fine article "Religious Consolation among Men and Women: Do Health Problems Spur Seeking?" Kenneth Ferraro and Jessica Kelley-Moore (2000, 232) included gender in their title and reported that "women are more likely than men to seek religious consolation," but they were silent as to why this might be. This neglect may occur because *everyone knows why:* that women are simply raised so as to be more open to religion. Perhaps. But as will be seen, what little research has been done does not offer much support to that claim. Thus, it is far past time that we seriously addressed the question.

Cross-Cultural Gender Differences

To begin, it will be useful to examine the extent and the cross-cultural scope of gender differences in religiousness by use of the World Values Surveys (WVS). These surveys are planned by an international committee of social scientists and then translated into local languages and conducted every few years by local polling organizations. The intent is to obtain fully comparable data from as many nations as possible, facilitating comparative research. The data are available to researchers from the various data archives.

Many years ago, after data were examined from elaborate sets of items concerning religious beliefs and actions, it was discovered that the best single measure of personal piety is simply to ask people how religious they are (Stark and Glock 1968). The English-language version of the WVS item is "Whether you go to church or not, would you say you are a religious person?" Table 4.1 compares men and women in forty-nine nations in terms of their answers to this question. In every instance, a higher percentage of women than men said they were religious persons. In all nations but Brazil, the differences were highly statistically significant. These results were fully replicated when based on other measures of religiousness (and these were significant in Brazil as well). The data in table 4.1 are primarily from 1995–96 surveys; data for some nations are from the 1991–92 surveys because the question was not asked in that country in 1995–96.

One may suppose that consistent cross-national gender differences of this magnitude on almost anything other than religiousness would have been the object of great interest and a lot of analysis. To the best of my knowledge, only on the commission of crime and delinquency are there comparable differences. Gender differences are virtually nonexistent in opinions about sex roles, for example. The primary reason that social scientists have ignored the gender differences in religiousness is probably because the majority of them have been mistakenly educated to believe that religion is of little interest, as it is soon to disappear. But that surely cannot explain why sociologists of religion have ignored gender effects, too.

Exploring the Religious Life

Table 4.1 Gender and Religiousness in the Christian World (Percent Who Say They Are "A Religious Person")

	Males	Females	Ratio of Females/Males
Europe			
Armenia (2000)[a]	58.4	73.9	1.27**
Austria (1281)	74.4	85.4	1.15**
Belarus (2092)	46.6	67.6	1.45**
Belgium (2483)	61.8	76.5	1.23**
Bosnia (1200)	62.3	71.0	1.14**
Bulgaria (1072)	37.9	57.0	1.50**
Croatia (1196)	67.2	74.8	1.11**
Czech Republic (1147)	34.3	46.7	1.36**
Denmark (965)	63.2	81.8	1.29**
Estonia (1021)	24.3	41.0	1.69**
Finland (987)	44.2	63.3	1.43**
France (950)	47.4	53.7	1.13**
Germany[b] (1017)	50.1	67.2	1.34**
Great Britain (1421)	49.6	64.1	1.29**
Hungary (645)	44.4	62.0	1.40**
Iceland (695)	66.0	83.5	1.27**
Ireland (987)	66.9	77.5	1.16**
Italy (1925)	78.8	89.4	1.14**
Latvia (1200)	49.5	69.1	1.40*
Lithuania (1009)	69.9	86.5	1.24**
Moldava (984)	74.7	84.7	1.13**
Netherlands (997)	53.1	66.8	1.26**
Norway (1127)	37.0	55.7	1.51**
Poland (1153)	88.0	93.3	1.06*
Portugal (1156)	65.1	83.5	1.28**
Romania (1239)	73.1	84.4	1.16**
Russia (2040)	45.8	67.9	1.48**
Serbia (1278)	52.3	59.0	1.13*
Slovakia (1095)	67.4	82.7	1.23**
Slovenia (946)	62.1	75.0	1.21**
Spain (1211)	57.4	76.8	1.34**
Sweden (1009)	25.0	38.1	1.52**
Switzerland (1212)	49.1	62.2	1.27**
Ukraine (2811)	46.7	65.6	1.41**
North America			
Canada (1682)	65.0	76.5	1.18**
Mexico (1488)	57.8	68.4	1.18**
United States (1502)	77.2	87.0	1.13**

(continued)

Table 4.1 *(continued)*

South America

Argentina (1054)	76.0	86.8	1.14**
Brazil (1149)	83.4	87.7	1.05
Chile (1000)	67.7	77.9	1.15**
Colombia (2996)	81.6	88.0	1.08**
Peru (1211)	74.5	79.8	1.07*
Puerto Rico (1143)	82.8	87.7	1.06*
Uruguay (1000)	40.7	61.0	1.49**
Venezuela (1178)	81.6	89.7	1.10**

Other

Australia (2013)	52.3	65.6	1.25**
New Zealand (1171)	42.6	52.5	1.23**
Philippines (1200)	80.0	87.2	1.09**
South Africa (2935)	75.7	86.8	1.15**

Source: World Values Surveys, 1991–92, 1995–97, Inter-University Consortium for Political and Social Research, Ann Arbor, Mich.
[a]( ) = number of cases
[b]West Germany and East Germany have been merged in proportion to their populations.
*$p < .050.$ **$p < .000.$

As with so much social science, the actual evidence of gender effects on religiousness has been limited to Western cultures—indeed, Walter and Davie (1998) explicitly limited their recent review of the literature to the "religiosity of women in the modern West." Consequently, much of the discussion has been concerned exclusively with Christianity. In this instance, however, that limitation is unnecessary and unproductive. As table 4.2 shows, substantial gender effects hold in non-Western societies as well. Since no similar data have been published before, I have not limited the table to the single item used in table 4.1 but have included other available items.

These data also are from the World Values Surveys conducted during 1995–97,[1] except for the Chinese data, which come from the 1991 survey. Unfortunately, some questions were omitted in some countries. In the instance at hand, I could not include Bangladesh and Pakistan in the Islamic group because many of the religion questions were not asked in their surveys and obvious coding problems mar the data for each. And I was forced to omit Nigeria because the codes provided indicate, quite

Exploring the Religious Life

absurdly, that there are more Jews (18.8%) and Eastern Orthodox Christians (22.5%) in Nigeria than Muslims (11.2%).

Turning to the table, four Asian nations make up the first group. In Japan, women are more likely to report religiousness than are men on all

Table 4.2 Gender and Religiousness in the Non-Christian World

	Males	Females	Ratio of Females/Males
Asia			
Japan (1054)[a]			
% who are "a religious person"	20.3	31.6	1.56**
% who "get comfort and strength from religion	29.4	39.5	1.34**
% who pray or meditate	84.8	89.6	1.06*
% who believe in an afterlife	38.6	56.3	1.46**
% who believe in God	48.4	66.3	1.37**
Taiwan (1452)			
% who are "a religious person"	70.1	76.8	1.10**
% who "get comfort and strength from religion	58.6	76.6	1.31**
% who believe in an afterlife	53.8	65.4	1.22**
% who say religion is important in their life	43.2	51.0	1.18**
% who believe in God	70.0	83.5	1.19**
China (1500)			
% who are "a religious person"	4.4	5.9	1.34*
% who pray or meditate	17.3	27.7	1.60**
% who say religion is important in their life	11.4	21.1	1.85**
South Korea (1249)			
% who say religion is important in their life	42.9	58.2	1.36**
% who belong to a religious organization	38.6	54.4	1.40**
India (2040)			
% who are "a religious person"	69.5	75.9	1.09**
% who "get comfort and strength from religion"	74.2	82.0	1.11**
% who pray or meditate	46.4	50.4	1.09**

(continued)

Table 4.2 *(continued)*

% who believe in an afterlife	38.9	48.4	1.24**
% who say religion is important in their life	76.3	82.0	1.08**
% who believe in God	91.6	95.9	1.04**

Islam

Albania (980)

% who are "a religious person"	35.5	51.5	1.45**
% who "get comfort and strength from religion	41.9	62.7	1.50**
% who believe in an afterlife	15.4	30.6	1.99**
% who say religion is important in their life	50.5	69.5	1.38**
% who believe in God	85.8	96.2	1.12**

Azerbaijan (2002)

% who are "a religious person"	81.0	86.3	1.07**
% who "get comfort and strength from religion	69.4	77.2	1.11**
% who believe in an afterlife	41.9	51.9	1.24**
% who say religion is important in their life	81.3	85.0	1.05*
% who believe in God	94.2	96.2	1.02*

Turkey (1907)

% who are "a religious person"	71.2	77.8	1.09**
% who "get comfort and strength from religion"	85.3	91.7	1.08*
% who believe in an afterlife	84.1	84.5	1.01
% who say religion is important in their life	89.0	92.6	1.04*
% who believe in God	95.5	98.9	1.03*

Source: World Values Surveys, 1991–92, 1995–97, Inter-University Consortium for Political and Social Research, Ann Arbor, Mich.

[a]( ) = number of cases

*p < .05. **p < .000.

five measures, and each difference is statistically significant. For example, while slightly fewer than half of the men in Japan say they believe in God, two-thirds of Japanese women believe. Similar differences exist in Taiwan—70 percent of Taiwanese men believe in God compared with about 84 percent of Taiwanese women.

Fewer measures of religiousness are available for China and South

Exploring the Religious Life

Korea, but in every instance women are significantly more religious than men. For example, whereas the Chinese are far less likely than the Koreans to say religion is important in their life, Chinese women are almost twice as likely as Chinese men to hold that view.

The second section of the table is based on the WVS survey of India. Although Indians in general are more religious than other Asians, here too women are more religious than men, and all the differences are statistically significant.

Finally, note the section on Islam. In Albania women are quite substantially more religious than men. The same holds in Azerbaijan. As for the five comparisons in Turkey, there is no sex difference on belief in life after death, but women are more religious than men on the remaining four items.

Thus, of 36 gender comparisons in non-Christian nations, women are significantly more religious on 35. It would, of course, be wonderful to have data on much less developed nations and on small, preliterate societies. However, the fact that data are available for most of the Western Hemisphere, all of Europe, and the major nations of Asia and that the gender effect holds in all of them suggests that what we are looking at is not limited but at least borders upon the universal.

The Search for Explanations

Despite the lack of attention given to gender differences in religious commitment, a number of explanations have been offered. Most of these are tautological, inconsistent with the evidence, or silly. In his much-admired study of the revivals that swept western New York during the nineteenth century, Whitney R. Cross attributed the greater "feminine susceptibility" to women's being "less educated, more superstitious, and more zealous than men" (1950, 178). Little did he know that gender differences in religiousness are as large or larger among the highly educated as among those with little or no schooling. As for superstition and zealousness, this is pure tautology, since Cross uses each as a synonym for religion.

The same can be said for explanations that attribute greater susceptibility to guilt feelings among women as the cause of their religiousness, since belief in sin is taken as a measure of guilt (Beit-Hallahmi and Argyle 1997). As for Freudian revelations that women turn to God because from childhood humans relate more closely to the opposite-sex parent, this is falsified by the lack of any credible evidence that children do relate more strongly to the opposite-sex parent and by the greater involvement of women than men in Goddess religions as well.

It also has been suggested that because many women do not work outside the home, they simply have more time to devote to religious activities (Azzi and Ehrenberg 1975; Iannaccone 1990; Luckmann 1967; Martin 1967), and it can be argued further that greater participation in religious groups also increases belief and private religious practice. This explanation fails because career women are as religious as housewives, and both are far more religious than their spouses or male peers (de Vaus and McAllister 1987; Cornwall 1988; Stark 1992a). Moreover, even among those who are equally active in church, women are more religious than men in other dimensions of faith. For example, using the 1998 General Social Survey, I calculated that among Americans who attended church once a month or more often, only 30 percent of men, compared with 47 percent of women, prayed more than once a day. Among those who never attended church, 6 percent of men and 14 percent of women prayed more than once a day.

Perhaps the most popular of all explanations proposes that women are socialized to be more religious than men. This takes many forms, but all of them involve discussions of women being raised to be more nurturant and submissive and then associating these traits with religious commitment (Mol 1985; Suziedalis and Potvin 1981). Indeed, it often is argued that religiousness is built into the role of mother (Walter and Davie 1998). However, research does not show that child-rearing is associated with greater female religiousness (de Vaus and McAllister 1987; Steggarda 1993). More generally, Marie Cornwall (1989) found that substantial gender differences in religiousness persist under a variety of controls for socialization.

The most compelling results in favor of the socialization explanation involved the use of a masculinity-femininity scale. Edward H. Thompson Jr. (1991) found that religiousness was associated with femininity *within* each gender. That is, feminine men and women were more religious than masculine men and women. These results strongly suggest that the basis for the gender and religiousness association lies deeply in gender per se. But Thompson had little to say about what that basis was or the reasons for what he found. An additional problem is that the findings are based on 385 New England undergraduates. However, Thompson's study soon prompted a spate of replications by Leslie J. Francis. All of these studies found substantial "femininity" effects that eliminated the effects of biological gender (Francis 1991, 1997; Francis et al. 2001; Francis and Wilcox 1996, 1998). But Francis also has been content to leave the fundamental source of these gender differences unexamined. Finally, using data on sexual partners included in the General Social Surveys, Darren Sherkat (2002) found that heterosexual females and homosexual males are far more religious than are heterosexual males or lesbian females.

Not only does the prior literature fail to sustain claims that differential socialization is the basis for the link between gender and religiousness, but furthermore, there is very little of that research, and two rather obvious hypotheses have not been tested.

Two New Socialization Hypotheses

If gender differences in religiousness are the result of differential socialization, then if sex-role socialization becomes less differentiated, the religious differences should decline too. From this it follows that *if* differential sex-role socialization has declined in the United States over the past generation, then *gender differences in religiousness should be smaller in the United States today than they were a generation ago.*

Table 4.3 is based on the General Social Surveys (GSS). Church attendance was the earliest item on religiousness asked by the GSS (in 1972, the first GSS conducted). There was a strong gender effect, but precisely the same effect exists in the 1998 survey. In 1973 the question on belief in life after death was asked for the first time. Women were more likely to believe. Twenty-five years later the gender difference is the same. When first asked in 1983, women were very much more likely than men to report frequent prayer. In 1998 the gender difference remains undiminished. The same lack of decline holds for denominational loyalty. These results fail to support the hypothesis.

Perhaps socialization has not changed sufficiently in a generation to show up in table 4.3. A second possibility is that those Americans who do not hold traditional sex-role attitudes may differ from those who do. In that case, *gender differences in religiousness will be significantly smaller among Americans with less traditional sex-role attitudes.*

Table 4.4 is based in the 1998 General Social Survey. Sex-role attitude was measured by the item "Most men are better suited emotionally for politics than are most women." Those who agreed were classified as traditionalists and those who disagreed, as liberals. The results show that, if

Table 4.3 Gender and Religiousness over a Generation (United States)

	Correlations (Gamma) with Gender	
	1972	1998
Church attendance	.19**	.18**
	1973	1998
Belief in life after death	.12*	.12**
	1974	1998
Denominational loyalty[a]	.19**	.17**
	1983	1998
Frequency of prayer	.37**	.33**

Source: General Social Surveys.
[a]Question: "Would you consider yourself a strong (Lutheran, Methodist, Catholic, etc.) or not very strong?"
*$p < .05$. **$p < .001$.

anything, the gender differences in religiousness are stronger among the liberals. Once again, results suggest that our hypothesis based on a traditional socialization argument must be rejected.

Of course, these results, like most others, are based only on the United States. In any one nation, the actual variations in socialization might be so limited that only the crudest and most extreme socialization effects can be detected. That is, the aspects of socialization that produce gender differences in religiousness may be too subtle to be adequately measured by the rather blunt research tools available to social science. Hence, until cross-cultural explorations of the possible socialization bases for the gender-religiousness relationship have been exhausted, it seems premature to count socialization out. Perhaps the socialization explanation still can be saved via cross-national research.

Testing the Role of Differential Socialization Cross-Nationally

The 1995–97 World Values Surveys (WVS) are based on national surveys conducted in fifty-four nations. The interviews asked similar questions in each nation, translated into the local language(s), although some items were omitted in some nations. Our first use of these data is to retest the second new hypothesis. Table 4.5 is based on more than seventy-three thousand respondents. Sex-role attitudes were measured by responses to the question "Do you think that a woman has to have children in order to be fulfilled or is this not necessary?" Traditionalists were those who

Exploring the Religious Life

responded that a woman needed children to be fulfilled; liberals were those who thought this was not necessary. Five measures of religiousness reveal very significant gender differences within both the traditionalist and liberal groups. As to magnitude, if anything there is a slight tendency for gender differences to be greater among the liberals. Once again this hypothesis is rejected.

If socialization is the basis for the gender differences, then the religious differences between women and men ought to be proportionate to the extent of differential socialization; hence, *the gender effects on religion ought to be greater in societies wherein more traditional sex roles prevail and women's primary roles tend to be limited to home and family than in societies where there is far greater gender equality.*

The dependent variable is the correlation (gamma) between gender and the percent who identified themselves as "a religious person." As shown in table 4.6, five measures of sex roles are available. The first of

Table 4.4 Gender, Religiousness, and Sex Role Attitudes (United States)

| | Correlations (Gamma) with Gender | |
	Traditionalists	Liberals
Frequencey of prayer	.34**	.42**
Belief in life after death	.11	.28**
Church attendance	.26**	.31**
Denominational loyalty	.24**	.26**
N =	(194)	(677)

Source: General Social Survey, 1998.
**$p < .001$.

Table 4.5 Gender, Religiousness and Sex Role Attitudes (World)

| | Correlations (Gamma) with Gender | |
	Traditionalists	Liberals
Belief in God	.28**	.32**
Belief in life after death	.16**	.23**
Belief humans have souls	.26**	.33**
Church attendance	.12**	.16**
"I am a religious person"	.23**	.25**
N =	45,534	27,906

Source: World Values Surveys, 1995–97, Inter-University Consortium for Political and Social Research, Ann Arbor, Mich.
**$p < .001$.

Table 4.6 Gender Effects and Sex Roles (55 Nations)

	Correlations (R) with the Strength of the Gender-Religiousness Correlations
Approval of single motherhood	.50**
Abortion rate	.42**
Fertility rate	−.46**
Percent of workforce that is female	.44**
Index of female empowerment	.40**

**p < .001.

these is the percentage of persons in each nation who answered "approve" when asked, "If a woman wants to have a child as a single parent but she doesn't want to have a stable relationship with a man, do you approve or disapprove?" If the gender-religiousness relationship is rooted in traditional sex-role socialization, then the gender difference ought to be larger where people disapprove of this sort of "liberated" behavior. But this hypothesis is not merely rejected; it is contradicted! The correlation is very strong and positive. Gender differences are stronger in nations where more people are willing to condone single motherhood.

The second measure of traditional sex-role socialization is the abortion rate. Once again, the correlation is strong and positive. The gender effect on religion is greater where the abortion rate is higher! Further confirmation is offered by the third correlation, which shows that gender affects religion least where the fertility rate is highest.

To explore a different facet of sex-role orientations of societies, the fourth correlation shows the percentage of the labor force made up by women. Once again the socialization hypothesis is contradicted. The final measure is of female empowerment (United Nations 1995). It too is highly positively correlated with gender differences in religiousness.

Results from the above tests are both perplexing and counterintuitive. Contrary to expectations, where female socialization is less traditional, the effect of gender on religiousness is actually greater! Given the intuitively appealing theoretical perspective that traditional female socialization patterns would lead to increased gender differences in religiousness and the wide range of societies being sampled, we expected to find at least modest support for a socialization argument. Furthermore, even if this perspective was wrong, and physiological rather than socializing influences were the cause, one would expect no correlation. However, neither of these results was obtained. Instead, we found a strong and consistent inverse relationship between traditional socialization and gender differences in religiousness. Moreover, not only were all of these correlations highly significant; when the scatter plots were examined, we found no distortion from outlying cases. The results are real. They also are really mysterious. It is one thing to find no support for socialization; it is something else to find a strong effect in the "wrong" direction.

Gender & Risk

At this point it is appropriate to consider Alan S. Miller and John P. Hoffmann's remarkable insight about gender and religion. They realized that, as so often is the case, we had been asking the wrong question. Rather than asking what it is *about women* that causes them to be more religious than men, they asked what it is *about men* that causes them to be less religious than women.

There is only one other gender difference similar to the one involving religion: males are far more likely than females to commit crimes. But unlike the effect on religion, this effect has attracted a great deal of scholarly attention. Here, too, differential socialization has been the favored explanation, and here, too, the facts have proved uncooperative. For one thing, the gender effects tend to be limited to impulsive, violent, physical, and dangerous actions having short-term gratifications: murder, assault, robbery, rape, and burglary. Sex differences are small or nonexistent on planned, "sit-down" offenses such as forgery, embezzlement, and credit card fraud. Moreover, remarkable data on homicides in France from early in the nineteenth century reveal that of persons charged with murder, only one of ten was a woman, but when poisoning was the method, women made up nearly half of the accused (Guerry 1833). What these data clearly show is that it is not socialization taking the form of conscience that prevents women from breaking the law, since it is the kind of crime, not generalized conformity, that produces the effect.

A second factor to consider vis-à-vis socialization is that the rates of "male crimes" tend to decline rapidly with age, and therefore gender differences attenuate as well. For example, in the United States, homicide and robbery rates are highest among males 16 to 19, they decline by about 50 percent for males 25 to 29, and men over 40 very seldom commit such offenses (Gove 1985; Stark 2000).

All explanations, whether or not they involve socialization, must deal with the fact that most of the impulsive, physical, and risky crimes are committed by young males who also engage in many other risky behaviors, legal or not. They get drunk, smoke, use drugs, don't wear their seat belts, speed, drive without a license, urinate in public places, skip school, often fail to show up for work, gamble compulsively, cheat on their wives and girlfriends, and engage in unprotected sex with strangers (Gottfredson and Hirschi 1990).

In their influential *General Theory of Crime*, Michael R. Gottfredson and Travis Hirschi (1990) concluded that the serious repeat offenders lack the self-control needed to defer gratifications — they simply can't or won't concern themselves with future consequences. The rewards of their risky behavior are immediate (including thrills and excitement), while the potential costs of their behavior are uncertain and not immediate. The habitual criminal population consists of those who are unable to resist temptations of the moment.

It was against this background that Miller and Hoffmann (1995, 64) drew their truly important conclusion that gender effects on religion and on crime *are different facets of the same phenomenon*. That is, to the list of risky behaviors engaged in by males, Miller and Hoffmann added irreligiousness: "one can conceive of . . . the rejection of religious beliefs as risk-taking behavior."

Miller and Hoffmann's logic is in accord with a classic argument in theology known as "Pascal's Wager" (Durkin and Greeley 1991). Blaise Pascal (1623–62), a French priest and philosopher, wrote that anyone with good sense would believe in God, because this is a no-loss proposition. He noted that God either exists or does not exist and people have the choice of either believing in God or not. This results in four combinations. Assuming that God exists, then upon death those who believe will gain all of the rewards promised to the faithful and escape the costs imposed on the unfaithful. In contrast, nonbelievers will miss out on the rewards and receive the punishments. Now assume there is no God. When they die, believers will simply be dead. But so will those who didn't believe. Therefore, Pascal reasoned, the smart move is to believe, for one has everything to gain and nothing to lose by doing so.

However, Pascal overlooked something. Faith is not free. Believers must give up some gratifications here and now, for various worldly delights are defined as sins. Consequently, if one is willing to take the risk of betting that God does not exist, one can enjoy many immediate gratifications prohibited by religion and in that sense come out ahead of the believer.

Exploring the Religious Life

Because many sins also are crimes, the interests of criminology and the social scientific study of religion converge on the same set of behaviors that overwhelmingly are committed by males. People who are willing to risk the secular costs of seeking immediate gratifications also are prone to risk the religious costs of misbehavior. Whatever it is that makes some men risk-takers also makes them irreligious. It seems appropriate to mention that only two groups have had significant success in resocializing serious criminals, both of them religious: the Prison Fellowship founded by Charles Colson and the various groups of Black Muslims (Stark and Bainbridge 1997).

When they analyzed appropriate data, Miller and Hoffmann found that within each gender, those scoring high on risk aversion were more religious. Moreover, when they compared men and women with a similar orientation toward risk, their religious behavior and beliefs were similar too. Further support has been lent to this finding by research showing that members of a sample of 1,148 newly ordained clergy in the Church of England scored well below the national average for English men on a scale of risk-taking (Francis et al. 2001). It also is consistent with findings that men tend to accept higher risks than do women when making financial investments (Glass and Kilpatrick 1998; Powell and Ansic 1997).

We propose to explore more deeply the religious aspects of risk and to place them within comparative religious contexts. That is, we propose that it is riskier to be irreligious within the terms of some religions than others and, consequently, that gender differences will be greater within the riskier religious contexts.

High-Risk Religions

Including irreligiousness on the list of risky behaviors dominated by men assumes that religious nonconformity carries the risk that if religious doctrines are true, then the consequences of irreligiousness will be very expensive, although perhaps not immediate. But that view of religion has a Western bias. Prospects of posthumous punishment are central to Christianity and Islam, as well as to Orthodox Judaism. However, as will be discussed at length presently, such notions are at most very peripheral to the major Eastern faiths. The point here is that in religious traditions wherein irreligiousness is not risky or not very risky behavior, gender differences should be far smaller and might consist of no more than modest effects of differential socialization vis-à-vis religion specifically. This might explain the mysterious findings, since the nations with great gender equality also are overwhelmingly Christian nations. Thus, to begin assessing this possible interpretation, we will examine data for the United States.

Christianity teaches that the primary risks of irreligion are located in "another" or a "next" world or life, where the fires of hell or the tedium of purgatory await a miscreant. Even those Christian denominations that deny hell accept that at the very least unbelievers will be denied access to heaven. Orthodox Judaism shares this view, offering a vivid portrait of Gehenna, where the wicked suffer eternal torment. However, when Reform Judaism arose in the nineteenth century, among the many Orthodox tenets it rejected were those concerning life after death. As the famous Pittsburgh Platform of 1885 explained, "Judaism [is] a progressive religion, ever striving to be in accord with the postulates of reason, [whereas] the Bible reflect[ed] the primitive ideas of its own age . . . We reject . . . the belief both in . . . Hell and Paradise" (complete text in Mendes-Flohr and Reinarz 1995). If this view is widespread among American Jews, then they should not perceive a substantial risk in irreligiousness. Table 4.7 shows that in fact, although the overwhelming majority of Protestants (both conservative and liberal) and Catholics believe in life after death, and only small minorities actually reject it, the majority of American Jews say they do not believe. Hence, *if perceived risk is the basis of gender differences in religiousness, then these effects ought to be strong among Protestants and Catholics but very weak or absent among Jews.*

Table 4.8 shows the effects of gender on five measures of religiousness. Strong, highly significant gender effects show up on all five among conservative Protestants, liberal Protestants, and Roman Catholics. Among Jews there are no gender effects on four of the measures and only a weak, but significant, correlation with prayer. As can be seen in the table, gender effects are far greater on prayer than on any of the other four measures. This may account for the fact that it even turns up among Jews. In any event, the hypothesis is strongly supported.

There is an even more stringent test of the risk hypothesis available in American data: *If perceived risk is the basis of gender differences in religiousness, then these effects ought to be strong among Orthodox Jews but should be very weak or absent among other Jews.*

Table 4.9 is based on the 1990 National Jewish Population Survey (Kosmin et al. 1991). It was conducted on the basis of an elaborate and

Table 4.7 Denomination and Belief in Life after Death (United States)

	Conservative Protestants	Liberal Protestants	Roman Catholics	Jews
"Do you believe in life after death?"				
Yes	78%	75%	71%	31%
Undecided	7	10	9	17
No	15	15	20	52
N =	(5,677)	(5,608)	(6,372)	(526)

Source: Merged General Social Surveys.

Table 4.8 Denomination and Gender Effects (United States)

	Correlations (Gamma) with Gender			
	Conservative Protestants	Liberal Protestants	Roman Catholics	Jews
Bible authority	.18**	.23**	.15**	.01
Bible reading	.26**	.31**	.13*	.07
Attendance	.17**	.15**	.18**	.03
Denominational loyalty	.16**	.18**	.15*	.01
Prayer	.37**	.40**	.37**	.15*
N =	(8,505)	(8,650)	(9,408)	(897)

Source: Merged General Social Surveys.
*p < .05. **p < .01.

effective method for locating everyone having a Jewish background, rather than relying on the more common, and very biased, method of sampling membership roles of synagogues and Jewish organizations (Stark and Roberts 2002). This is the only reliable national sample of Jews that includes sufficient cases to compare Jewish "denominations." Unfortunately, the researchers took an extremely narrow view of Jewish religion, as consisting entirely of practice. The only thing approaching a belief item was a question asking whether the Bible was the inspired word of God or merely an ancient book. This question revealed a very strong gender effect among the Orthodox but none among conservative or Reform Jews or among those who claimed no denominational preferences, saying they were "just Jewish." The same strong and significant gender pattern holds among the Orthodox for keeping Kosher, lighting candles on Friday nights, and lighting Hanukkah candles, but no gender effects exist among other Jewish groups. More than a third of American

Faith & Gender

Jews say they always or often have Christmas trees. This is not related to gender among most Jews, but it is, very strongly, among the Orthodox. Finally, only among the Orthodox is there a gender effect on synagogue attendance, but it is negative. Not surprisingly, given the very peripheral role of women in Orthodox synagogues, men are more likely than women to attend frequently. With this one qualification, the hypothesis is very strongly supported.

Of course, non-Orthodox Judaism is not the only major faith that attaches a low risk to irreligiousness. Buddhism, Confucianism, and Shintoism project very mild (if any) penalties for irreligiousness (Miller 2000). In contrast, Islam is the equal of Christianity and Orthodox Judaism in terms of the fate believed to be in store for the unfaithful. However, this is not how these faiths compare in terms of commitment to traditional sex roles. Here the Eastern faiths truly excel, as do Islam and Orthodox Judaism. Although there is some overlap in these orderings, they are sufficiently different to permit a clear contrast between predictions vis-à-vis sex-role socialization and risk. *If risk is the basis for the gender effects on religiousness, the effects ought to be greatest among Christians, Muslims, and Orthodox Jews and least among Buddhists, Confucianists, Shintoists, and non-Orthodox Jews.*

Conversely, *if gender socialization is the basis for gender differences in religiousness, then gender effects ought to be the most pronounced among Muslims, Orthodox Jews, Buddhists, and Hindus, whereas the differences ought to be substantially smaller among Christians and non-Orthodox Jews.*

To test these hypotheses, we used nations as the units of analysis, as shown in table 4.10. The data support the risk interpretation: the gender effects are strongly, significantly, and *positively* correlated with the percent

Table 4.9 Gender Effects within American Judaism

| | Correlations (Gamma) with Gender | | | |
	Orthodox	Conservative	Reform	"Just Jewish"
Bible authority	.39**	.08	.10	.09
Keep kosher	.53**	−.04	.03	−.14
Light candles Friday night	.32**	.09	.12	−.07
Light Hanukkah candles	.36**	.10	.12	−.08
No Christmas tree	.42**	.07	.01	−.18
Synagogue attendance	−.34**	−.04	.06	−.17

Source: 1990 National Jewish Population Survey.
**$p < .01$.

Table 4.10 Gender Effects and Religions (40 Nations)

	Correlations (R) with the Strength of the Gender-Religiousness Correlation
Percent Christian	.40**
Percent Muslim[a]	.35*
Percent Buddhist	−.31*

[a]Turkey, Albania, and Bulgaria removed as deviant cases.
*p < .05. **p < .001.

Christian and with the percent Muslim, while significantly *negatively* correlated with the percent Buddhist (there were insufficient cases to permit analysis of the percent Hindu). We already have seen that gender differences are strong among Orthodox Jews and absent among non-Orthodox Jews. Thus, the hypothesis concerning risk is supported; the hypothesis concerning socialization is rejected.

So risk-taking does seem to be the basis of the gender difference in religiousness, just as it is in the commission of crimes. But to say that merely reformulates the fundamental question; it does not solve the puzzle: Why are some men (and very few women) shortsighted risk-takers? Although virtually everyone who has considered the matter has assumed that socialization provides the answer, substantial and repeated efforts by criminologists to find such socialization effects have been unavailing. For example, many studies have attempted to account for gender differences in delinquency by controlling for gender differences in attachments to parents and in degree of parental supervision, without significant success (Gottfredson and Hirschi 1990). Meanwhile, however, some progress was being made on the gender and criminality front from an entirely different direction.

Physiology & Nonconformity

The male tendency to criminality does not appear to be a continuous variable. That is, a small percentage of young men commit many crimes, while most men of any age commit none. The famous study of a Philadelphia male birth cohort revealed that 6 percent committed about half of all offenses and two-thirds of the violent crimes (Wolfgang, Figlio, and Sellin 1972). A subsequent longitudinal study in England got precisely the same results—a very criminal 6 percent (Farrington 1988). This points to a precipitating factor that is not present in varying degrees in all men;

it is present only in some and absent in most. The same applies to that tiny percentage of women who commit "male crimes."

The idea that biology plays an essential role in criminality has had a long and controversial career in criminology. Late in the nineteenth century, the Italian criminologist Cesare Lombroso proposed that the most vicious and habitual criminals differed from others who committed crimes by being genetic "throwbacks" to our more primitive ancestors. As he described them, the "born criminal" is "an atavistic being who reproduces in his person the ferocious instincts of primitive humanity and inferior animals" (Lombroso-Ferrero [1911] 1972). Lombroso's fundamental point has never really been falsified by data. Indeed, although the textbooks cite the work of Charles Goring as providing trustworthy data to refute Lombroso, they uniformly fail to report that Goring was fully convinced that his data showed that indeed there are "born criminals": "our evidence conclusively shows that, on average, the criminal in English prisons is markedly differentiated by . . . physique . . . by defective mental capacity . . . and by an increased possession of anti-social proclivities" (Goring 1913, 370).

The disappearance of biology from academic criminology and sociology was not based on empirical findings. Rather, nature was "outlawed" by virulent attacks based on the new ideology of nurture. Emile Durkheim was among the most strident of these critics, proclaiming that crimes were committed by entirely normal individuals who were compelled to crime by social forces beyond their comprehension or control. Consequently, Durkheim wrote, "crime must no longer be conceived of as evil" ([1894] 1982, 102).

Fortunately, most biologists, including physical anthropologists, were content to shrug off this sort of sociological counsel. Writing in 1939, Earnest Hooten remarked, "The anthropologist who obtrudes himself into the study of crime is an obvious ugly duckling and is likely to be greeted by the lords of the criminological dung-hill with cries of 'Quack! quack! Quack!'" (3). Undeterred, Hooten offered some remarkable work on the biological characteristics differentiating criminals from noncriminals, including indications that it was a difference in general physique, not in specific bodily anomalies, that mattered. These conclusions by Hooten launched a continuing and significant line of study. Thus, in 1940 W. H. Sheldon found that persons having a husky or mesomorphic body build are far more likely then others to commit risky crimes of impulse.

This was confirmed by Epps and Parnell in 1952, by the Gluecks in 1956, by Cortés and Gatti in 1972, and by a number of other researchers.

Another line of research pursued the question of heredity and crime through studies of twins and adoptees. The first of these involved 13 pairs of identical (MZ) twins and 17 of fraternal (DZ) twins located in Germany by Johannes Lange (1931). Among the MZ twins, if one of the pair had a criminal record, so did the other in 10 of the 13 pairs. Among the DZ twins (who are no more closely related than ordinary siblings), in only 2 of the 17 pairs were both criminals. These findings were confirmed in at least five studies during the 1930s, followed by a lapse of twenty years. Then in 1962 twin studies resumed as Yoshimasu found a high concordance in the criminality of MZ twin pairs compared with the concordance among DZ pairs (all in Christiansen 1977). All of these studies suffered from small numbers of cases. However, in 1977, Karl O. Christiansen assembled data on 3,586 Danish twin pairs and found that for identical twins, if one had a criminal record, the odds were fifty-fifty that the other twin did, too. But among dizygotic twins, if one twin was criminal, the odds were only one in five that the other twin had a record. It follows that the difference reflects a biological effect, since both kinds of twins shared environments. Soon, other researchers found that in terms of criminal records, adoptees far more closely resembled their biological than their adoptive parents (Mednick, Gabrielli, and Hutchings 1984).

Finally, in 1985, Walter Gove, a sociologist, proposed that the combination of the well-known gender and the age effects on crime clearly point to physiology. Many crimes require strength, agility, aggression, and self-confidence. This is why males, and especially big, strong males, excel in these offenses, while gender differences are much less on "sedentary crimes" such as embezzlement or poisoning. Gove also noted that the traits that give males advantages in committing violent and risky crimes are very age-related. Hence, just as athletes must retire at a rather early age, so too do criminal males become too old to keep on doing it. Of course, Gove's theorizing does not address the issue of why only a few of the strong young males commit crimes.

Then came breakthrough studies of testosterone and crime, and these not only were fully compatible with Gove's analysis but also began to account for the narrow range of susceptibility.

Beginning in the 1970s, the widespread abuse of anabolic steroids (synthetic testosterone) by athletes and bodybuilders lent credence to the view that hormones can greatly influence behavior. Users as well as observers soon noticed that those taking large doses seemed unusually prone to rapid mood swings, to uncontrollable fits of temper, to outbursts of violent behavior, and to greatly increased sexual appetites. From this it seemed to follow that men having unusually high natural levels of testosterone might be prone to violent and impulsive behavior.

The first scientific studies of the effects of testosterone offered very strong support for this view. Not only were men with high levels of testosterone more likely to offend; so, too, variations in testosterone levels influenced antisocial behavior among women (Dabbs et al. 1987, 1988; Daitzman and Zuckerman 1980; Julian and McKenry 1989; Udry 1988). Like the early twin studies, however, this research suffered from being based on quite small numbers of cases, seldom more than 100. But in 1985 the Veteran's Administration conducted a huge health study of 4,462 men who had served in Vietnam during the period 1965–71. In addition to several days of examinations and testing, extensive interviews were conducted concerning social behavior. And every vet's testosterone level was measured. These data have produced a wealth of testosterone research. Those with the highest levels do behave in quite impulsive, violent, risky ways: they get into fights, commit crimes, abuse drugs and alcohol, are promiscuous, beat their wives, get divorced, and have poor work records (Booth and Dabbs 1993; Dabbs 1992; Dabbs and Morris 1990). Unfortunately, nothing is known of their religious behavior. It should be noted that men with high levels of testosterone also tend to have husky (mesomorphic) builds and that levels of testosterone normally decline with age.

Since these breakthrough studies, there have been many other studies linking physiology and risky behavior. For example, it recently was learned that a group of men who engaged in "anti-social" behavior had significantly less prefrontal gray matter than did a control group (Raine et al. 2000). Even more compelling is a study that found that boys identified by their peers and by their records as guilty of persistent antisocial behavior were quite deficient in the cortisol level found in their saliva after they had been subjected to stress (McBurnett et al. 2000). Cortisol is produced by the body in response to fear and anxiety. What the data show is that there exist boys who do not have normal fear reactions. In effect, they cannot be deterred.

So here we are. It appears that scientists are closing in on substantial physiological sources of criminality that explain the very substantial gender differences. If we assume with Miller and Hoffmann that irreligiousness is simply another form of risky behavior to which certain kinds of men are given, then there seem to be grounds for proposing a link between physiology and faith.

Conclusion

In conclusion let me offer several qualifications concerning gender and biology. First, socialization must have some effect on gender differences, too. It is not only risk-taking males who are irreligious, and some gender differences no doubt remain even when women are compared to men of more normal physiology. Indeed, this is likely to occur in part because of peer influences, which not only may exaggerate the genetic potential of the afflicted men but may well tend to generalize their behavior to other males. Assuming that there are males genetically predisposed to be violence-prone, fearless risk-takers, they will serve as undesirable role models, setting quite excessive standards for masculinity: "Real men take what they want." "Only wimps go to church." It seems likely that normal male genetics and socialization make men rather vulnerable to these excessive standards. That is to say, I am willing to accept the claim by evolutionists that there is high survival value for the species if males are biologically programmed to be aggressive. However, it is absurd, even within the most doctrinaire evolutionary perspective, to propose that normal males are so inherently violent and aggressive as to be almost beyond the reach of calming socializing influences, just as it is absurd to claim that women function by different, "nonlinear" logical principles. Normal men can feel and normal women can think.

To the extent that there is a genetic basis for the inability of some males to control their antisocial impulses and resist immediate gratification, it is a genetic abnormality not shared by the majority of males. One is very tempted to mention the mark of Cain.

How Are Revelations Possible?

Jews, Christians, Muslims, and Mormons believe God speaks: that the Torah, the Bible, the Qur'ān, and the Book of Mormon derive from revelations, from the actual thoughts of God conveyed to selected recipients. If we would truly understand these faiths, it is necessary to ask, *"How do revelations occur?"*

Despite being *the* question, it seldom has been raised, and the ongoing empirical research on revelations and various other aspects of "the sociology of mysticism takes place within a theoretical vacuum" (Hood 1985, 287). The reason for this theoretical neglect has been that the "causes" of revelations have seemed obvious to most social scientists: those who claim to have received revelations—to have communicated with the supernatural—are either crazy or crooked, and sometimes both. Even many social scientists who will assume the rationality of more mundane religious phenomena find it quite impossible to accept that *normal* people can *sincerely believe* they have communicated with the divine. No reviewer flinched when in the third sentence of his book *Mystical Experience*, Ben-Ami Scharfstein (1973, 1) revealed that "mysticism is . . . a name for the paranoid darkness in which unbalanced people stumble so confidently."

Although scholars often are more circumspect than Scharfstein, it long has been the orthodox position that the world's major religious figures, including Moses, Jesus, and Muhammad, as well as thousands of more recent revelators such as Joseph Smith Jr., Bernadette Soubirous, and Sun M. Moon, were psychotics, frauds, or both. When Bainbridge and I

A previous version of this chapter appeared as "A Theory of Revelations," *Journal for the Scientific Study of Religion* 38 (1999): 286–307.

(1979) surveyed the literature on revelation more than twenty years ago, we found that although the topic had been little covered, the psychopathological interpretation was the overwhelming favorite, with conscious fraud treated as the only plausible alternative.

In that essay, Bainbridge and I reworked this slim literature and analyzed our own field observations to propose three models of revelation. The first gives systematic statement to the *psychopathology* model. Here revelations are traced not simply to mental illness, but also to abnormal mental states induced by drugs or fasting. The second model substitutes chicanery for psychopathology and characterizes some religious founders as *entrepreneurs*. Finally, we proposed a *subcultural-evolution* model of revelation wherein a small group, interacting intensely over a period of time, assembles a revelation bit by bit, without anyone being aware of the social processes taking place. Here, at least, we made room for revelations involving neither craziness nor corruption.

After the publication of that article, it became increasingly clear to me that these three models fail to account for many cases of revelations—especially the most significant ones. There have been precious few examples for which there is any persuasive evidence that the founder of a new religious movement had any symptoms of mental problems.[1] Of course, lack of visible signs is no impediment for Freudians and others who are entirely willing to infer psychopathology from religious behavior per se (Capps and Carroll 1988; Carroll 1987; Freud [1927] 1961; La Barre 1969; Schneiderman 1967). But for those lacking confidence in Freud's revelations, the apparent normality of scores of well-documented cases ought to stimulate new approaches. Moreover, it seemed equally clear that few of the apparently sane recipients of revelations were frauds. Too many made personal sacrifices utterly incompatible with such an assessment. Finally, the subcultural-evolution model will not take up the slack, for the majority of cases seem not to fit it either. The need for a new approach was patent. Consequently, I devoted several papers to exploring how normal people could talk with God (Stark 1991, 1992b, 1997). In this chapter I greatly revise and extend that work into a general model of revelations.

The inspiration for pursuing such a model came from reading an account of how Spencer W. Kimball, president of the Church of Jesus Christ of Latter-day Saints, received the revelation that Africans and those of African descent should be admitted to the Mormon priesthood (Mauss 1981). Kimball reported no voices from beyond, no burning bushes, and no apparitions. He spoke only of the many hours he spent in the "upper room of the temple supplicating the Lord for divine guidance." The actual process by which he received his revelation would seem to involve nothing more (or less) than achieving a state of complete certainty about what God wanted him to do.

Or consider an account by Sun M. Moon, founder of the Unification Church, of the method by which *The Divine Principle,* the scriptural basis of his movement, was revealed to him. "God will not tell you outright. Therefore you have to search, to find out by yourself" (in Barker 1984, 71). So Moon studied and reflected in search of new religious truths and then used prayer to test each answer. If you are wrong, Moon explained, God lets you sense that fact. "You immediately know that is not right. It is something else."

If these episodes can be considered revelations, then it is entirely clear that normal people can, through entirely normal means, believe they communicate with the divine. Moreover, as I pursued the matter in greater depth, I saw that this assumption can be extended even to cases involving voices and visions—as I plan to demonstrate.

Although the model is, of necessity, limited to the human side of revelations, it is inappropriate to rule out the possibility that revelations actually occur. Unfortunately, as Ralph Hood (1985) has pointed out, even the most unbiased social scientists typically have been unwilling to go further than to grant that the recipients of revelations have made honest *mistakes,* that they have *misinterpreted* an experience as having involved contact with the divine. This is taken as self-evident on the grounds that any real scientist "knows" that real revelations are quite impossible. Scientists "know" no such thing: it is entirely beyond the capacity of science to demonstrate that the divine does not communicate directly with certain individuals. Therefore, provision will be made for the possibility that revelations are real, although this is not, and ought not to be, a *necessary* assumption of the model.

Keep in mind that insights gained through meditation, such as when Zen Buddhists gain enlightenment, are *not* revelations, because a revelation is not an insight or an inspiration. A revelation is a *communication.* Neither Kimball nor Moon thought they had found truth within themselves but that *God had placed it there.* As defined in chapter 1, a revelation is *a communication believed to come from a God.*

With this definition to guide us, I will illustrate each element in my model by drawing on the four most important cases of revelations in

Western history. I make considerable use of the case of Joseph Smith Jr. (1805–44), not only because his revelations launched the most impressive new religious movement in centuries, but also because of the extraordinary amount of reliable detail that is available. The second primary case is that of Muhammad (570?-632), whose life and activities also are very well documented. Jesus (c. 5 B.C.E.–30) is the third case I will draw upon; I was very relieved to discover that the mists of unrecorded history are far less dense than I had feared. The fourth case is Moses (c. 1400 B.C.E.), and here my analysis will be limited, since the mists are thick indeed.

The Context of Revelations

If not all conceptions of the supernatural can be the source of revelations, not all sociocultural contexts can sustain revelatory activity (Stark 1965b). Hence, the first two principles in the model specify the context necessary for revelations to occur. The first applies to the general context: revelations will tend to occur when and where there exists a *supportive cultural tradition* of communications with the divine. The second is more specific: the recipient of revelations will have had *direct contact with a role model,* with someone who has had such communications.

As will be seen, people routinely experience many things they *might* define as communication with God (Hood 1985), but to actually define something as a revelation, they must assume that such communication is possible. This assumption can be supported by the religious culture in general, but revelations are far more likely for those who know and respect someone who already has had such encounters. This holds in all four major cases.

JOSEPH SMITH JR.

At the age of eighteen, when he had his first encounter with the Angel Moroni, Joseph Smith Jr. lived in Palmyra, New York, a small town in the heart of a region that came to be known as the "Burned-over District" because of its responsiveness to revivals and for giving rise to so many religious movements. Thus, in addition to the general Christian tradition of revelation, Smith lived in a local environment in which people were accustomed to reports of revelations (Ahlstrom 1972; Brodie 1945; Cross 1950), and Joseph Smith's family took revelations for granted, as did most of their neighbors. Local people frequently reported having vivid religious experiences, including Smith's father, Joseph Smith Sr., who often had dreams that he defined as "visions" (Arrington and Bitton 1979; Brodie 1945; Bushman 1984). Seven of these visions were regarded as so significant that they are recounted in detail in his wife's memoirs, published years later (Smith [1853] 1996). These visions, which always involved healing and salvation, were well known to all family members. Consequently, the son was prepared for visions of his own, and when they occurred, the first thing he did was to tell his father, who "expressed no skepticism. Having learned himself to trust in visions, he accepted his son's story and counseled him to do exactly as the angel said" (Bushman 1984, 63). LaMar C. Berrett (1988, 37) noted that the senior Smith was "the first person to have faith in Joseph's experience with Moroni" and "showed respect and trust to his son concerning an experience that would cause most fathers to question, criticize, or disregard."

MUHAMMAD

Revelations were taken for granted in Arabic culture in Muhammad's time. In part, this was a result of the constant and close contact with Christians and Jews. Communities of both faiths existed all over the Arabian peninsula in these days, and there were sizable Jewish populations in both Mecca and Medina. In fact, at the start of his prophetic career, Muhammad assumed that Christians and Jews would embrace his revelations, since he believed himself to be the last in a line of prophets beginning with Abraham and including Jesus. There also was an indigenous Arabic tradition of revelation. This was especially well developed among a group known as the *hanif*, who seem to have been a monotheistic sect in Arabia that included elements of both Christianity and Judaism — possibly a refuge for heretics from both (Bowker 1997). Scholars now generally accept that the *hanif* reflected the existence of "a national Arabian monotheism which was the preparatory stage for Islam" (Fück [1936] 1981, 91).

Muhammad was directly influenced by two of the four founders of the *hanif* movement. One of these was his cousin Ubaydallah ibn Jahsh, who also was among Muhammad's early converts, and the other was his wife's cousin Waraqa ibn Naufal, a famous ascetic, whom Muhammad may have known since early childhood (Peters 1994, 104). Waraqa had visions of his own and had long been predicting the coming of an Arabian prophet. Consequently, he authenticated Muhammad's earliest

Exploring the Religious Life

visions and spurred him on in pursuit of more revelations (Armstrong 1993; Farah 1994; Payne 1959; Peters 1994; Rodinson 1980; Salahi 1995; Waines 1995; Watt 1961).

JESUS

There is much uncertainty about the actual revelations on which Christianity is based. Jesus did not leave a "book," and his fundamental message, let alone what he actually said, always has been in dispute—there is no Islamic or Mormon apocrypha. That aside, the story is much the same.

Has there ever been a time and place where revelation and prophecy were more taken for granted than Palestine in this period? Indeed it is the combined legacy of Judaism and early Christianity that provided the cultural basis for the revelational activities of Muhammad and Joseph Smith. As for a role model, according to Luke 1:36, John the Baptist and Jesus were cousins, and John A. T. Robinson (1985) made a persuasive case that they were close friends from childhood (also see Metford 1983, 92, 144) and that Jesus and several of his apostles began as followers of the Baptist. Moreover, the Baptist's father Zacharias was a high priest, whose revelation from the Angel Gabriel concerning his son's conception was known far and wide (Luke 1:5–22), and the most famous among John's revelations is the one in which he is told that Jesus is the promised messiah and son of God. A case might be made that Mary also served as a role model. Although the New Testament says surprisingly little about the mother of Jesus (she is not even named in the book of John),[2] the account in Luke 1:26–56 tells of her revelation concerning her conception of the "Son of God" and also reports her discussions with Elizabeth, mother of John the Baptist, concerning the divine source of that miraculous pregnancy as well. Granted, many scholars deny that there is any historical reality behind this passage. But of course, they make the same claim about most of the Bible—despite a century of archaeology that strongly demonstrates otherwise (Dodd 1963; Finegan 1992; Robinson 1985). Moreover, it never seems to occur to these scholars that even if they are correct that revelations don't actually occur, that doesn't falsify *reports* about people who believe they communicated with the divine. When scholars claim that because *they* "know" that there was no virgin birth, therefore Mary could not have perceived an encounter with the Holy Spirit, they express a non sequitur, despite all of the academic apparatus within which it usually is wrapped. We do not know whether Mary was or was not "a teenage prophetess who sang hymns of joy when she became pregnant with Jesus" (Allen 1998, 36). *All* we know is that Luke says she was and that when her son grew up, he believed that he spoke to God.

MOSES

Admittedly, an attempt to draw upon the case of Moses to illustrate the model pushes the limits of scripture and tradition (Ginzberg [1911] 1939; Klugel 1997; Philo, *On the Life of Moses,* c. 25). I can make no claim that any particular portion of these traditions is true. I cannot even refute revisionists who claim that Moses never lived—Burton Mack called him a "legendary prophet-king" (1996, 67). However, like Mack, most of these writers are so militantly antireligious as to disqualify their claims. Moreover, were the whole story of Moses mythical, it would seem curious that the account in the Pentateuch is so entirely consistent with the other three cases—the "mythmakers" had no model to guide them in these respects. All that said, let's see what the tradition tells us.

However it was that the Israelites got to Egypt and whatever their actual status under the pharaohs, it appears that they took the idea of revelation for granted, as the story of Abraham attests. Scripture reports no skepticism when Moses and Aaron confided the Lord's message to all the assembled "elders of the people of Israel" (Exod. 4:29–31). Closer to home, Moses' wife is presented as having been entirely supportive: she not only agreed to accompany him back to Egypt, but she also is reported to have circumcised her eldest son along the way in order to protect him from God (5:20–26). As the daughter of Jethro, who is identified as the "priest of Midian" (2:16; 3:1), she may have been accustomed to such episodes. We do not know whether Jethro had visions or otherwise served as a role model, but it is a worthy supposition and entirely consistent with his enthusiastic support of his son-in-law's claims and plans (Exod. 18). In addition, Moses' brother Aaron also had a revelation at this time, directing him to join Moses. Finally, in Exodus 15 Moses' sister Miriam is identified as "the prophetess." Since she was older than Moses, depending upon when she began to prophesy, she too could have served as a role model. As Yehezkel Kaufmann (1960, 227) put it, Moses "seems to have grown up among a family of . . . seers." In any event, Moses did not have to invent the idea of revelation.

Exploring the Religious Life

Let us now focus more closely on the phenomenon of revelation as such.

The "Mystical" Majority

Revelations are merely the most intense and intimate form of religious or mystical experiences—those episodes involving perceptions and sensations that are interpreted as communication or contact, however slight, with the divine (Glock 1959). As I have noted, such episodes differ greatly according to the intensity and intimacy of the contact (Stark 1965b). But even the least intense form of religious experience contains the potential for more intense encounters. Indeed, the ordinary, frequent, and very widespread act of prayer has often been the springboard for revelations. This is how it all began for Muhammad. With this in mind, consider remarks by an American Catholic interviewed as part of Margaret Poloma and George Gallup Jr.'s national survey on prayer (1991, 28): "There are times when I need to make contact with God, but he seems very far away. During those times I'll force myself to recite the rosary—and somehow he'll just become present. After I finish the decades I can go on to talk with him in my own words. I don't understand how it works, I just know that it does." This respondent did not report revelational experiences, and most people don't. But for those who pray often and talk with God in their own words, the possibility is always there. Given that well over 80 percent of Americans pray quite regularly and nearly all do so in their own words, the wonder is that revelations aren't rife. And perhaps they are. As will be discussed, most revelations do not involve anything new and thus do not require recipients to report them. Most revelations simply provide recipients with personal confirmation of the reality of God (Stark 1965a, 1965b).

Although religious experiences do occur among the mentally ill and sometimes are caused by fasting or drugs, overwhelmingly they occur among normal, sane, sober people (Stark and Bainbridge 1997, 129–55). There is an immense body of evidence suggesting that quite ordinary mental phenomena can be experienced as some sort of mystical or religious episode involving contact with a supernatural being (Hood 1985) and that many (perhaps even most) people in most societies have such experiences (Gallup International 1984; Greeley 1975). Hence, *many common, ordinary, even mundane mental phenomena can be experienced as contact with the divine.*

Most of the time, these contacts do not produce revelations but provide an experiential validation of faith, or what I have called a "confirming experience" (Stark 1965b). Thus, for example, Catholics often report seeing the Madonna, but seldom is she reported to speak. Moreover, even when the contact does involve a communication, this usually will be interpreted in support of the prevailing religious culture. Such revelations are the kind Ernst Troeltsch ([1912] 1931) defined as dogmatic mysticism, in that they support the current orthodoxy. Troeltsch contrasted these with revelations of the nondogmatic variety, which do challenge orthodoxy and can lead to protest movements. Evelyn Underhill ([1911] 1942, 95) made the same point, noting that mysticism "is most usually founded upon the formal creed which the individual mystic accepts . . . he is generally an acceptor not a rejector of such creeds . . . The greatest mystics have not been heretics but Catholic saints."

The far greater prevalence of the confirming or dogmatic variety of religious experience is the result of two factors. First, religious organizations typically come to recognize the risks involved in uncontrolled mystical activity among their adherents. As James S. Coleman (1956, 50) noted: "[O]ne consequence of the 'communication with God' is that every[one] who so indulges . . . can create a new creed. This possibility poses a constant threat of cleavage within a religious group." Consequently, religious organizations take pains to filter, interpret, and otherwise direct such activities so that the communications enhance and even revive conventional faith. Indeed, orthodoxy has been the standard against which Christianity has tested revelations, as stated clearly in 1 John 4:1–3: "Beloved, do not believe every spirit, but test the spirits to see whether they are of God; for many false prophets have gone out into the world. By this you know the Spirit of God: every spirit which confesses that Jesus Christ has come in the flesh is of God, and every spirit which does not confess Jesus is not of God. This is the spirit of antichrist, of which you heard that it was coming, and now it is in the world already." In addition to institutional control, the second reason that most people who communicate with the supernatural bring forth orthodox revelations is that most such people are deeply committed to a prevailing orthodoxy and few are possessed of the creativity needed to generate new culture. This leads to the third element of the model: *most episodes* involving contact with the divine will merely *confirm the conventional religious culture,* even when the contact includes a specific communication or revelation.

Most revelations are utterly boring and clearly uninspired, as is easily discovered at the nearest occult bookstore. In contrast, some revelations seem genuine in the sense that the material is so culturally impressive as to be worthy of divine sources. For example, entirely apart from its status as a sacred text, Islamists never cease to praise the Qur'ān for its extraordinary literary merit, particularly the rhyming, rhythmic stanzas of the earliest sûrahs. As Robert Payne (1959, 3) put it, in the Qur'ān the Arabic "language reaches its greatest heights. Muhammad, who detested poetry, was the greatest poet to come out of Arabia." How could this happen?

Suppose that someone with the literary gifts of William Shakespeare underwent a series of mental events that he or she interpreted as contact with the supernatural. Would it not be likely that the revelations produced in this way would be messages of depth, beauty, and originality? The question is, of course, How can geniuses mistake the source of their revelation? That is, how could they not know that they, not the divine, composed it?

The psychopathological model explains their mistake as delusional. The entrepreneurial model claims that there is no mistake but merely conscious fraud. Nevertheless, it seems likely that such a mistake could easily be made by an entirely rational and honest individual.

Most composers *compose*. That is, they write music slowly, a few notes at a time. But this is not the way all composers work. For Mozart and Gershwin, melodies simply came to them in completed form—they did not compose tunes, they simply played what they heard and later wrote down what they had heard (although they often polished what they had originally heard). And both of them seemed to regard the sources of their music as somehow "out there," as external. In a letter to Isaac Goldberg, Gershwin described the genesis of his *Rhapsody in Blue:* "It was on that train, with its steely rhythms, its rattlety-bang that is so often stimulating to a composer—I frequently hear music in the heart of noise—I suddenly heard—and even saw on paper—the complete construction of the rhapsody from beginning to end . . . All at once I heard myself playing a theme that must have been haunting me inside, seeking outlet. No sooner had it oozed out of my fingers than I knew I had it" (in Peyser 1993, 80–81).

Compare this with the report by the great first-century Jewish mystic Philo of Alexandria:

> Sometimes when I have come to my work empty, I have suddenly become full; ideas being in an invisible manner showered upon me, and implanted in me from on high; so that through the influence of divine inspiration, I have become greatly excited, and have known neither the place in which I was, nor those who were present, nor myself, nor what I was saying, nor what I was writing; for then I have been conscious of a richness of interpretation, an enjoyment of light, a most penetrating insight, a most manifest energy in all that was to be done; having such an effect on me as the clearest ocular demonstration would have on the eyes. (in James [1902] 1958, 364)

The similarity between artistic and religious creation has long been remarked. According to Evelyn Underhill (1911, 63), "[i]n all creative acts, the larger share of the work is done subconsciously: its emergence is in a sense automatic. This is equally true of mystics, artists, philosophers, discoverers, and rulers of men. The great religion, invention, work of art, always owes its inception to some sudden uprush of intuitions or ideas for which the superficial self cannot account; its execution to powers so far beyond the control of that self, that they seem, as their owner sometimes says, to 'come from beyond.'"

Of course, most of what comes "from beyond" to most people is banal or a confused muddle, just as most music from beyond is dreadful and most such literature is trash. But even if true genius occurs only once in 50 million births, or even less often, it happens. And scriptures that come to a genius "from beyond" can be awesome. Suppose that splendidly expressed and profound new scriptures suddenly flooded into one's consciousness? How easily one might be convinced by the quality and content of these revelations, as well as their sudden arrival, that they only could have come from the divine.

It seems instructive here to examine briefly how Muhammad received the Qur'ān. The founder of Islam told his followers that an angel spoke the text to him and he, in turn, repeated it so scribes could take it down. Much of this dictation took place in front of audiences. Obviously, then, Muhammad could not have appeared to his listeners to be composing the Qur'ān as he went along. If he actually was repeating the words spoken to him by an angel, there would have been no false starts, no second attempts, no backing up and starting over as would be the case with normal approaches to prose composition. This does not mean that he didn't edit—Muhammad often rearranged material after it had been revealed, and he sometimes received an emending revelation at a later time (Watt 1961). But it does mean that when he was receiving a revelation, Muhammad's performance would have been more like someone reading than like someone composing scripture. Of course, Muhammad could neither read nor write, and that too would have made him prone to mistake his own creations for external products.

Indeed, in his distinguished study of Muhammad, W. Montgomery Watt (1961, 18) reported that in his first two revelational experiences, Muhammad had seen "the glorious Being," but that "this was not the normal manner in which he received revelations." Watt then noted: "In many cases it is probable that he simply found the words in his heart (that is, his mind) in some mysterious way, without his imagining that he heard anything. This seems to be what originally was meant by 'revelation' (*wahy*) [in the Qur'ān]."

Is it not more plausible to cast Muhammad in the role of literary and religious genius who produced the Qur'ān without realizing he was doing so, than to argue that he was psychopathological or a fraud? It is hard to imagine a man with either defect behaving as he did. Here, too, Watt (1961, 17) puts the case most forcefully: "[Muhammad] must have been perfectly sincere in his belief. He must have been convinced that he was able to distinguish between his own thoughts and the messages that came to him from 'outside himself.' To carry on in the face of persecution and hostility would have been impossible for him unless he was fully persuaded that God had sent him . . . Had he known that these revelations were his own ideas, the whole basis would have been cut away from his religious movement."

The case of Joseph Smith Jr. is remarkably similar. He did not simply one day produce a copy of the Book of Mormon. Instead, he began dictating it page by page to his assembled family. Soon, Oliver Cowdery, a young schoolmaster who was rooming with Joseph Smith's parents, took over the job of scribe, writing down the scripture as Smith spoke it. As in the case of Muhammad, the prose came smoothly (Bushman 1984, 98) and impressed many as being far too sophisticated to be the creation of someone with so little education. When Sidney Rigdon, one of the most colorful characters in nineteenth-century American religious history, and quite learned, discovered that Joseph Smith hardly had a common-school education, he remarked, "[I]f that was all the education he had, he never wrote the book" (Van Wagoner 1994, 60).

In any event, there seems to be sufficient evidence that an absolutely rational person could utter spontaneous prose, just as Muhammad and Joseph Smith Jr. seemed to do, and quite easily externalize the source.

However, as mentioned before, there is another possibility that cannot be dismissed: that Muhammad and Joseph Smith could spontaneously produce remarkable scripture because they were merely repeating what they had read or heard. Since science cannot disprove that possibility, provision must be made. The question arises, If revelations really come from divine sources, why doesn't everybody experience them? Or why did these specific people receive them rather than some other people? Having access only to the human side of the phenomenon, one must speculate. There are several possibilities. Perhaps only some people have the capacity to receive revelations or the willingness to do so. Evelyn Underhill (1911, 76) suggested that just as "artists . . . [have a talent for] receiving rhythms and discovering truths and beauties which are hidden from other men, so th[e] true mystic . . . lives at different levels of experience from other people." In addition, perhaps many more people receive revelations than report them, perhaps because they are quickly silenced—a matter taken up subsequently. And perhaps God moves in mysterious ways.

In any event, a fourth principle may be stated: certain individuals will have the capacity to *perceive revelations,* whether this is an *openness or sensitivity* to real communications or consists of *unusual creativity enabling* them to create profound revelations and then to externalize the source of this new culture.

As noted, most such episodes will produce orthodox religious culture. The primary interest, of course, lies in novel revelations, the sort that get identified as heresies. Several factors limit the kinds of people likely to produce a novel revelation and define the times and places in which they are likely to do so. Just as people without interest in music probably don't have melodies come to them, people without abiding interests in religion probably do not receive revelations. And people are very unlikely to receive heretical revelations unless they are concerned about shortcomings in the prevailing religion. That is, *novel* (heretical) *revelations* will most likely come to persons of *deep religious concerns* who perceive *shortcomings* in the *conventional faith(s).*

Exploring the Religious Life

Of course, people will be more likely to find fault with conventional religions under certain social conditions than under others. Hence, the probability that individuals will perceive shortcomings in the conventional faith(s) *increases during periods of social crisis.*

Crisis & Heresy

Frequently in human history, crises produced by natural or social disasters have been translated into crises of faith. Typically this occurs because the crisis places demands on the prevailing religion that it appears unable to meet. This inability can occur at two levels. First, the religion may fail to provide a satisfactory explanation of why the disaster occurred. Second, the religion may seem to be unavailing against the disaster, which becomes truly critical if or when all secular responses also prove inadequate, for then the supernatural remains the only plausible source of help. In response to such failures of their traditional faiths, societies frequently have burst forth with new ones—often based on the revelations of one individual. A classic instance is the series of messianic movements that periodically swept through the Indians of North America in response to their failures to withstand encroachments by European settlers (Mooney 1896). An immense number of similar movements in Asia and Africa have been reported by Bryan Wilson (1975).

In a famous essay, Anthony F. C. Wallace (1966) argued that *all* successful religious movements arise in response to crises. Although that clearly is untrue, religions frequently are discarded and new ones accepted in troubled times. Keep in mind that such new faiths often are efficacious, which is why Wallace called them revitalization movements. This name indicates the positive contributions such movements often make by revitalizing the capacity of the culture to deal with a crisis. How do they revitalize? Primarily by effectively mobilizing people to attempt collective actions. Thus, the Ghost Shirt movement initially revitalized American Indian societies by greatly reducing drunkenness and despair and then by providing the means to join fragmented bands into a cohesive political unit capable of concerted action.

Of course, a crisis need not afflict a whole society in order to provoke religious innovations. That may be why the incidence of messianic movements is so high among oppressed minorities—from the Jews of the Diaspora (Sharot 1982) to blacks in the New World (Bastide 1978; Simpson 1978).

Another principle now can be added: during *periods of social crisis,* the number of persons who receive novel revelations and the number willing to accept such revelations is *maximized.*

This principle certainly applies to all four major cases. Joseph Smith Jr. grew up in a time and place of immense upheaval and disorder. His home was only a short walk from the Erie Canal—described by contemporaries as Satan's sewer. This area of western New York was the most rapidly growing, transient, booming, crime-ridden, drunken, and socially disorganized area in the United States at that time, and so productive of revelations and new religions that it has prompted an immense literature (Barkun 1986; Cross 1950; Thomas 1989). Muhammad came to maturity in an environment overshadowed by the climax of the long and immense struggle between the Byzantine and the Persian empires and agitated locally by bitter clan and ethnic conflicts among Arabs as well as chronic grievances involving nearby Jews and Christians. During Muhammad's boyhood, the public consciousness had become pregnant with impending religious expectations that soon the Arabs, too, would have a prophet (Hodgson 1974; Payne 1959; Peters 1994; Watt 1961). In the time of Jesus, Palestine seethed under Roman misrule, corrupt vassal kings, and all manner of religious controversy, while angry prophets and millenarian expectations abounded (Horsley 1989; Mathews 1921; Neusner 1975, 1984). And Moses, of course, was born to a people held in bondage in a land of the unchosen.

Keep in mind that I do not suppose that revelations (or religious movements for that matter) require social crises. As clarified in chapter 2, such movements often occur when nothing special is going on in societies. Nevertheless, revelations will be more frequent during times of stress, and the probability that a revelation will be heretical also rises at such times.

Social Support

People typically are somewhat reluctant to divulge a revelation, especially one that is heretical—which is further evidence of their sanity. As will be seen, at first Muhammad was "assailed by fears and doubts" and apparently wondered whether he was mad (Watt 1961, 21). It took a lot of initial encouragement from his wife and her cousin for him to fully believe in his mission. In similar fashion, Jesus did not begin his ministry with messianic claims but only revealed them slowly and in confidence.

Exploring the Religious Life

The reason for such reluctance and worry is obvious. Human beings, at least those not afflicted with mental illness, are greatly influenced by the reactions of those around them. The more extraordinary one's claims, the greater the perceived likelihood of rejection and ridicule. And, as Watt (1961, 21) said, "[f]or a man in remote seventh-century Mecca thus to believe that he was called by God to be a prophet was something stupendous." Had his wife rejected his claims, Muhammad may well have remained unknown to history.

Two additional principles are appropriate here:

First, an individual's *confidence* in the validity of his or her revelations is reinforced to the extent to which *others accept* these revelations.

Second, a recipient's ability to convince others is proportionate to the extent to which he or she is a respected member of *an intense primary group*.

Imagine yourself living a life of solitary contemplation. One day new truths are revealed to you by a divine being—a revelation that does not simply ratify current religious conceptions but which adds to or departs from these conceptions to a significant degree. Having imparted a heterodox revelation, the divine being directs you to communicate it to the world, which means you must found a heretical religious movement. Having no close friends to reassure you or to help spread the word, somehow you now must find someone who will believe you, and then another, and another. It is a daunting prospect.

But what if, instead of living a solitary life, you are a respected member of an intense primary group? It would seem far less difficult to share your revelation with people who love and trust you than to convince strangers. Moreover, if members of your immediate social network can be converted, they constitute a ready-made religious movement.

Revelations cannot be sustained and transformed into successful new religions by lonely prophets; they are invariably rooted in preexisting networks having a high level of social solidarity. Indeed, new religious movements based on revelations typically are *family* affairs—profound achievements of what rational choice economists would call household production (Becker 1964; Iannaccone 1990). Whether or not a religious founder's primary group is based on kinship, what is important is that it is a durable, face-to-face network with very high levels of trust and affection. It could even happen that a lonely prophet is able to hook up with such a network and establish the needed bonds of faith, although that does not apply to any of these famous instances.

The principle concerning the role of primary groups in sustaining a religious founder would appear to contradict the New Testament, which attributes these words to Jesus upon his return to Nazareth: "A prophet is not without honor, except in his own country, and among his own kin, and in his own house" (Mark 6:4). The same statement also appears in Matthew 13:57 and John 4:44. Nevertheless, I am prepared to argue that both history and theory testify that a prophet without honor among his own kin and in his own house is probably a prophet silenced. I suggest that if Jesus actually said these words, they were not directed toward his immediate family at all, but perhaps toward the neighbors and more distant relatives—which is another matter entirely. As will be seen, Jesus was honored by his family, at least some of whom seem to have been his earliest and most ardent followers. Centuries of Christian art to the contrary, the "Holy Family" did not consist of three, but of at least nine members (and probably many more). Indeed, all four of the great revealed faiths were solidly rooted in Holy Families.

The Mormon Holy Family

In 1823, in a farm home just outside Palmyra, New York, lived Joseph Smith Sr.; his wife, Lucy Mack Smith; their six sons, Alvin (25), Hyrum (23), Joseph junior (18), Samuel (15), William (12), and Don Carlos (7); and their three daughters, Sophronia (20), Catharine (11), and Lucy (2). They were, by all accounts, a close and loving family, greatly given to religious discussion and experimentation, having switched denominations repeatedly (Backman 1988; Berrett 1988; Bushman 1988; Smith [1853] 1996). The Smiths provide the quintessential example of household religious production.

In September of that year, Joseph Smith Jr. had a vision during which the Angel Moroni revealed to him the existence of a set of golden plates on which was written a "Record" of events concerning Christ's visit to the New World, known today as *The Book of Mormon: Another Testament of Jesus Christ*. Following the episode, almost the first thing Joseph did was to tell his father, who encouraged him to do as the angel instructed. According to Joseph Smith, the next day he found the plates in the place identified by Moroni. But having done so, he then disobeyed Moroni's injunction not to look directly upon the plates and suffered a severe physical shock. At this point, the angel reappeared, rebuked him for touching the plates, and told him he was forbidden from "bringing them forth"

Exploring the Religious Life

until he had demonstrated his willingness "to keep the commandments of God." What did he do then? His mother (Smith [1853] 1996, 110) tells us: "When Joseph came in that evening, he told the whole family all that he had made known to his father in the field and also of finding the record, as well as what passed between him and the angel while he was at the place where the plates were deposited." How did his family respond? According to his mother (111–12):

> We sat up very late and listened attentively to all that he had to say to us . . . and every evening we gathered our children together and gave our time up to the discussion of those things which he instructed to us. I think that we presented the most peculiar aspect of any family that ever lived upon the earth, all seated in a circle, father, mother, sons, and daughters, listening in breathless anxiety to the religious teachings of a boy eighteen years of age who had never read the Bible through by course in his life. For Joseph was less inclined to the study of books than any child we had, but much more given to reflection and deep study.
>
> We were convinced that God was about to bring to light something that we might stay our minds upon, something that would give us a more perfect knowledge of the plan of salvation and redemption of the human family than anything which had been taught us heretofore, and we rejoiced . . . The sweetest union and happiness pervaded our house.

Several months later, Alvin, the eldest Smith son, died. As the family gathered at his bedside, Alvin used much of his ebbing strength to encourage Joseph junior to obtain the plates. Four years later he did, bringing them home inside a locked trunk, which could not be opened because, as he reminded everyone, to look directly upon the plates could be fatal. He also claimed to be able to read the plates through the trunk and to translate them by looking through two transparent stones, known as the Urim and Thummim. So Smith began to translate the Book of Mormon, usually doing so orally in front of the family, which now included his wife Emma. The family responded enthusiastically, and everyone was eager to hear each new installment. Soon after the translating began, Joseph and Emma established their own household, and others outside the family began to learn about his activities. Among them were Martin Harris, Joseph's longtime friend, neighbor, and sometime employer, and Oliver Cowdery, a young schoolteacher who was rooming in the home of the senior Smiths. Twenty years earlier, in Vermont, Cowdery's father, William, had participated with Joseph Smith Sr. in a religious group that used divining rods as a medium of revelation (Quinn 1994). Cowdery learned about the ongoing translation process from long conversations with the prophet's mother, Lucy, who subsequently introduced him to her son, whereupon Cowdery volunteered to serve as his scribe to write down the translation as Smith dictated it.

Soon after meeting Joseph Smith Jr., Cowdery formed a close friendship with David Whitmer. As work on the translation progressed, Cowdery sent Whitmer "a few lines of what they had translated" (Porter 1988, 75). David Whitmer shared these with his entire family, who responded with very great interest. Subsequently, Smith, Cowdery, and Smith's wife Emma moved into the Whitmer home, where the manuscript was completed late in 1829. During this stay, Cowdery got to know Elizabeth Ann Whitmer, whom he later married. Consequently, at the start of 1830, the first 23 Mormons (counting in-laws) consisted of 11 Smiths, 10 Whitmers, Martin Harris, and Oliver Cowdery.

The Muslim Holy Family

Muhammad was about forty when he first began to have visions. They occurred in the month of Ramadan,[3] during which he had for several years secluded himself in a cave on Mount Hiraa. Here "Muhammad spent his days and nights in contemplation and worship. He addressed his worship to the Creator of the universe" (Salahi 1995, 62). This practice may have been prompted by "the old visionary Waraqa" (Payne 1959, 15), who had converted to Christianity, is thought to have known Hebrew, and who, as mentioned, had long been predicting the coming of an Arabian prophet (Armstrong 1993; Farah 1994; Peters 1994; Rodinson 1980; Salahi 1995; Watt 1961). Eventually Muhammad began to have vivid dreams involving angels and to experience mysterious phenomena such as lights and sounds having no source (Salahi 1995, 62). These upset him, and he feared he was losing his sanity or that he had been possessed by an evil spirit. So he confided in his wife Kahdījah. She gave him immediate reassurance. She also hurried to consult Waraqa, who accepted these as signs that greater revelations would be forthcoming (Payne 1957, 16). Subsequently, when Kahdījah brought Muhammad to consult him, Waraqa cried out, "If you have spoken the truth to me, O Kahdījah, there has come to him the greatest *namus* who came to Moses aforetime, and lo, he is the prophet of his people" (Salahi 1995, 85). Later, when he encountered Muhammad in the marketplace, Waraqa kissed him on the forehead as a mark of his mission as the "new prophet of the one God" (85). Indeed, Waraqa "serves as a kind of John the Baptist in the accounts of Muhammad's early revelations" (Peters 1994, 123).

Thus reassured, Muhammad now accepted his mission and expected to receive major new revelations—and soon did so. Through all that was to come, Kahdījah's support remained constant. M. A. Salahi (1995, 73) commented: "It was indeed a blessing that [she] should readily accept the new faith. She was to give the Prophet unwavering support, and comfort him in the years to come when opposition to his message was to increase in ferocity and wickedness."

As a reward for her steadfastness, the Angel Gabriel came to Muhammad telling him to convey Allah's greetings to Kahdījah and to "give her the happy news that she had a special home in heaven where she would enjoy total bliss and happiness."

But Kahdījah was not alone in her faith in Muhammad. Let me briefly enumerate the members of the Muslim Holy Family. After Kahdījah, first among them was, of course, Waraqa, who was Kahdījah's cousin and who also may have known Muhammad since childhood (Peters 1994, 104). Muhammad was an orphan, who seems to have had little contact with his siblings; otherwise, those family members probably would have been part of the founding core of Islam, just as Joseph Smith's parents and siblings were prominent early Mormons. Despite this, Islam began as a family affair. Kahdījah bore Muhammad two sons, both of whom died in early childhood. Perhaps partly as a result, Muhammad and Kahdījah adopted two sons. The first was Muhammad's cousin Ali, and the second was Zayd ibn-Hārithah, whom they originally had purchased as a slave. These adopted sons became Muhammad's third and fourth converts (after Kahdījah and Waraqa). Kahdījah also bore four daughters, Fātimah, Zaynab, Ruqayya, and Umm Kulthūm, each of whom also converted. In addition, three of Muhammad's cousins accepted his message (including the famous *hanif* Ubaydallah), as did Asmar, wife of his cousin Ja'far. Muhammad's aunt also was an early convert, as was his freed slave Umm Ayman, a woman who had cared for him in infancy.

The second convert from outside Muhammad's immediate family, and the fifth to accept the new faith, was Abū-Bakr, Muhammad's oldest and closest friend. Occupying a bridge position in the network,[4] as Oliver Cowdery did in the early Mormon network, Abū-Bakr in turn brought the new faith to "a group of five men who became the mainstay of the young [movement]" (Watt 1961, 35). These five young men were close friends and business associates. One of them was Abū-Bakr's cousin, and another was the cousin of Muhammad's wife Kahdījah. Abū-Bakr had great sympathy for slaves and throughout his life spent much of his income to purchase and free people from bondage. Two of the earliest converts to Islam were slaves freed by Abū-Bakr, including Bilāl, who gained lasting fame as the first muezzin (or crier) to call the faithful to prayer. So there they are, the first twenty-three Muslims.

The Christian Holy Family

The New Testament is so remarkably silent on the subject of the family of Jesus that it seems quite likely that the early texts were expurgated. Even Mary is seldom mentioned, and her portrait is further obscured by confusing references to several "other" Marys, who sometimes might not be "others" at all (Bauckham 1990). As for the siblings and other close relatives of Jesus, they barely made it into the scriptural canon. In Mark 6:3 we learn that Jesus had four brothers—"James, Joses, Judas, and Simon," and unnamed "sisters." In Matthew 13:55–56 Joses is called Joseph, and reference is made to "all his sisters." Mark 15:40 identifies one of Christ's sisters as Salome and again mentions his brothers James and Joses, the latter being named again in Mark 15:47. And in I Corinthians 9:5, Paul refers to "the brothers of the Lord" and claims that they were accompanied by their wives as they traveled with "the Lord." In the expert opinion of Wolfgang A. Bienert (1991, 471), because Paul claims personal acquaintance with "bodily brothers," who still lived at the time in which he was writing to others who would have known of them, the existence of these siblings "must be treated as historically reliable."

In addition to biblical references, Epiphanius of Salamis (*Panarion,* 78.8; *Anacoratus,* 60) mentions Salome as well as another sister of Jesus, named Maria or Mary. The *Gospel of Philip* (CG II, 3), a Coptic text from the Nag Hammadi collection, also identifies a sister of Jesus as Mary. The apocryphal *History of Joseph the Carpenter* (2) names Jesus' half brothers as "Judas, Justus, James, and Simon" and his two half sisters as "Assia and Lydia."

Of the siblings, James is by far the best documented. Paul acknowledges him as an apostle and as head of the church, having been so designated by his brother Jesus (Gal. 1:19; 2:9). In Acts 12:17 James also is confirmed as the brother of Jesus and, at least by implication, as head of the church. James also appears in respectable noncanonical sources. Josephus (*The Antiquities of the Jews,* 20.9.1) reported the execution of "the brother of Jesus, who was called Christ, whose name was James." In the fragment of the *Gospel of the Hebrews* quoted by Jerome (*De viris inlustribus,* 2), which may date from the middle of the first century, James is placed at the Last Supper and Jesus is quoted as calling him "My brother." In the *Gospel of Thomas,* which also may date from the first century, we read:

> (12) The disciples said to Jesus, "We know that you will depart from us. Who is to be our leader?
>
> Jesus said to them, "Wherever you are, you are to go to James the right-eous, for whose sake heaven and earth came into being."

This is also what Clement of Alexandria reported (in the fragment quoted by Eusebius, 2:1): "Peter, James and John, after the Ascension of the Sav-iour, did not claim pre-eminence . . . but chose James the Righteous as Bishop of Jerusalem." Of course, Eusebius himself several times identi-fied James as "the Lord's brother" (2.23). Finally, in another work that survives via Eusebius (2.20), Hegesippus identified James as "the brother of the Lord." He also reported that the grandsons of Judas, "who was said to be His brother, humanly speaking," were brought before Do-mitian, who freed them once they had convinced him that the "King-dom" promised by Christianity was not of this world.

Elsewhere, however, Hegesippus identified James, Judas, Simon, and Joseph as *cousins* of Jesus, a view later supported by Jerome (Eisenman 1997, xxviii). Others redefined the "brothers and sisters" of Jesus as half brothers and half sisters, being children of Joseph by a prior marriage. Still others have resorted to the confusion over the various Marys to claim that this brood belonged to another Mary, the wife of Alphaeus (Metford 1983, 54).

These contradictory kinship identifications bring into view the reason it is necessary to ransack the sources in pursuit of the family of Jesus: the doctrine concerning the *perpetual* virginity of Mary. Since this doctrine ruled out the possibility that Jesus could have actual siblings, what is re-markable is not that these people became obscure but that verses identi-fying them as actual siblings survived in the official canon at all. Perhaps they did so only because the doctrine of perpetual virginity is of theo-logical origins and therefore developed slowly. Thus, even at the end of the second century, Tertullian (*Against Marcion,* 4.19) vigorously defended the position that the "Lord's brothers" were his blood brothers, born of Mary and sons of Joseph, against those, including Marcion, who proposed that Jesus had not actually undergone physical birth or was otherwise beyond biology. A generation later, however, Origen (*Commentary on Matthew*, 10.17) noted that "some say . . . that the brethren of Jesus were sons of Joseph by a former wife, whom he married before Mary. Now those who say so wish to preserve the honour of Mary in virginity to the end." By the fourth century, Eusebius seems to have found the whole matter confusing but did take pains to note that Jesus was not the son of Joseph (2.1). Eventually, this became another matter of dispute between Protestants and Catholics, the former accepting the interpretation that Jesus had biological brothers and sisters. Recently, many Catholic scholars have come to this view as well (Bienert 1991, 470).

For my purposes, of course, it doesn't matter whether these were the actual brothers and sisters of Jesus, half brothers and sisters, or cousins. What matters is whether they constituted an intense primary group that served as a committed group of initial followers, which is, of course, specifically denied by scriptural passages quoted earlier. But here, too, revisionist hands left sufficient evidence to the contrary.

Recall that Paul mentioned that "the brothers of the Lord" traveled about with him. Is it reasonable to suppose that siblings who rejected Jesus would have accompanied him on his ministry or, indeed, that they would have been permitted to do so? In the same line of thought, R. E. Brown (1966, 112) commented (vis-à-vis John 7:5) that "it is curious to find the 'brothers' of Jesus following him along with his mother and disciples who believed in him." Moreover, in the same verse it is reported that "the brothers" urged Jesus to show his miracles to the world.

Tertullian (*Against Marcion*, 4.19) believed the famous denial of his family by Jesus reported in Mark 3:33 was a misinterpretation. When, told that "Your mother and your brothers are outside, asking for you." Jesus is quoted as responding "Who are my mother and my brothers?" Then, gesturing to those who sat listening to him, Jesus added, "Here are my mother and my brothers. Whosoever does the will of God is my brother, and sister, and mother." Tertullian explained that Jesus used this as a device to stress the kinship of faith, not to deny his family feelings. The more significant aspect here is that such an important early church father was committed to traditions of family support for Jesus.

In addition, Origen dismissed as figurative the claim that "a prophet is not without honor, but in his own country, and among his own kin." He noted (*Commentary on Matthew*, 10.18) that if taken literally and generally, "it is not historically true." As proof he listed many prophets of the Old Testament who were honored in their local communities. He continued, "But, figuratively interpreted, it is absolutely true for we must think of Judea as their country, and . . . Israel as their kindred." Origen then reasoned that the facts that the people needed repeatedly to be censured, that they sometimes persecuted prophets, and that all remained sinful were proof of the figurative truth, for had "their country" and "their kin" truly honored Moses, Elijah, Samuel, or Jeremiah, things would have been entirely different.

Surely there is nothing in the Marian traditions that would suggest that she was less than ardent in her support of Jesus. Likewise, it seems undeniable that Jesus did designate his brother James to lead the church and that he was among the most important of his brother's followers — perhaps the most important (Ward 1992; Eisenman 1997). It is less certain, but likely, that Simon also played an important role in his brother's movement and that, like James, he was put to death as a result (Eisenman 1997). Finally, there is no plausible reason to suppose that only three family members accepted Jesus while the others scoffed. What seems more plausible is that the stoning of James and some of his associates and the subsequent destruction of Jerusalem following the failed uprising against Rome obliterated Jerusalem Christianity, and with it went most remaining relatives of Jesus and the memory of their significant roles in the movement. This is entirely consistent with Helmut Koester's evaluation of the Epistle of Jude. The author of this book of the New Testament identifies himself as "Jude, brother of James." Koester (1982, 246–47) noted that he meant "without any doubt not an 'apostle,' but a brother of Jesus . . . The use of this pseudonym would have made sense only at an early date, as long as there was still some memory of the significance of such members of Jesus' family."

It was not until I circulated a draft of this chapter among historians of the early church that I learned of Richard Bauckham's extensive monograph (1990) on the part played by the relatives of Jesus in the early church.[5] Had I known of it sooner, I would have been spared a great deal of scrutiny of unfamiliar primary sources, since most of what I report above is laid out carefully and clearly in Bauckham's first two chapters. Bauckham also argues persuasively that Jesus' brothers and sisters were active and well known in the early church. He suggests that there may have been a brief period when several of the brothers were not part of Jesus' entourage but concludes that they did travel with him during much of his ministry, noting that "Paul includes the brothers of the Lord within the general category of apostles" (59).

The Jewish Holy Family

Like Muhammad, Moses did not have a revelation until he was in his mature years, having fled Egypt after achieving fame as a military leader and becoming a favorite of the pharaoh. Moses had settled in Midian, married Zipporah, and fathered several sons before God spoke to him from a burning bush. This first revelation was quite elaborate, as were others yet to come.

It seems clear that Moses' family played a major role in his religious career. His father-in-law and his wife were active, loyal supporters. His brother Aaron was his comrade and confidant and invites comparisons with James; his sister Miriam also seems to have played a prominent part. Although two of Aaron's sons (Nadab and Abihu) were killed by God for offering an improper sacrifice (Lev. 10:1–2), his other two sons (Eleazar and Ithmar) became priests and major figures during the second generation of the movement (Num. 3). Moses' son Gershom also gained considerable prominence (Exod. 2:22; Num. 3), and Moses' other sons, whose names are unknown, may have done so too. If this was not the first Holy Family, it is the earliest one about which anything is known.

Heresy Amplified

Holy Families do more than accept revelations; they encourage a recipient to have (or report) additional revelations. One of the first things Waraqa is said to have told Muhammad is to expect further revelations, and subsequently, as his audience responded to each new additional portion of the Qur'ān, he was encouraged to seek more. The same is true in the case of Joseph Smith Jr. Hence, the greater the *reinforcement received,* the more likely a person is to have *further* revelations.

This is, of course, nothing more than elementary exchange theory. Behavior that is rewarded tends to be repeated, and that not rewarded tends to disappear. However, I now wish to develop a rather more subtle and less obvious implication of how reinforcement influences revelations.

Close examination of the available reports on successful religious

Exploring the Religious Life

founders reveals a most interesting pattern: revelations tend to become more novel (heretical) over time. That is, the earliest revelations reported by a "prophet" tend to be substantially more conventional than do their later ones.

Let us consider Joseph Smith Jr. His early revelations represented at most a very modest shift from conventional Christianity. In fact, the Book of Mormon contains none of the religious doctrines that now separate Mormons and conventional Christians. Most of these were received by Smith in Nauvoo, Illinois, nearly two decades after his initial revelation. The same principle applies to Muhammad. His earliest teachings tended to be quite general and highly compatible with Arab paganism. Maxime Rodinson (1980, 96) summed this up:

> There was nothing at all revolutionary or shocking in [Muhammad's initial] message—or not, at least, at first sight. It did not appear to involve any major religious innovations . . . Strangely enough, in fact, Muhammad's Lord did not, in his first revelations, attempt to deny either the existence or the power of the other divinities. He was content merely to ignore them. There are no denunciations as there are in later messages of "those who would assign companions to Allah," no insistence on the uniqueness of the supreme deity . . . Criticism of the "complacency" of the rich and of their conviction that their wealth entitled them to "be independent" of all authority was perfectly acceptable in moderation. Insistence on the necessity of almsgiving was nothing out of the ordinary . . . There was nothing in all of this unacceptable to the Meccans.

The distinctive Islamic faith Muhammad eventually taught was revealed to him progressively. In similar fashion, Jesus only slowly revealed the full scope of his mission. We do not know, of course, whether this reflected a progression in his awareness of his mission or in his willingness to break the news—a caveat that also applies to Muhammad, Joseph Smith, and other revelators. Finally, Moses' first revelation was entirely devoted to instructing him to return to Egypt and lead his people to freedom—no doctrine was involved at all. That came after the Exodus.

What is to be made of this pattern? I suggest that the interaction between a successful founder and his or her followers tends to *amplify heresy*. Given that successful founders typically will be confronting a social crisis and the need for a new religion, there will be sufficient motive to move in new doctrinal directions. However, the initial revelations will tend not to be too heretical, because there is a selection process by which the initial credibility of founders is established. Had Joseph Smith Jr. begun his career with revelations favoring polygamy and teaching that humans become Gods, it seems very likely that he would have been rejected. But once a credible relationship exists between a founder and a set of followers, the stage is set for more daring innovations. The greater the amount of *reinforcement* received and the *more revelations* a person produces, the more *novel* (heretical) *subsequent revelations will become.*

At this point, of course, the model of normal revelations has become linked to the subcultural-evolution model. For now, the pattern of social interactions between founder and followers may play a major role in shaping revelations, bit by bit, in ways that go absolutely unnoticed. This will be facilitated when the process of revelation is public, as in the case of Muhammad and Joseph Smith Jr.

It should be noted that this principle does not necessitate any assumptions concerning the conscious withholding of revelations, nor does it require the assumption that reinforcement is shaping the revelations. An entirely plausible theistic interpretation is that God does not overwhelm the human capacity to assimilate and comprehend revelations.

Finally, revelations do not continue indefinitely. If for no other reason, as movements grow and develop more ramified organizational structures, pressures build up against further revelations, for *organizations* are served best by a *completed* faith. Often the antirevelational forces do not make substantial headway until the founder is gone. In any event, a movement cannot long sustain constant doctrinal revision, nor can it permit unrestricted revelation. Therefore, as they *become successful,* religious movements founded on revelations will attempt to *curtail revelations* or to at least *prevent novel* (heretical) revelations.

Max Weber's work ([1922] 1993) on the routinization of charisma obviously applies here. Weber regarded charismatic authority as suited only for "the process of originating" religious movements and as too unstable to sustain an organized social enterprise. Moreover, upon the death or disappearance of the prophet, a new basis for authority is required in any event. Several options exist. The movement can take the position that the age of revelations is ended, for all necessary truths have been told. This has been the usual Protestant stance. Or the capacity to reveal new truths may be associated with the leadership role—the charisma of the prophet is replaced by charisma of office, in Weber's terms. This has been the Roman Catholic and the Mormon choice. In either

Exploring the Religious Life

case, however, doctrine is stabilized sufficiently to sustain a changeover from prophetic to administrative leadership.

On Charisma

Since I already have mentioned it above, it seems appropriate to include a brief discussion of charisma, especially since my views are quite heretical. Max Weber borrowed this Greek term meaning "divine gift" to identify a form of authority that is seen as legitimate because it is attributed to divine sanction. Quite obviously, then, the founders of religions based on revelations have, or at last claim, such authority, and it might be useful to have a name to identify this phenomenon. Trouble arises when we forget that *charisma* is merely a *name,* just as *pope* is merely a name. *Names explain nothing.* Thus, it is as circular and silly to say Muhammad's early followers believed his authority came from God because Muhammad had charisma, as it is to say that John Paul II is the leader of the Roman Catholic Church because he is the pope.

Unfortunately, most scholars who use the term *charisma* forget that it is only a name describing a form of authority, and they use it as a trait of individuals that *explains why* others believe that their authority is God-given. That is, charisma becomes a mysterious power that enables people to impose their authority on others. But even this application is no more than a name, and thus to say Jesus had charisma is merely to substitute one mystery for another. Why did the disciples believe in Jesus? Because he had charisma. What is charisma? A kind of power that makes people believe in you.

Weber was as guilty of this circularity as anyone else. Having discussed the "extraordinary powers" often attributed to religious adepts, Weber ([1922] 1993, 2) wrote, "We shall henceforth employ the term 'charisma' for such extraordinary powers." In subsequent discussions, when, for example, Weber wrote, "We shall understand 'prophet' to mean a purely individual bearer of charisma" (46), he said nothing more than that charismatics have charisma. And when he went on to claim that prophets hold authority on the basis of "charismatic authentication" (47), Weber again answered this most fundamental question with a tautology. We still are presented with no *explanation* of what this power is or how anyone gets it. Unfortunately, Weber's authority (charisma?) has been such that generations of scholars have been content to attribute the accomplishments of various individuals to their charisma.

I am entirely comfortable with the observation that successful religious founders have *something*. They do seem able to form and maintain very intense emotional bonds with other people (Stark and Roberts 1982). There is nothing wrong with identifying that something as charisma, or "magnetism," or even as "it," so long as we never mistake the name for an explanation.

Frankly, I don't find even the concept of personal charisma to be nearly as interesting as the group process by which charisma is *attributed* to leaders. Holy Families not only reinforce the founder's confidence; more importantly, their testimony generates faith among potential and new converts. Followers effectively attribute charisma to their leader, and this can, to a considerable extent, be independent of the actual traits or behaviors of the leader. That is, charisma may exist primarily in the eyes of the inner circle and in the accounts they provide to those who are less well situated. Followers love to relate incidents of their leader's amazing capacities, especially to those who can have no similar tales to tell. Thus, early Mormon missionaries who knew Joseph Smith did not limit themselves to discussing passages in the Book of Mormon but also gave substantial testimony concerning their prophet's amazing gifts.

Conclusion

This chapter has attempted to explain how it is that normal people can talk to the Gods, while retaining a firm grip on rational thought. This is not to suggest that only sane (or sober) people receive revelations. Nor is it to suggest that "revelations" are never rooted in conscious fraud. In religion, as in any other sphere of life, delusion and deception exist. But it does not seem the more reasonable choice to attribute truly profound religious culture to such disreputable sources. I close by acknowledging that in his classic monograph on Muhammad, W. Montgomery Watt (1961, 238) anticipated several central elements of my model:

> I would begin by asserting that there is found, at least in some [persons], what may be called "creative imagination" . . . Prophets and prophetic religious leaders, I should maintain, share in this creative imagination. They proclaim ideas connected with what is deepest and most central in human experience, with special references to the particular needs of their day and generation. The mark of the great prophet is the profound attraction of his [or her] ideas for those to whom they are addressed.

Where do such ideas come from? Some would say "from the unconscious." Religious people say "from God" . . . Perhaps it could be maintained that these ideas of the creative imagination come from that life in a man [or woman] which is greater than himself [or herself] and is largely below the threshold of consciousness.

※6※

Spirituality & Unchurched Religions in America, Sweden & Japan

With EVA HAMBERG and ALAN S. MILLER

Debates concerning secularization often confuse faith and practice. Many who are committed to the reality of secularization point to low or declining levels of participation in organized religion in Britain and parts of western Europe as proof that religion is doomed in the modern world. Their opponents point out, however, that belief remains high in most of these same places; many people in Britain and western Europe have become "believing non-belongers," as Grace Davie (1994) would have it. Assuming that *both* claims are true, what do they mean? Is religion disappearing, or is it simply changing?

Moreover, what about those from Christian or Jewish backgrounds who no longer profess Christian or Jewish beliefs and reject any imputation that they have a religion? Are they the "enlightened" rationalists anticipated by the secularizationists? Or have they merely embraced other sorts of supernatural convictions? When Anthony F. C. Wallace (1966, 265) pronounced the inevitability of secularization, he did not limit himself to predicting the demise of the churches or even of Christianity; he asserted that "belief in supernatural powers is doomed to die out, all over the world." When people switch their commitment from Jehovah to "the

A preliminary version of this chapter was published as Rodney Stark, Eva Hamberg, and Alan S. Miller, "Spirituality and Unchurched Religion in America, Sweden, and Japan," *Journal of Contemporary Religion,* in press.

Goddess," that is not secularization but a shift from one religion to another.

The task of properly understanding the religious situation in modern nations and correctly gauging future possibilities requires that we know what unaffiliated and self-styled "unreligious" people actually believe. Are most of them irreligious, or do they pursue relatively unorganized religions? If the latter, then they give importance to many aspects of the nature and capacities of such faiths.

This chapter begins by defining several needed terms and then elaborates the concept of *unchurched religion,* developing a conceptual scheme to identify its major forms. Subsequently, this scheme is used to guide case studies of the significance of unchurched religions in the United States, Sweden, and Japan. The chapter concludes with a few observations comparing the fundamental strengths and weaknesses of churched and unchurched religions.

Creeds & Congregations

Religions based on revelations usually sustain **creeds,** *a specific set of beliefs to which all members of a religious group are expected to assent.* That is, when a religion is based on revelations, it tends to follow that a particular set of beliefs are of divine origin and therefore not subject to human choice. Brutal fights often occur within religious groups over what precisely is the creed, but this only serves to emphasize the importance placed on the creed and its acceptance. In contrast, although most Godless religions sustain quite elaborate religious culture and foster a common wisdom, they tend not to have formal creeds of the kind associated with Roman Catholicism or Islam. Instead, a great deal of picking and choosing is permissible. Moreover, as will be seen, not all Godly religious groups, not even all organized forms of Godly religions, sustain creeds.

Although religion is defined in chapter 1 as a set of beliefs, religions exist outside of sacred texts only as *social or collective phenomena.* Purely idiosyncratic faiths are only found, and then very rarely, among the mad or (perhaps) singular prophets—even ascetic hermits pursue a collective faith. One reason religions are social is that it is a difficult task to create a plausible and satisfying religious culture. Therefore, any given religion usually is the product of many contributors (even those religions attributed to a single founder). For this same reason, religions are most effectively sustained by dedicated specialists. The second reason religions are social is that the universal problem of religion is *confidence*—the need to convince people that the religion's teachings are true and that its practices are effective. Since the ultimate proofs of religious claims typically lie beyond direct examination, it is through the testimony of others that people gain confidence in a religion. Organized religious groups maximize the opportunity for people to reassure one another that their religion is true. Among followers of Godly religions, in addition to asserting their personal certainty about otherworldly rewards, people often enumerate miracles—how they recovered from cancer, how they overcame alcoholism or drug abuse, how they became reliable and faithful spouses, how they survived a catastrophic accident, or how their prayers for a dying child were answered. In this way people demonstrate that a religion "works," that its promises come true. Thus, religions tend to generate *congregations,* groups of *adherents* who *meet regularly* for religious reasons.

Magic & Spirituality

Recall that magic is excluded by the definition of religion, since it does not concern itself with ultimate meaning and typically does not offer explanations even of its own mechanisms, let alone of more profound matters. In addition, magic is essentially Godless. *Magic* refers to all efforts to *manipulate or compel* supernatural forces *without reference to a God or Gods* or to *matters of ultimate meaning.* Put another way, magic is *limited to impersonal conceptions of the supernatural.*

Recently, discussions of popular religion have been dominated by spirituality, a label that is applied to an immense variety of beliefs, feelings, and practices concerned with things of the spirit as opposed to the material (Fuller 2001; Jacobson 1997; Marler and Hadaway 2002; Roof 1993, 1999; Wuthnow 1998; Zinnbauer et al. 1997). Although seldom defined in any precise way, all forms of *spirituality* assume the *existence of the supernatural (whether Gods or essences)* and that *benefits can be gained from supernatural sources.* The term also connotes that these beliefs are *not necessarily associated with organized congregations* and *often do not constitute creeds,* for all that exponents often freely pick and choose from an array of creedlike bodies of doctrine. Indeed, this picking and choosing reflects that many who regard themselves as involved in spirituality define it as *a highly personal search* for what Christopher Clausen (2000) has so tellingly called "conformist individualism." As will be seen, many people who say they have no religion are deeply involved in spirituality.

Much that is called spirituality these days is not religion but magic, as in the case of astrology, crystals, reflexology, alchemy, rebirthing, tarot, aroma therapy, tantric sex, divination, candles, intuitive medicine, biorhythms, numerology, telepathy, pyramids, and essential oils. Other forms of spirituality involve Godless religion, as in the instance of people who say that they do not believe in a personal God, but in some sort of "higher power," and in the popularity of Eastern religions in this milieu. But many forms of spirituality involve Godly religions—they assume the existence of conscious supernatural beings. The difference is that, within the realm of spirituality, these Godly religions often lack congregations or creeds, and sometimes both.

Against this background, religions can be distinguished on the basis of variations in their degree of organization and in their commitment to a creed.

Churched & Unchurched Religions

Although all religions are social, there is substantial variation in their organizational character, so that some can be identified as *churches,* and others fall far short of any legitimate definition of that term. A *churched religion* has a relatively stable, organized *congregation* of lay members who acknowledge a *specific religious creed*—thus we include both sects and churches as churched religions. An **unchurched religion** typically lacks such a congregational life, usually existing as relatively free-floating culture based on loose networks of like-minded individuals who, if they do gather regularly, do not acknowledge a specific religious creed, although they may tend to share a common religious outlook. However, even among unchurched religions, there is a great deal of variation, thus generating the typology developed in figure 6.1.

Type 4 is the most prevalent and socially important form of religion, but it is of least interest in this chapter. Included in type 4 are all of the *churched religions,* groups having formal congregations and creeds. All three other types are *unchurched religions.* As will be noted in the discussion of type 2 (client religions), *practitioners* of these faiths often accept creeds and form organized bodies (priestly guilds or monasteries) and thus approximate type 4. But their clients do not form congregations, and most do not limit their religious portfolios to any one of these faiths.

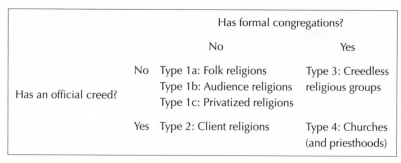

	Has formal congregations?	
	No	Yes
Has an official creed? No	Type 1a: Folk religions Type 1b: Audience religions Type 1c: Privatized religions	Type 3: Creedless religious groups
Yes	Type 2: Client religions	Type 4: Churches (and priesthoods)

Fig. 6.1. A typology of churched and unchurched religions

To begin, consider type 1, which is the polar opposite of type 4: religions having neither organizations nor creeds, some of which acknowledge a God and some of which settle for a divine essence. There is sufficient additional diversity within this type to warrant the specification of three subtypes.

TYPE 1A: FOLK RELIGIONS

Most medieval Europeans had little contact with the Church, and their religion was without organization or creed, being a loose and somewhat inconsistent set of pagan and Christian notions and practices with a very large component of magic. As was written in the Icelandic *Landnámabók,* Helgi the Lean "was very mixed in his faith; he believed in Christ, but invoked Thor in matters of seafaring and dire necessity" (in Brønsted 1965, 306). In addition to invoking a jumble of supernatural beings and entities, the medieval European masses took part in various sacred celebrations and festivals not authorized or sponsored by the Church, were obsessed with "luck," made pilgrimages to various sacred wells and groves (some Christianized, many not), and made constant use of incantations, potions, and charms—often hiring local specialists to supply such objects or perform these procedures (Kieckhefer 1989; Thomas 1971). Although much of this popular religious culture had originated in organized religions—in classical paganism, tribal religions, Judaism, and Christianity—it lived on in decayed and heterodox forms as part of a free-floating folk culture, for although many parish priests embraced much or most of this same culture, they were insignificant as to its maintenance and transmission. That is, local priests did not learn this culture from the Church (which often opposed portions of it), but like everyone else, they had

Exploring the Religious Life

simply grown up with it (Stark 2003). Faiths of this sort can best be identified as *folk religions,* lacking both creeds and congregations.

Folk religions are not limited to premodern societies. For example, although Iceland has a Lutheran State Church, folk religion is so potent there today that planned highways are sometimes rerouted so as not to disturb various hills and large rocks wherein may dwell *huldufolk,* or hidden people, such as elves, trolls, gnomes, and fairies; and people planning to build a new house often hire "elf-spotters" to ensure that their site does not encroach on huldufolk settlements (Nickerson 1999; Swatos and Gissurarson 1997). All of this goes on in what has been called the first fully secularized nation on earth (Tomasson 1980). As will be seen, very similar activities take place in Japan.

Moreover, when a churched religion has passed through several generations of nonparticipants, it effectively becomes a folk religion. In the absence of congregational life and organized religious socialization, creeds grow hazy, problematic, and heterodox. Thus, when asked if she believed "in a God who can change the course of events on earth," an English respondent answered, "No, just the ordinary kind" (Davie 1994, 1). To the extent that "believing" nonbelongers are common in Europe, folk religion thrives.

There is also an important variation on folk religions that is limited to modern societies: religions sustained by the mass media.

TYPE IB: AUDIENCE RELIGIONS

In all modern societies, an immense array of proponents of unchurched supernaturalisms (both magical and religious) vie for public attention through the general mass media and countless specialized publications, Web sites, and public lectures: Wicca, astral travel, astrology, Goddess worship, channeling, biorhythms, "walk-ins," ascended masters, and the like. A survey conducted by the National Science Foundation in 2001 found that 60 percent of Americans believe some people have psychic powers, 50 percent think astrology is scientific, 30 percent believe that the earth is being visited by aliens (another 13 percent aren't sure), and 68 percent think magnetic therapy is based on science (NSF 2002). As noted, much of this is magic and of interest only to refute claims that we live in an enlightened age in which science has vanquished all forms of superstition. Some of these are religions, which, as in the case of Goddess worship, offer a general perspective on matters of ultimate meaning based on supernatural assumptions. However, many people who are deeply engrossed in various of these faiths never gather in pursuit of their interests, except sometimes for public lectures or book-signings; they are audiences, not congregations. And although some among them do seem to become committed to a single selection, most have many interests and express their belief in many faiths, including sets that would seem to be utterly contradictory. This catholicity is facilitated by the fact that most who are active in the world of audience religions identify themselves as "students" of occult, metaphysical, and spiritual subjects. Indeed, given the immense array of available cultural options, it is likely that many people have their own peculiar blend.

The following quotations come from an Internet spirituality site devoted to personal ads seeking lovers and companions. Each was asked to include her or his "spiritual interests":

> Female, 42: "Self-awareness, Astrology, Tarot, UFOs, Reiki, Channeling, Meditation."
> Male, 45: "astrology, aquarian gospel and christianity."
> Female, 27: "Finding the spiritual path, earth energies, shamanism, ecologist."
> Male, 47: "healthfood, yoga, astrology, Ascended Masters, meditation."
> Female, 52: "Meditation, channeling, Rebirthing, anything to keep me connected to self."
> Male, 47: "Spiritualism, Tarot, Astrology, Metaphysical, UFOs."
> Female, 48: "Walk-ins, astrology, channeling, Edgar Cayce's information, paganism."
> Male, 35: "The Celestine Prophesy, Reiki Healing, Unity, Science of Mind, Stephen R. Schwartz, OSHO, Adi Da, gurus, metaphysics, Eckhart Tolle, Conversations with God."
> Female, 30: "Astrology, past lives, crystals, tarot, dreams, angels, egyptology, spirit guides, fairies, mermaids."
> Male, 45: "I am both a Christian and an alien abductee."

People are encouraged to select and sustain such splendid jumbles of supernaturalism by the dominant theme in this milieu: that religion or spirituality is a wholly private matter—some devotees even claim that such things can only be experienced, not expressed (see Roof 1999).

TYPE IC: PRIVATIZED RELIGIONS

In recent decades many social scientists have claimed not only that churched religions are doomed but that a major step in that direction is the "privatization" of faith (Luckmann 1967; Berger 1967). Of course, not only did the predicted rapid privatization of religion fail to appear on time, but it is not clear that there is anything really new about privatization. It can be argued that privatization was quite prevalent even in medieval times. Whether or not that is so, clearly many people today do prefer to shield their religiousness from others and to pursue it only in private (Roof 1999; Roof and McKinney 1987; Fuller 2001; Miller 1995; Wuthnow 1998). This will be evident in the examination of unchurched religion in America.

Keep in mind that *privatize* is a verb, not a noun. What is distinctive about privatized religions is how they are acquired and pursued, not their contents or origins. As noted, people do not create their own religions. Although there will be some degree of idiosyncrasy when people do not rely on organizations and clergy to define their beliefs and practices, the contents of privatized religion will be well known, deriving from folk religions and from the organized and professional sources that sustain audience religions. For example, a twenty-seven-year-old divorced woman described her spiritual interests as "Buddhism, Wicca, Divination, Runes, Astrology, Meditation, and Yoga." Each of these "interests" is firmly rooted in well-organized, professional sources.

TYPE 2: CLIENT RELIGIONS

A major form of unchurched religion involves exponents of elaborate creeds who operate without congregations, their relations with the laity taking the form of practitioner-client. Emile Durkheim observed that this was typical of magic. He began by pointing out that magic may be as widely believed as religion but that magical notions "do not bind men who believe in them to one another . . . *There is no Church of magic*" ([1912] 1995, 42, his emphasis). "Between the magician and the individuals who consult him," Durkheim continued, "there are no durable ties that make them members of a single moral body, comparable to the ties that join the faithful to the same god or the adherents of the same cult." Rather, "the magician has a clientele, not a Church, and his clients may have no mutual relations, and may even be unknown to one another.

Indeed, the relations they have with him are . . . analogous to those of a sick man with his doctor." Just as with doctors, when magicians form societies, they "encompass only the magicians. Excluded from them are the laity."

Modern societies abound with magicians and their clients, as is evident in the many "interests" expressed in the ads quoted above. The practitioner-client relationship is far less common when religions are involved, especially monotheistic religions; usually proponents of these faiths can assemble congregations. "Initiation religions" tend to be the exception. Thus, the early Christian Gnostics could not sustain congregations because their creeds prevented them from ever being more than a loose network of individual adepts, each pursuing secret knowledge through private, personal means (Pagels 1979). Moreover, within the realm of unchurched spirituality, even many proponents of fully developed religions (especially of the Godless variety) must settle for clients and audiences. In the United States, Canada, and Europe, most Zen masters must support themselves by holding classes in meditation, and most exponents of Hinduism end up giving lessons in Yoga. Hence, although the practitioners may have elaborate creeds, they are unable to assemble congregations.

TYPE 3: CREEDLESS RELIGIOUS GROUPS

The final type of unchurched religion is sustained by (weak) congregations but is quite lacking in creeds. An apt example was provided by Melinda Bollar Wagner (1983, 49) in her revealing study of the Spiritual Frontiers Fellowship (SFF). As one member explained, the most attractive aspect of membership in SFF is that "you can look at these things [various teachings] with an open mind, believe what you want to believe and take the best from each one of them." SFF "leaders are advised that each member should feel free to work out a personal interpretation." Another example of creedless religious groups is the UFO-oriented religious organization studied by Christopher Bader (1999). The central concern of this group is with the activities of aliens, including their frequent abduction of earthlings. Most participants believe that they have been abductees, a fact known to them only through memories "recovered" during hypnosis. As they conceive them, aliens have supernatural powers and know truths about the meaning of life and the universe toward which earthbound religions are merely groping: the aliens are

Exploring the Religious Life

Gods on a par with most deities found in polytheistic systems. Nevertheless, the group is so lacking in a coherent creed that members appeared not to notice when what seemed to have been a firmly held prophecy concerning the arrival of an alien space fleet failed to take place. No one but the sociological observer seemed to have been aware when the deadline passed uneventfully, let alone to have given the failure any importance.

Although they gather regularly and sometimes even pay dues, groups such as these are more like discussion groups than real congregations. Solid congregations of committed believers require creeds to give them unity and purpose, as many ultraliberal Christian groups seem to be discovering the hard way (Stark and Finke 2000).

This conceptual scheme now serves as a basis for close-up examinations of spirituality and unchurched religion in the United States, Sweden, and Japan.

Unchurched Religions & Spirituality in America

The percentage of Americans who say they have no religion is said to have increased in recent decades. In 1973 the General Social Survey found that 5 percent of the nation's adults answered "none" when asked their religious affiliation. In 1983 this had inched up to 7 percent. In 1993, 9 percent said they had no religion. The survey done in 2000 found 14 percent with no religion. These may be real increases, or they may only be an artifact of the steep decline in the response rate to surveys, given that higher-income and more-educated people increasingly are very underrepresented in surveys and are, of course, those least likely to have no religious affiliation. Assuming that the increase in the percentage of "nones" is meaningful, some observers have long associated this trend with the secularization thesis, interpreting it as proof that people are increasingly rejecting not only organized religions "but also their ideological components" (Condran and Tamney 1985, 422). Others have been less willing to draw this conclusion. Stark and Bainbridge (1985, 47) noted nearly twenty years ago that "the premise that the 'nones' are irreligious is itself false . . . the majority of people who say they have no religious affiliation express considerable belief in the mystical and supernatural," and they suggested that this was the group most easily converted to deviant religious perspectives. Wade Clark Roof and William McKinney (1987, 99) reached a similar conclusion, noting that what most "nones" lacked was not belief in "the supernatural and the mystical" but "interest in organized religion." However, despite the seeming importance of the matter, as will be seen, there is only a very slim research literature on the religious beliefs and activities of the "nones."

Table 6.1 supports the claim that the "nones" are not the vanguard of secularization but that most of them pursue privatized religion. Two out of five of these "nones" pray daily or weekly, and only 4 percent never pray. Atheists are few; the majority believe in God, and many of the rest believe in a "higher power." Indicating their taste for magic, about half of the "nones" believe that "[a]strology—the study of the star signs—has some scientific truth." Religious they may be, but the "nones" over-whelmingly are unchurched. Two-thirds say they never attend church, and nearly another third say they go no more than once or twice a year. Three percent attend weekly.

The number of "nones" probably substantially underestimates the extent of unchurched spirituality in the United States. Many who give a specific denominational preference when asked do not in fact actually belong to that group. The best estimate is that about a third of Americans are effectively unchurched (Finke and Stark 1992). But they are not unreligious. Limiting the data to those who claim a religious affiliation but are not actual members, most nonmembers pray weekly, all of them pray at least occasionally, and there are no atheists among them (General Social Survey, 1988).[1] But like the "nones," these Americans very seldom, if ever, attend a conventional church. Many of them are involved in unchurched religions and no doubt prefer the label "spiritual" to that of "religious." This is in close accord with Roof's results when he asked the 14 percent of his respondents who said "no" when asked, "Do you con-sider yourself to be in any way religious?" whether they considered them-selves to be "a spiritual person." Two-thirds of these not-religious people answered yes.

So how many Americans are best described as involved in spirituality? Here the problem arises that the overwhelming majority of churched Americans say they are spiritual, too! Based on a national sample, Scott (2001) reported that 61 percent of Americans said they were both reli-gious and spiritual, 20 percent selected spiritual only, and 8 percent said they were only religious. That agrees with Roof's estimate (1993) that the spiritual but not religious constitute about 19 percent of the population.

There is both confusion and controversy as to whether there is a trend toward spirituality and away from churched religions, or whether there

Exploring the Religious Life

Table 6.1 The Religion of Americans Who Gave Their Religious Preference as "None"

Prayer
At least once a day	22%
At least once a week	17%
Sometimes	57%
Never	4%
	100%
	N = (213)

God
Atheists	14%
Agnostics	17%
"Higher Power"	18%
Believe in God	51%
	100%
	N = (142)

Astrology
True	45%
Perhaps	8%
False	47%
	100%
	N = (260)

Church Attendance
Never	65%
Once or twice a year	29%
Monthly	3%
Weekly	3%
	100%
	N = 377

Sources: For Prayer, god, and Church Attendance, General Social Survey, 2000; for Astrology, General Social Surveys, 1993–94.

always has been a substantial unchurched segment in American religious life. Although they try to be carefully circumspect, Marler and Hadaway (2002) cannot restrain their enthusiasm for seeing a progressive switch to spirituality and, indeed, to regard this as a harbinger of eventual religious decline. If they are right, if there is a substantial trend toward spirituality, it will have quite significant implications, not just for organized religion, but for the culture in general (see the last section of this chapter). But it is entirely plausible that there is no trend one way or the other. There always has been a substantial demand for unchurched religion (spirituality) in America. It was, after all, in the nineteenth century that spiritualism boomed, as did such nearly unchurched faiths as Unitarianism and Universalism. There are many similar examples, as Lippy (1994) has demonstrated in his study emphasizing the continuity of nineteenth- and twentieth-century American "popular" religions.

Trend or not, the conclusion must be drawn that between religion and spirituality and various combinations thereof, the overwhelming majority of Americans are accounted for, offering no visible support for Anthony F. C. Wallace's prediction that belief in supernatural powers is doomed. Of course, since Americans are thought to be among the most religious people on earth, these findings concerning the religiousness and spirituality of the unchurched may not reflect what is going on in other nations. Perhaps in Sweden and Japan, when people say they are not religious, they are denying all forms of supernaturalism. Or perhaps not.

Unchurched Religions & Spirituality in Sweden

If one examines data on Christian beliefs and practices, Sweden appears to be among the most secularized nations in western Europe. According to the 1995 World Values Survey, only 10 percent of Swedes attend church as often as once a month, and only 16 percent express confidence in the existence of a personal God.[2] However, before proposing Sweden as the vanguard of a secular future, we should note that 46 percent affirmed the existence of "some kind of spirit or life force," and 18 percent said they simply didn't know what to believe. Thus, looked at from the other end of the distribution, one could say that "only" 20 percent of Swedes reject God.

Responses given in a survey (Hamberg 1990) that asked Swedes to answer in their own words what they believed about God suggest that it is not rampant secularity but a kind of jumbled and unchurched spirituality that characterizes the majority view:

> Male, 18: "There is something. Perhaps God or some superior power, don't know."
>
> Female, 18: "Believe that there's something, not exactly a God, but something else. Cannot say what."
>
> Female, 64: "I believe in something, I don't quite know what."
>
> Female, 69: "Believe that there's something divine or spiritual, but don't know what."

Thus, the pressing question is whether what is happening in Sweden is religious *decline* or religious *change*. Is Sweden undergoing a transition from faith to secularity, or are Swedes mainly abandoning what they perceive as a moribund state church and adopting an unchurched spirituality? Many new surveys suggest that it is the latter, that in the place of conventional Christian commitment, most now describe themselves as "Christians in their own personal way," and many other Swedes advocate a whole range of New Age and Eastern spiritualities.

To begin, however, it is important to know that Sweden may never really have shifted from folk to churched religion: it is not clear that the ordinary Swedes ever were fully Christianized. The "official" Christianization of Sweden involved little more than the baptism of the royal house and the upper nobility. At that time, very little was done to convert the people, most of whom seem to have been content to add Jesus and a few saints to the pantheon of Norse folk religion and to observe some Christian holidays while continuing to celebrate pre-Christian holidays as well (Stark 2001, 2003; Stark and Finke 2000). This explains how King Gustavus I (1496–1560) was able to expel the Catholic Church and replace it with a Protestant state church without arousing any popular outcry (Latourette 1975; Roberts 1968). Catholic or Protestant? Apparently the public didn't care, probably because most of them were neither. Nor did the Swedish Catholic clergy protest—they quickly professed to be Protestants and remained in the same churches offering pretty much the same services, only in Swedish rather than Latin. Subsequently, there was no need for the Swedish Lutheran clergy to stir up public support— all Swedes were, by law, members and were required to pay church taxes sufficient to keep the clergy in style.

Thus was created a classic example of the monopoly church. Rather than to rely on evangelism to overcome the prevalence of folk religion, the Church Law of 1668 was content to demand conformity. Henceforth the local clergy were required to hold home "examinations," in which all competent members of each household were required to demonstrate knowledge of the Ten Commandments, the Apostle's Creed, the Lord's Prayer, and elements of Luther's catechism. Passage of these examinations was to be recorded along with records of births, baptisms, and the like. The home examinations continued into the nineteenth century, when the responsibility for religious education was shifted to the schools. However, it is certainly not clear that, even if enforced, this policy would produce belief rather than rote learning. It seems pertinent that all students in the former Soviet Union were required to study Scientific Atheism at every grade level, but after seventy years of such instruction there were very few atheists (WVS 1995). One supposes that efforts to force conformity to religious standards might not be much more successful and that Swedish folk religion remained quite unscathed.

In any event, in the past century the Swedish State Church has been in no position to demand conformity to a traditional Christian creed, since many of its clergy no longer embrace a creed. Rather, in recent decades the Swedish Church has been partly controlled by a liberal or very liberal clergy: the current archbishop is frequently accused of being evasive about theological matters such as whether one can reject the idea that Jesus is the Son of God and is merely a man who set a moral example and still qualify as a Christian (*Svenska Dagbladet* (Stockholm), March 3, 2002, 31). Nor have the state church clergy resisted government intervention even in theological matters (Gustafsson 1990). Parliament recently adopted a law that defines the expression of religious opposition to homosexuality from any pulpit (state church or not) as illegal "hate speech."

If one assumes that people attend church primarily from religious motives, it is not surprising that the state churches appear to be nearly empty shells. Only about 3 percent of those claiming affiliation with the state church attend weekly (another 6 percent say they go at least once a month), which does little to fill the pews in church buildings constructed to hold far larger crowds—whether or not they ever actually did so. With members of the small evangelical "free churches" added in, about 4 percent of Swedes attend weekly and another 6 percent go at least once a month. However, church attendance does not tell us much if the most basic aspect of current Swedish religion is a shift to unchurched faiths. It seems very revealing that Swedes are *far* more likely to pray than to attend church—only 38 percent say they never pray (Hamberg 2001). In addition, most Swedes (69%) say they are concerned about "the meaning and purpose of life," and 59 percent believe that each individual has a soul (WVS 1995).

It is not metaphorical to call the Swedish State Church a shell, since one of its major functions is as a physical site for "unchurched" religious activities. Thus, the churches often are used for life-cycle events such as funerals and weddings, although the actual religious orientation of those involved often closely resembles the folk religion of their medieval forebears, and the Swedish Church "willingly offers such services to non-

Exploring the Religious Life

members" (Hamberg and Pettersson 1994, 214). In addition, the state churches offer meeting space for various "unchurched" faiths—what Granqvist and Hagekull (2001, 527) describe as a "smorgasbord" of spirituality. Indeed, many have noted a rapid increase in New Age activities and beliefs in Sweden during recent years, both within and outside the state church (Frisk 1998; Sjödin 2002). About one Swede in five believes in reincarnation (WVS 1995). Another recent national survey showed that 33 percent believed in nontraditional medical treatments such as "healing crystals," one in five said they would consider purchasing a personal horoscope, 10 percent would consult a medium, and nearly two of five believe in ghosts (Bråkenhielm 2001).

The question of how religious (or how secularized) Sweden is produces quite different answers if one examines beliefs rather than church attendance, and especially if one explores non-Christian beliefs. It also is crucial to know not only that the popularity of nontraditional spirituality and New Age notions has been increasing in recent years, but also that these beliefs are substantially more prevalent among the young than among older people. The young are especially given to belief in paranormal phenomena such as premonitions and UFOs. A similar penchant to embrace esoteric and magical beliefs has been reported for students in Germany and Austria (Höllinger and Smith 2002), as well as in the Netherlands (Houtman and Mascini 2002). In any event, using supernatural beliefs as the criterion, Ulf Sjödin (2002, 83) concluded that 78 percent of "young Swedes are religious" and only 13 percent are not.

To sum up: religiousness has not disappeared in Sweden; it simply is not to be found in church. Faith lives on as privatized, unchurched spirituality—"a kind of private or invisible religion" (Sjödin 2002, 84). And being undisciplined by creeds or congregations, the supernaturalism most popular in Sweden is infused with a lot of "paranormal" convictions and is about as skeptical of science as it is of organized religion (Sjödin 2002). Surely this is not what the secularization theorists had in mind.

Unchurched Religions & Spirituality in Japan

At first glance, Japanese religion is a confused muddle. Statistics on what Westerners call religious affiliation add up to far more than 100 percent of the population. That's because, on one hand, many Japanese claim several affiliations, Shinto and Buddhism being the common pair. On the other hand, as shown in table 6.2, only 5 percent of Japanese say they are active in a church, 77 percent say they were not raised "religiously," and 76 percent do not consider themselves to be religious. Such statistics have led many to cite Japan as a "postreligious" or secularized society (Eades et al. 1986; Fukutake 1981; Ikado 1972; Wilson 1977). However, the last two items in table 6.2 challenge that conclusion. The majority (57%) believe in the supernatural. Almost two-thirds (63%) believe that humans have souls. But to conclude from these data that the Japanese are, like the British, "believing non-belongers" is to miss the primary aspects of Japanese religious life. The Japanese turn out to be deeply and very *actively* religious if unchurched religion and spirituality are examined. Unfortunately, as translated into Japanese, the word *religious* excludes these forms of faith.

Consider that in 88 percent of their households, the "irreligious" Japanese maintain Buddhist altars, which are believed to shelter the spirits of their deceased ancestors (Miller 1992). Most Japanese perform frequent rites before these altars and offer gifts (including food) to the spirits. In addition to a Buddhist altar, nearly all Japanese homes contain a *kami-dana,* or Shinto home shrine, before which they perform rituals each morning and evening. Japanese life outside the home is also drenched in religious assumptions and practices. When one buys a new car, it is customary to drive to the nearest Shinto Temple to have the vehicle blessed by a priest (Nelson 1992). Everyone who seeks a loan to build a house will be sent a form by the government Home Loan Office, listing normal "closing" expenses. Here is a translation of part of this list, with estimated costs converted into U.S. dollars:

- transfer of ownership paperwork $2,600
- filing legal documents $1,200
- earthquake insurance $890
- religious ceremony to purify land $1,200

One may be able to persuade a lender to forgo the religious ceremony, but few Japanese would consider doing so—nor would most be willing to inhabit a home built without such a ceremony. Should it be necessary to remove a tree, it is assumed that no action will be taken without a religious service to appease the spirit of that specific tree. This, too, requires the services of a Shinto priest and does not come cheap.

In truth, Japan is an unreligious society only if that term is under-

Table 6.2 Japanese "Religion"

1. "Are you active in a church?"	
Not a member	88%
No, inactive	7%
Yes, active	5%
2. "Were you raised religiously?"	
No	77%
Yes	23%
3. "Do you consider yourself religious?	
No	76%
Yes	24%
4. "Do you believe in the supernatural?"	
Yes	57%
No	43%
5. "Do you believe in a human soul?"	
Yes	64%
No	37%

Sources: For questions 1–3, World Values
Survey, 1992; for questions 4–5, World Values
Survey, 1995. Inter-University Consortium for
Political and Social Research, Ann Arbor, Mich.

stood to refer to churched religions. With the possible exception of Sōka Gakkai, the only real churched religions in Japan are mission faiths of foreign origin. About 4 percent of Japanese are Christians, and some profess to be Muslims or Hindus, which matches the 5 percent who say they are active in a church (Barrett, Kurian, and Johnson 2001). The traditional organized Japanese faiths are *client* religions, and the average Japanese mixes these with large doses of *folk* and *audience* religions and with *privatized spirituality.*

Japan's two major traditional faiths—Buddhism and Shintoism—do not sustain congregations. They are more like firms engaged in a service industry (Miller 1992). For a fee, they provide a variety of rites, such as funeral services and the pacification of spirits as noted above. There is no emphasis on regular participation, nor do these faiths seek to impose a creed, although each sustains a full-time priesthood that does embrace a creed. As for the laity, both Buddhist and Shinto priests assume that individuals will mix and match to their own satisfaction. The results are clear in table 6.3.

Most Japanese (75%) regularly visit their family grave site. Few (26%) doubt that a person's spirit remains with the family after death. About

Table 6.3 Unchurched Spirituality in Japan

"Do you regularly visit a family grave at least several times a year?"
Yes	75%
No	25%

"After death, a person's spirit remains with the family."
Agree	58%
Unsure	16%
Disagree	26%

"Do you pray on certain occasions when you need assistance?"
Yes	64%
No	36%

"Have you visited a temple recently to pray for a positive outcome in your life?"
Yes	54%
No	46%

"Do you keep a good luck charm or amulet around?"
Yes	63%
No	37%

"Do you feel that rivers and mountains have spirits?"
Yes	59%
No	41%

"Do you think palm reading is a reliable way to tell the future?"
Yes	53%
No	47%

"When a person is born and when a person dies are predetermined."
Agree	73%
Unsure	8%
Disagree	19%

"Without reference to any established religion, do you believe it is important to have spiritual beliefs?"
Yes	72%
Unsure	14%
No	14%

Source: Tenth Annual Japanese Character Study, Institute of Statistical Mathematics (Sakamoto 2000).

two-thirds (64%) say they pray when they need assistance. More than half (54%) have recently visited a temple in order to pray for "a positive outcome" in their lives. Nearly two-thirds (63%) use good luck charms and amulets. Three out of five (59%) believe rivers and mountains have spirits. Over half (53%) think palm reading is "a reliable way to tell the future," and almost three-fourths (73%) accept predestination.

Finally, the Japanese overwhelmingly believe that it is important to

Exploring the Religious Life

have spiritual beliefs—only 14 percent say no. Rather than being one of the most secularized societies (if such there be), Japan is among the most religious—if care is taken to distinguish between churched and unchurched religions. Those who do not consider themselves to be religious are as "religious" or more so than other Japanese in terms of their beliefs and activities. For example, 86 percent of those who do not consider themselves to be religious believe it is important to have spiritual beliefs (not shown). What sets Japan apart from the United States and Sweden is that the Japanese are not *turning toward* unchurched religion; they have pursued unchurched religions all along. Consequently, Japan offers an opportunity to observe some of the possible consequences should there be a shift elsewhere from churched to unchurched religions.

Religion & Authority

Unchurched religions lack authority, both moral and intellectual. *Creedless* religions impose no standards: individuals truly are expected to be their own philosophers or theologians, and the concept of *sin* is either very vague or absent entirely. Religions without *congregations* cannot exert social pressure to observe the moral order, even if they maintain a creed. Hence, the lack of creeds or congregations causes unchurched religions to have little or no social impact. Put another way, where unchurched religions predominate, religion plays, at most, a very peripheral role in the culture. This is clear in Japan. Religion may provide divine car insurance and protect against unsettled spirits, but it plays no part in defining or sustaining the moral order. As will be seen in chapter 7, neither religious beliefs nor religious practices are correlated with disapproval of criminal acts among the Japanese. That is, in Japan attitudes toward buying stolen goods or engaging in a hit-and-run auto accident are uncorrelated with the importance placed on God or the frequency of temple visits, of prayer, or of meditation. The same lack of religious effects exists in China, too, where religion also is primarily of the unchurched variety. In contrast, strong correlations obtain in all of the nations of "Christendom," including Sweden, where the legacy of churched religion still is decisive. Hence, the sociological "law" that "religion functions to sustain the moral order" is limited to churched religions.

Moreover, the lack of religious authority extends to a variety of more distant cultural matters, including respect for science. Just as the fundamental commitment of Christian theologians to reason explains why science arose only in Europe (Grant 1996; Jaki 1986; Stark 2003), unchurched religions, and especially those engaged in celebrating spirituality, tend to reject not only creeds but also commitment to rationality. They often condemn the very idea that there are *rules* of logic and evidence (Houtman and Mascini 2002). In contrast, studies based on Sweden (Sjödin 2002), Canada (Orenstein 2002), and the United States (Bainbridge and Stark 1980) demonstrate that churched religion offers a very substantial barrier to belief in magic and various forms of pseudoscience—it even seems to be far more supportive of conventional science than is education.[3] Conversely, as young Swedes embrace spirituality, they express skepticism about science. Expressions of hostility to science are rife on Internet spirituality sites, where little is so disdained as the "dead grip of linear thought" and the "materialist dogmas of science."

When Bainbridge and Stark (1980) first published their findings about the incompatibility of evangelical religion and "superstitions" in the *Skeptical Inquirer,* a journal founded to oppose magic and pseudoscience (but quite as hostile toward religion), many readers went into extreme denial. Dozens wrote to explain why it must be impossible that students who claimed to be "born again Christians" could be far less accepting of UFOs as alien visitors, of ESP, astrology, Tarot, séances, and Transcendental Meditation than students who said they had no religion. A prominent American humanist leader put it rather good-naturedly: "Am I supposed to agree that secularity is a mixed blessing?" The answer would seem to be yes.

Conclusion

This is not the proper occasion to pursue the many social implications of the lack of authority of unchurched religions. Here the concern has been to delineate the concept of unchurched religion and to demonstrate that the apparent irreligiousness of many people in the United States, Sweden, and Japan is an illusion caused by a failure to define religion with sufficient breadth and nuance: to say that most Japanese are irreligious is to ignore the extraordinary spirituality of their daily lives. The Japanese are overwhelmingly unchurched, however, and that matters a great deal, too. Only where most people lack an anchorage in a churched religion could a new religious movement such as Sōka Gakkai enroll a million homes in a decade. After more than twenty years of effort in the United States, Herff Applewhite had only thirty-seven followers when his Heav-

Exploring the Religious Life

en's Gate cult committed mass suicide, but it took Asahara Shōkō less than half that long to attract about ten thousand followers to Aum by the time the group released nerve gas in a Tokyo subway (Kisala and Mullins 2001).

Finally, other things being equal (which often they are not), it should be expected that churched religions will tend to be more popular than unchurched religions, having far more to offer—even if they also demand more (Iannaccone 1994; Stark and Finke 2000). However, for those unable or unwilling to be churched, unchurched religions seem to fill a basic human need. Irreligion appears to be the least stable of all "religious" conditions. At least, a substantial body of well-known research shows that it is extremely difficult to pass secularity along to one's offspring (summarized in Stark and Finke 2000).

7

Gods, Rituals & the Moral Order

Religion functions to sustain the moral order. This classic proposition, handed down from the founders, is regarded by many as the closest thing to a law that the social scientific study of religion possesses.

In his Burnett Lectures, W. Robertson Smith explained that "even in its rudest form Religion was a moral force, the powers that men revered were on the side of social order and moral law; and the fear of the Gods was a motive to enforce the laws of society, which were also the laws of morality" (1889, 53). Emile Durkheim, of course, argued that religion exists *because* it unites humans into moral communities and that, although law and custom also regulate conduct, religion alone "asserts itself not only over conduct but over the *conscience.* It not only dictates actions but ideas and sentiments" ([1886] 1994, 21). And according to Bronislaw Malinowski, "every religion implies some reward of virtue and punishment of sin" (1935, viii).

In one form or another, this proposition undoubtedly appears in every introductory sociology and anthropology text on the market. But as will be seen, it's wrong. Moreover, it wasn't even handed down from the founders, at least not unanimously! The founder of British anthropology, Edward Tylor, and the founder of British sociology, Herbert Spencer,[1] both took pains to point out that only *some kinds* of religions have moral implications.

Tylor ([1871] 1958, 446) reported:

To some the statement may seem startling, yet the evidence seems to justify it, that the relation of morality to religion is one that only belongs in its rudiments, or not at all, to rudimentary civilization. The comparison of savage and civilized religions bring into view . . . a deep-lying contrast in their practical action on human life . . . the popular idea that the moral government of the universe is an essential tenet of natural religion simply falls to the ground. Savage animism [religion] is almost devoid of that ethical element which to the educated modern mind is the very mainspring of practical religion. Not, as I have said, that morality is absent from the life of the lower [cultures] . . . But these ethical laws stand on their own ground of tradition and public opinion, comparatively independent of the animistic beliefs and rites which exist beside them. The lower animism is not immoral, it is unmoral.

Spencer (1896, 2:808–9) also noted that many religions ignore morality, and he went even further by suggesting that some religions actively encourage crime and immorality: "At the present time in India, we have freebooters like the Domras, among whom a successful theft is always celebrated by a sacrifice to their chief god Gandak."

Although little noticed, this dissenting view has continued among anthropologists. In 1922 J. P. Mills noted that the religion of the Lhotas includes no moral code: "Whatever it be which causes so many Lhotas to lead virtuous lives it is not their religion" (121). In his distinguished study of the Manus of New Guinea, Reo Fortune (1935, 357) contrasted the moral aspects of their religion with that of the typical tribe, agreeing that "Tylor is entirely correct in stating that in most primitive regions of the world religion and morality maintain themselves independently." Ruth Benedict (1938, 633) also argued that to generalize the link between religion and morality "is to misconceive" the "history of religions." She suggested that this linkage probably is typical only of "the higher ethical religions." Ralph Barton (1946) reported that the Ifugaos impute their own unscrupulous exchange practices to their Gods and seize every opportunity to cheat them. Peter Lawrence (1964, 27) found that the Garia of New Guinea have no conception whatever of "sin," and "no idea of rewards in the next world for good works." And Mary Douglas (1975, 77) flatly asserted that there is no "inherent relation between religion and morality: there are primitives who can be religious without being moral and moral without being religious."

Tylor's observation that not all religions support the moral order always should have been obvious to anyone familiar with Greek and Roman mythology. The Greco-Roman Gods were quite morally deficient. They were thought to do terrible things to one another and to humans as well—sometimes merely for amusement. And although they were quite likely to do wicked things to humans if the humans failed to propitiate them, the Gods had no interest in anything (wicked or otherwise) that humans might do to one another. Instead, the Greek and Roman Gods only concerned themselves with direct affronts. For example, no religious sanctions were incurred by young women who engaged in premarital sex *unless* they immersed themselves in sacred waters reserved for virgins (MacMullen 1981, 58). Because Aristotle taught that the Gods were incapable of caring about mere humans (53), he could not have concurred that religion serves the function of sustaining and legitimating the moral order. Indeed, classical philosophers would have ridiculed such a proposition as peculiar to Jews and Christians—and they would have been correct (MacMullen 1981; Meeks 1993; Stark 1996a). As will be seen, the proposition about the moral functions of religion requires a particular conception of supernatural beings as being deeply concerned about the behavior of humans toward one another. Such a conception of the Gods is found in many of the major world faiths, including Judaism, Christianity, Islam, and Hinduism. But it appears to be largely lacking in the supernatural conceptions prevalent in much of Asia and in animism and folk religions generally.

It would seem to follow that the moral behavior of individuals would be influenced by their religious commitments *only* in societies where the dominant religious organizations give clear and consistent expression to divine moral imperatives. Thus, for example, were proper survey data available, they should show that those who frequented the temples in Greco-Roman times were *no more* observant of the prevailing moral codes than were those who were lax in their religious practice (with the exception of members of the ascetic sects noted in chapter 3). As Tylor pointed out, this is not to suggest that societies in antiquity lacked moral codes but only that these were not predicated on religious foundations.

When and why, then, did social scientists get it so wrong? It was when Durkheim and the other early functionalists (including Robertson Smith and Malinowski) dismissed Gods as unimportant window-dressing, stressing instead that rites and rituals are the fundamental stuff of religion. In a long review of part 6 of Herbert Spencer's *Principles of Sociology*, Emile Durkheim ([1886] 1994, 19) condemned Spencer for reducing religion "to being merely a collection of beliefs and practices relating to a supernatural agent." Seen from the perspective of "real sociology" (i.e., French functionalism),

Exploring the Religious Life

[t]he idea of God which seemed to be the sum total of religion a short while ago, is now no more than a minor accident. It is a psychological phenomenon which has got mixed up with a whole sociological process whose importance is of quite a different order . . . We might perhaps be able to discover what is thus hidden beneath this quite superficial phenomenon . . .

Thus the sociologist will pay scant attention to the different ways in which men and peoples have conceived the unknown cause and mysterious depth of things. He will set aside all such metaphysical speculations and will see in religion only a social discipline.

Thus began a new social science orthodoxy: it is only through participation in rites and rituals that people are bound into a moral community. Eventually this line of analysis "bottomed out" in such absurdities as Rodney Needham's denial (1972) of the existence of *any* "interior state" that might be called religious belief and S. R. F. Price's claim (1984) that religious belief is a purely Christian invention, so that when "primitives" pray for things, they don't really mean it. In any event, it long has been regarded as self-evident that all religions consist of rites and rituals designed to sustain the moral order.

In this chapter I will more fully develop the thesis that it is particular conceptions of God, *not* participation in rites and rituals, that empower religions to sustain the moral order. Of course, participation in rites can greatly reinforce and vivify divine influences, but it is the attributes of Gods that determine the forms that such influences take. I will formulate my views as specific hypotheses, which I will test on appropriate cross-cultural and cross-national data.

Gods & Morality

Divine essences do not issue commandments. The Tao does not advise humans to love one another, nor does the "First Cause" tell us not to covet another's spouse. The "ground of our being" is not a *being* and consequently is incapable of having, let alone expressing, moral concerns. Only Gods can desire moral conformity. Even that is not sufficient. Gods can only lend sanctions to the moral order if they are *responsive*—that is, if they are concerned about, informed about, and act on behalf of humans. Moreover, to promote virtue among humans, Gods must themselves be virtuous—they must *favor good* over evil. Finally, the greater their *scope*—that is, the greater the diversity of their powers and the range of their influence—the more effective Gods will be in sustaining moral precepts. All-powerful, all-seeing Gods ruling the entire universe are the ultimate deterrent. "Can any hide himself in secret places that I shall not see him? saith the Lord. Do not I fill heaven and earth? saith the Lord" (Jer. 23:24, King James Version).

This analysis does, of course, imply that there is progress from less to more complex cultures and that the linkage between religion and morality reflects such a progression. In a colorful passage, Ruth Benedict (1938, 633) wrote that moral concerns *become* a central value of "religion in man's history just as the pearl constitutes the value of the oyster." But, she noted, just as oysters must develop pearls, religions must develop moral engagement.

The discussion can be summed up in four hypotheses:

1: *In many societies, religion and morality will not be linked.*
2: *This linkage will tend to be limited to more complex cultures.*
3: *The effects of religiousness on individual morality are contingent on images of Gods as conscious, morally concerned beings; religiousness based on divine essences or unmoral Gods will not influence moral choices.*
4: *Participation in religious rites and rituals will have little or no **independent** effect on morality.*

The remainder of the chapter is devoted to testing these hypotheses.

Religion, Morality & "Progress"

Both Tylor and Spencer believed that the connection between religion and morality was a mark of cultural progress—that it was something to be found in the religions of more "advanced" peoples. They based this conclusion on their immense knowledge of ethnographic reports. However, a less impressionistic evaluation of this proposition became possible with the advent of quantitative cross-cultural studies, pioneered by George Peter Murdock (1949, 1981; Murdock and White 1969) and his colleagues following World War II. In *The Birth of the Gods* (1960) Guy E. Swanson selected 37 premodern societies from Murdock's then-current set of 556 and coded them as to whether or not the supernatural was believed to impose sanctions on "immoral" behavior. Even though his criteria for coding the presence of such sanctions were very generous, Swanson found no such sanctions in a fourth of these societies. He interpreted this as evidence against Tylor, noting that "Contrary to Tylor's formulation, a considerable proportion of the simpler peoples do make a connection between supernatural sanctions and moral behavior" (174).

As is obvious, Swanson's study suffered from including only a very small number of cases. In addition, here as in his study of the Reformation, Swanson's theoretical approach was relentlessly psychological, and this led him to try to relate the presence of supernatural sanctions to various possible sources of "tension" affecting the individual. Most of these turned out not to be correlated significantly with the presence of supernatural sanctions, but five, including the prevalence of personal debts, the existence of social classes, private property ownership, primogeniture, and the presence of cereal agriculture, were significantly correlated with supernatural sanctioning. Swanson took this as mixed support for his hypothesis concerning tension as the basis for the link between the Gods and morality. But of course, Tylor and Spencer would have noticed that the variables yielding significant results all measure aspects of cultural and social complexity, or what they called civilization. Thus, Swanson's discovery that each of the above variables was significantly positively associated with divine sanctions was confirmation of hypothesis 2. Although Swanson was one of the few contemporary social scientists who was aware of Tylor and Spencer's views, if he recognized these implications of his results, he chose to ignore them. A somewhat abortive attempt to replicate Swanson's study, based on seventy-two Native North American societies, also ignored the matter (Peregrine 1996).

For more than twenty years, it has been possible to test hypotheses 1 and 2 on a very large selection of cases (although I can find no indications that anyone has done so). When Murdock published the *Atlas of World Cultures* (1981), he responded to Swanson's earlier work by coding whether or not the "High Gods" in each of 427 societies were "active, and specifically supportive of human mortality" (there was no concept of a High God in 183 of these societies). Moreover, for more than a decade these and other of Murdock's "samples" have been available in a carefully cross-checked, electronic format from the MicroCase Corporation,[2] and that is the version I have used.

The results show that only a fourth (23.9%) of these societies acknowledged a "High God" who was concerned with human morality, thus confirming Tylor and Spencer's judgment that most premodern societies *do not* link religion and morality. However, some of the Gods in societies lacking high Gods might also promote human morality—that was not

Table 7.1 Correlations between Cultural Complexity and Moral Gods

	Correlations with the Presence of Moral Gods
Dairy herds	.898**
Domesticated large animals	.876**
Existence of the state	.790**
Metal working	.777**
Weaving	.718**
Cereal-based agriculture	.689**
Pottery making	.655**

N = 427
**Significant above .000.

part of the coding scheme. But even if we omit all societies without high Gods, the high Gods in 58 percent of the remaining 244 societies *do not* support human morality. Either way, in keeping with hypothesis 1, a lack of connection between religion and morality is common in premodern societies.

But what about hypothesis 2, that this linkage develops as societies become more culturally sophisticated? Table 7.1 offers very striking confirmation. The presence of "moral Gods" is very highly correlated (gamma) with seven measures of cultural complexity. Thus, it seems that the linkage between religion and morality generally is limited to the more "advanced religions," just as the early anthropologists claimed.

Conceptions of God & Morality

I devote the remainder of this chapter to testing hypotheses 3 and 4 in various societies that differ in their general conceptions of God.

GOD AND MORALITY IN THE UNITED STATES

Because of the extent and variety of the available data, I will begin with data from surveys of the United States before examining data for other nations. A suitable measure of conformity to the moral order is a question about having been picked up by the police, included in some early General Social Surveys, most recently in 1984. After a filter question to screen out traffic offenses, respondents were asked, "Were you ever picked up, or charged, by the police for any (other) reason whether or not you were guilty?" In 1984, 13 percent acknowledged having been picked up. In that same survey, respondents were asked, "How close do you feel to God most of the time?" Thirty-one percent said they felt "extremely close," another 54 percent said "somewhat close," 14 percent said "not close" or "not close at all," and 1 percent said they didn't believe in God.

In keeping with hypothesis 3, *the closer they feel to God, the less likely people are to have been picked up by the police.*

The hypothesis is strongly supported. Only 8.7 percent of those who felt extremely close to God had ever been picked up, compared with 13.1 percent of those who felt somewhat close and 19.4 percent who did not feel close to God. The relationship is significant beyond the .001 level.

Although it seems generally true that belief in God helps to sustain the moral order in the United States, this result may be masking important variations related to how people think about God. Of particular relevance here are objections often raised by conservative Christians that liberal portrayals of God as a nonjudgmental, easy-going "friend" not only are bad theology but are inimical to morality. As revival preachers are fond of reminding their audiences, "God did not give Moses the Ten Suggestions."

These views are entirely testable because, from time to time, Andrew Greeley has provided funds to include a battery of questions about God in the General Social Surveys, and fortunately that battery was included in 1984. It was introduced as follows: "When you think about God, how likely are each of these images to come to your mind?" Twelve one-word images were used, and four response categories were provided, ranging from "Extremely likely" to "Not likely at all." The images easily can be divided into two groups: those reflecting God as *powerful* and those reflecting God as *affectionate.* Hence, consistent with the third proposition, *powerful images of God will sustain moral conformity; affectionate images will not.*

Table 7.2 shows the correlations (gamma) between images of God and the item on having been picked up by the police. In order to avoid biasing the effects of variations in contrasting images of God, respondents who said they did not believe in God have been excluded. The results are striking. A powerful God sustains the moral order; an affectionate God does not! Indeed, the contrast between the image of God as Father

Table 7.2 Images of God and Moral Conformity (United States)

	Correlations with "Picked up by the police"
Powerful God	
Father	−.37**
Redeemer	−.37**
Healer	−.34*
Liberator	−.30*
Master	−.29*
Creator	−.29*
Judge	−.26*
King	−.17
Affectionate God	
Mother	.01
Lover	.04
Spouse	.18
Friend	−.14

**Significant above .01. *Significant above .05.

(−.37**) and as Mother (.01) could hardly be more dramatic. Seven of the eight powerful images of God are significantly negatively correlated with having been picked up (that is, the more a person thought of God as powerful, the less likely he or she was to have been picked up). None of the four affectionate images is significantly correlated with having been picked up.

Unfortunately, these items are available only for the United States. However, items available from the World Values Surveys include some that are adequate for testing the relationship between images of God and the moral order.[3] These surveys consist of national polls conducted in many nations, using the same questions (translated into the local language) in each. Although not all items were asked in each nation, most were, making it possible to replicate findings in a great variety of cultures and social settings. In the 1990–91 surveys, respondents in most nations were presented with a battery of items asking whether they approved or disapproved of various kinds of immoral and illegal behavior. Most of these behaviors lacked cross-cultural consensus—in at least a few nations the majority did not disapprove. These included items concerning prostitution, abortion, homosexuality, divorce, lying, euthanasia, and sui-

Exploring the Religious Life

cide. Eventually I selected three, each of which was judged as unjustified by a substantial *majority* in *each* nation.

> Please tell me for each of the following statements whether you think it can always be justified, never be justified, or something in between.
> Buying something you knew was stolen (Stolen Goods).
> Failing to report damage you've done accidentally to a parked car. (Hit/Run)
> Taking the drug marijuana or hashish (Smoke Dope).

Respondents were asked to rank the statements on a scale of 1 to 10, with 10 being always justified, and 1 being never justified.

In similar fashion, respondents were asked, "How important is God in your life?" and asked to place themselves on a scale from 1 ("not at all") to 10 ("very important"). Table 7.3 shows that in the United States the importance placed on God is very significantly negatively correlated (gamma) with each of the three measures of tolerance for immorality.

No doubt Durkheim would propose the counterhypothesis that the real basis for these correlations is participation in collective religious rituals, as these sustain *both* belief in the supernatural and commitment to the moral order. However, this claim is refuted by the second row of correlations, which report the effects of ritual, measured as church attendance. Attendance is on an eight-point scale, ranging from 8 ("More than once a week") to 1 ("Never, or practically never"). Both belief and atten-

Table 7.3 God, Church Attendance, and the Moral Order in the United States

	Stolen Goods	Hit/Run	Smoke Dope
Correlations with			
Importance of God	−.30**	−.23**	−.38**
Correlations with			
Church Attendance	−.20**	−.15**	−.26**

Regression Analysis			
	Standardized Betas		
God	−.138**	−.085**	−.243**
Church Attendance	−.040	−.052	−.038
R^2 =	.026**	.015**	.163**

**Significant above .01. *Significant above .05.

Gods, Rituals & the Moral Order

dance are correlated with morality, but in all three comparisons, the ritual effect is notably weaker than the God effect. Moreover, when entered into a regression analysis, the God variable eliminates all effects of church attendance. Contrary to Durkheim's revisionism, it appears that Tylor and Spencer were right that ideas about God, rather than rituals, are the most fundamental basis of religion. Thus, hypotheses 3 and 4 are strongly supported by American data.

In the remainder of this chapter, I will use items from the World Values Surveys to assess the link between God and morality in thirty-three nations. Because the nature of God is left unspecified in the item, I will depend upon cultural contexts to define God. For societies where God generally is conceived of as a conscious being who imposes moral demands, hypothesis 3 anticipates negative correlations between the importance placed on God and willingness to condone moral violations. But in societies that generally regard God(s) as unconcerned about morality or as impersonal essence, no correlations should exist between the importance placed on God(s) and willingness to condone moral violations. And, in accord with hypothesis 4, the effects of ritual participation should be weaker than and contingent on images of God(s). I shall proceed on the basis of appropriate geocultural blocs.

GOD AND MORALITY IN THE WESTERN HEMISPHERE

Table 7.4 shows the correlations between the importance of God in one's life and the three measures of adherence to the moral order in five nations of the Western Hemisphere: Canada, Mexico, Brazil, Chile, and Argentina. Although these nations differ greatly in many ways, they share a general conception of God as an active, divine being who imposes moral standards. Therefore, the correlations with the importance of God should be negative, and they are. Each of the 15 correlations is negative and highly statistically significant. Hypothesis 3 is strongly confirmed. The table also includes the correlations with church attendance. In 14 of the 15 comparisons with the God effects, the church attendance effect is weaker— usually substantially weaker. Only in Argentina on smoking marijuana does this generalization not hold, and that probably can be dismissed as a random fluctuation. Again, hypothesis 4 is confirmed.

By Durkheim's definition, many nations of Western Europe are quite irreligious, church attendance being so low that few people are involved in collective religious rituals. But as *religious* is defined by Tylor and Spencer, most people in Western Europe are religious nonetheless. Atheists are few (seldom more than 5%), and the great majority consider themselves to be "a religious person"—they are "believing non-belongers," as Grace Davie (1994) so aptly put it. Moreover, the prevailing conception of God is the conventional Christian deity. These nations of Western Europe make it possible to examine the effects of God on morality in settings where belief is not confounded with participation in religious rituals, as it is in the Western Hemisphere, where both belief and church attendance are high. In accord with hypothesis 4, within the European context the correlations ought to be as strongly negative in Scandinavia, where religious participation is extremely low, as in southern Europe, where participation is high.

Table 7.5 powerfully confirms these expectations. Of the 48 correlations shown, all are negative, and only one falls short of statistical significance (smoking dope in Sweden). Moreover, the correlations are about of equal strength in Scandinavia and in southern Europe. In addition, in only 7 of the 48 comparisons does the church attendance correlation (not shown) equal or exceed the God effect. As in the Western Hemi-

Table 7.4 God and the Moral Order in the Western Hemisphere

	Correlations with Importance of God		
	Stolen Goods	Hit/Run	Smoke Dope
Canada	−.24**	−.19**	−.34**
Mexico	−.17**	−.11**	−.25**
Brazil	−.39**	−.22**	−.50**
Chile	−.29**	−.11**	−.38**
Argentina	−.37**	−.20**	−.30**
	Correlations with Church Attendance		
Canada	−.19**	−.09*	−.25**
Mexico	−.04	−.08	−.13**
Brazil	−.22**	−.17**	−.39**
Chile	−.12**	−.08*	−.26**
Argentina	−.30**	−.16**	−.41**

**Significant above .01. *Significant above .05.

Gods, Rituals & the Moral Order

Table 7.5 God and the Moral Order in Western Europe

	Correlations with Importance of God		
	Stolen Goods	Hit/Run	Smoke Dope
Great Britain	−.29**	−.23**	−.31**
Ireland	−.43**	−.29**	−.45**
Northern Ireland	−.59**	−.39**	−.57**
Scandinavia			
Norway	−.37**	−.21**	−.41**
Sweden	−.24**	−.27**	−.12
Finland	−.31**	−.20**	−.25**
Denmark	−.30**	−.16**	−.31**
Iceland	−.37**	−.21**	−.41**
Northern Europe			
West Germany	−.35**	−.24**	−.33*
Netherlands	−.23**	−.13**	−.32**
Belgium	−.22**	−.17**	−.26**
Switzerland	−.26**	−.24**	−.32**
Southern Europe			
France	−.24**	−.15**	−.29**
Italy	−.35**	−.10**	−.38**
Spain	−.21**	−.18**	−.35**
Portugal	−.30**	−.20**	−.37**

**Significant above .01. *Significant above .05.

sphere, the church attendance correlations typically were substantially lower, lending support to hypothesis 4.

GOD AND MORALITY IN EASTERN EUROPE

Thus far I have been hypothesizing negative correlations between the importance placed on God and acceptance of moral violations because of the conception of God prevalent in the nations examined. For parts of eastern Europe, I do not anticipate such effects, in part because Eastern Orthodoxy stresses rite and ritual, icons and incense, and has remarkably little to say about sin: "The emphasis is not so much on truth and justice as on beauty and love" (Weaver 1998, 76). Consequently, Orthodoxy projects a comparatively remote and nonjudgmental image of God. Unfortunately, in the nations available for analysis, this religious factor is partly confounded with a long history of Communist repression of religion and with the collaboration of most Orthodox Churches with their repressors (Filatov 1994). Both of these factors also ought to have weakened the link between religion and morality.

Compared with Christianity in the West, Eastern Orthodoxy far more closely fits the model of religion proposed by Durkheim and the functionalists, in that it is a religion of collective ritual and rite, putting far greater emphasis on the sacraments than on a direct relationship with God. An indication of this is the virtual absence of any discussions of sin and the almost exclusive focus on sacraments in the few discussions of sin that do appear in recent summaries of Orthodox theology (cf. Ware 1997, 1979; Clendenin 1995). Indeed, Orthodox writers stress that confession of sins (if sincere) *automatically* results in complete forgiveness, and they are very critical of the "Latin church" for "teaching of penalties and punishments," including the concept of purgatory, "all of which the Orthodox church most strenuously rejects" (Karmiris 1973, 29). Nicolas Zernov (1959, 101) offers this contrast: "In the Roman Church the role of the priest in the confessional is that of judge . . . In the East the priest is not a judge, but a witness."

However, rather than emphasizing a personal relationship between the penitent and God, this Orthodox approach to confession seems to have quite the opposite effect of making the process impersonal. Moreover, the distaste for punishment of sin (and even the concept of sin) carries over into Orthodox teaching about salvation. Bishop Kallistos (Timothy) Ware (1997, 262) explained that in the Orthodox view, although "[h]ell exists as a final possibility . . . several of the Fathers have none the less believed that in the end all will be reconciled to God. It is heretical to say that all *must* be saved, for this is to deny free will; but it is legitimate to hope that all *may* be saved." As Nikos Kokosalakis (1994, 143) noted, "[t]here is a remarkable flexibility, approaching permissiveness, in the Orthodox Church."

Orthodoxy also stresses the collective nature even of salvation. Aleksei Khomiakov (1895, 216) explained that "no one is saved alone." Nicolas Zernov (1959, 98) drew this contrast: "Orthodoxy starts with community, and sees the individual as a member thereof. Western Christianity begins with the individual, and interprets the community as the outcome of a decision made by individuals to act together." The greater emphasis on the individual in the West may have originated in (or may have been greatly increased by) the Reformation and the Counter Reformation, neither of which had any impact on Orthodoxy. In any event, the emphasis on collectivity and ritual shows up in prayer, as Orthodoxy discourages attempts to establish a direct, personal relationship with God of the sort typical of the devotional life in the West (although there are denominational differences in the West, too).

These differences in doctrine may seem subtle, but they are quite apparent as the religion is experienced by the laity: from the pew, God seems remote and rather inactive. However, I would only expect this aspect of the Orthodox conception of God, in and of itself, to *reduce*, not eliminate, the link between the individual's commitment to God and his or her moral conformity. That is, I would expect negative, significant, *but substantially weaker* correlations in Orthodox nations than in the West. Unfortunately, as mentioned, there are also the confounding effects of Communism to consider.

In the wake of the Russian Revolution, the Communist regime imposed brutal and unrelenting religious repression. On orders from Lenin (Troyanovsky 1991), thousands of priests and nuns were murdered, often in bizarre ways after extended torture (Pospielovsky 1988). Party squads also looted all the churches, many of which had very valuable artwork and altar vessels; even all the church bells were confiscated and melted down for scrap (MacKenzie 1930). Most church buildings also were seized, and some of the most famous and beautiful were converted into museums of scientific atheism. Following the initial campaign of terror, repression was sustained at a somewhat less ferocious level throughout the Communist era. Millions were exiled to labor camps for persisting in religion, especially for practicing non-Orthodox religions. Millions of others were discriminated against (excluded from the party, from better jobs, and from higher education) because they were known to be or suspected of being religious (Pospielovsky 1988). At the start of the Revolution, there were more than 80,000 Orthodox churches in what became the Soviet Union. By 1939 there were only about 1,000 (Barrett 1982). Similarly, in 1917 there were more than 1,200 Orthodox monasteries; a decade later there were none—some had been converted into prisons (Timberlake 1995). In response to the need for national unity following the German invasion, Stalin slightly eased the repression, only to increase it somewhat again at the war's end (Anderson 1994; Pospielovsky 1997). During the 1980s there were about 5,000 Christian churches in the USSR (not counting secret Protestant congregations), or about 1 per 50,000 people (Barrett 1982). Islamic groups also endured intense repression. In the former Soviet of Dagestan, for example, there were more than 1,700 mosques in 1917. By 1988 there were only 12, to serve a far larger population than in 1917 (Bobrovnikov 1996).[4] Buddhists were not spared, either (Snelling 1993). Although the antireligious campaign was not directed against them until 1930, by 1936 all Buddhist monasteries had been destroyed, and "Molotov could rejoice in the liquidation of the 'parasitical lama class' as one of the achievements of Soviet Policy" (243).

Even so, throughout the Soviet Union the police (and on holidays, volunteers from Communist youth groups) prevented anyone but elderly, regular members from entering a church or mosque to attend services. In addition to closing churches and mosques and persecuting religious people, the Soviet regime conducted a constant program of atheistic education, making it a regular part of the primary and secondary school curricula. One of the primary goals of this campaign was to disconnect morality and religion, and the schools devoted considerable effort to moral education combined with attacks on religion.

Following Word War II, when the USSR imposed Communist regimes on many nations of eastern Europe, attempts were made to impose similar levels of religious repression. Compared with the early terror campaign in Russia, far fewer clergy were murdered (although a substantial number were in Albania), but large numbers were imprisoned, many churches were seized, and many others were closed. However, the effectiveness of these efforts varied depending on the level of local cooperation, which was far higher in nations dominated by the Orthodox Church than in Roman Catholic nations.

We now know that these Communist efforts to stamp out religion were not very successful in the sense that belief in God remains widespread in eastern Europe. Even in Russia only 8 percent identified themselves as atheists in 1991. But repression did greatly diminish religious participation, and especially religious education. Moreover, a side effect of religious repression was to discredit "the Church" in most nations where the Eastern Orthodox Church predominates. For a variety of reasons, the national Orthodox Churches were successfully co-opted by local Communist regimes to such an extent that clergy frequently informed on non-Orthodox religious activities and even on religious dissidents within their own ranks. Worse yet, some Orthodox clergy were willing to ratify views such as "God is identical with the Marxist concept of history" (Pásztor 1995, 27) or to defend government prohibitions on church attendance by young people because "religious instruction of underage children promotes prejudices" (Johansen 1983, 15). (Romania is a notable exception, as will be seen.) In contrast, in the non-Orthodox nations, the churches, particularly the Roman Catholic Church, managed to preserve their honor and to be beacons of resistance.

I anticipate that each of these factors—repression, collaboration, and a more distant image of God—will tend have an effect, as formulated in these subsidiary hypotheses:

1. *Communist efforts to weaken the link between religion and morality will show up in substantially weaker correlations in the non-Orthodox nations of eastern Europe than those found in western Europe.*
2. *Within eastern Europe, the more remote Orthodox conception of God will result in correlations that are weaker in Orthodox nations than in the non-Orthodox nations. In combination with the effects of Communist repression, this will result in a lack of any significant correlations between God and morality in the Orthodox nations, except for Romania.*

As can be seen in table 7.6, the first of these subsidiary hypotheses is strongly supported. Although significant negative correlations obtain in 10 of the 11 instances, they do tend to be weaker than in table 7.5. For example, all three correlations are much higher in the former West Germany than in the former East Germany. Only the correlations in Poland resemble the magnitudes typical in western Europe, but, of course, nowhere in eastern Europe was the church so effective in resisting the regime as in this nation that produced the first non-Italian pope in many centuries. As for hypothesis 4, in 10 of the 11 comparisons, the church attendance effect (not shown) is substantially weaker (most correlations are not significant) than the God effect.

The second subsidiary hypothesis also is strongly supported by table 7.6. In Russia, all three of the correlations are minuscule. In another sample, based only on the population of Moscow, again none of the three correlations is significant. Nor are there any significant correlations in Bulgaria. There are two small, significant correlations in Belarus, but they are in the wrong direction! That is, the more importance Belorussians place on God, the *more* willing they are to condone immorality. I suspect that this is a meaningless finding.

Then there is Romania. It, too, is an Orthodox nation, and it, too, long endured Communist rule. But all three correlations are strong, negative, and highly significant. Why? Part of the answer would seem to lie in the effective resistance of the Romanian Orthodox Church, which,

Exploring the Religious Life

Table 7.6 God and the Moral Order in Eastern Europe

	Correlations with Importance of God		
	Stolen Goods	Hit/Run	Smoke Dope
Non-Orthodox Nations			
Poland	–.17*	—	–.21**
East Germany	–.19**	–.11**	–.12**
Hungary	–.15**	–.08*	–.12**
Slovenia	–.03	–.14**	–.19**
Orthodox Nations			
Russia	.02	–.06	.04
(Moscow)	.07	.03	–.04
Bulgaria	–.07	–.07	.00
Belarus	.09*	.05	.10*
Romania	–.26**	–.22**	–.31**

— Question not asked.

**Significant above .01. *Significant above .05.

unlike the Orthodox Church in Russia,[5] never was subservient to the state—for a time in the 1930s the Romanian Orthodox patriarch also was the prime minister. But perhaps the major reason behind these correlations can be traced to the idiosyncrasies of that strange tyrant Nicolas Ceauşescu, who ruled the nation from 1965 until he was executed by revolutionaries on Christmas Day 1989. It is uncertain what Ceauşescu's private religious views may have been, although after taking power he did provide a religious funeral for his father. But from the beginning of his rule, he established very friendly, personal relationships with the heads of all religious bodies in Romania, including Protestants and Jews. Following the overthrow of the Ceauşescu regime, some have condemned these relationships as collaboration (Tökés 1990). Perhaps so, but they also resulted in a religious climate unlike that in any other Communist state. For example, rather than demanding that Communist Party members be staunch atheists, Ceauşescu merely required that party members not hold religious offices—many party members were openly active Christians. In addition, under Ceauşescu the government gave extensive financial subsidies to all of the churches and exempted all seminarians and clergy from military service. Most important of all, the churches were freely permitted to operate a huge system of Sunday schools (Barrett 1982). Thus, in Romania, moral education remained religious education. Writing about fifteen years after Ceauşescu took over, Earl A. Pope (1981, 4) reported that "there appears to be a very important resurgence of religious faith in Romania. Paradoxical as it may seem, the rise of Marxism has led to the inner strengthening of religious communities. In certain respects, some of them appear to be healthier now than they were in an earlier era—despite the limitations and restrictions imposed." Granted, Ceauşescu did not tolerate opposition from anyone, including church leaders. But the fact remains that the religious situation in Romania was unique among Communist states (Barrett 1982; Pope 1981, 1992).

I am unable to document that the image of God portrayed in these Romanian Sunday schools, including those that were Orthodox (as most of them were), was more vigorous and morally relevant than was sustained in other Orthodox nations such as Bulgaria, Belarus, or Russia, but that seems likely, given that the Romanian Orthodox Church recently welcomed World Vision, one of the leading evangelical Protestant world mission agencies, to help with the "spiritual recovery" of Romania. In fact, the majority of staff and board members of World Vision Romania are provided by the Orthodox Church (Athyal 1998). This partnership with World Vision is unique among Orthodox Churches in eastern Europe or the former Soviet Union. The other national Orthodox Churches have become militant opponents of all possible competitors, especially "outsiders" such as World Vision.

Given the great emphasis on ritual in the Orthodox Church, Durkheim surely would propose a counterhypothesis. However, the data (not shown) offer no support for the ritual alternative, being entirely consistent with hypothesis 4. Only one of the 12 correlations with church attendance is significant, and it is in the wrong direction! Religion, either as God or as ritual, fails to support the moral order in these Orthodox nations.

God & Morality in Turkey

Muslims believe that the God of the Torah and of the New Testament is the same God who gave the Qur'ān to Muhammad, the final prophet in a line beginning with Abraham. "He hath revealed unto thee (Muhammad) the Scripture with truth, confirming that which was (revealed) before it, even as He revealed the Torah and the Gospel" (Qur'ān 3:3). Not surprisingly, the Muslim image of God's nature is very similar to that of traditional Judaism and Christianity: an all-seeing, all-powerful, eternal, conscious, virtuous, morally concerned *being*. "Allah! There is no God

Table 7.7 God, Mosque Attendance, and the Moral Order in Turkey

	Stolen Goods	Hit/Run	Smoke Dope
Correlations with importance of God	−.45**	−.31**	−.44**
Correlations with mosque attendance	−.19**	−.12*	−.12

Regression Analysis	Standardized Betas		
God	−.184**	−.138**	−.162**
Mosque attendance	−.051	−.036	−.027
R^2	.042**	.024**	.030**

**Significant above .01. *Significant above .05.

save Him, the Alive, the Eternal. Lo! nothing in the earth or in the heavens is hidden from Allah" (Qur'ān 3:2, 5). As for morality, the Qur'ān is entirely clear about how humans are to behave toward one another, the immense rewards awaiting the virtuous, and the eternal sanctions to befall those who fail to conform.

Consequently, Muslims who place the greatest importance on God ought to be most opposed to moral transgressions. Table 7.7 strongly supports hypothesis 3: all the correlations between God and tolerance of immorality are negative, significant, and of a magnitude comparable with the highest found elsewhere. The second row of correlations shows that here, too, Durkheim's ritual alternative fails quite badly. As predicted by hypothesis 4, the correlations with mosque attendance are far weaker, and one even falls short of significance. In fact, regression analysis eliminates all traces of a mosque attendance effect.

God & Morality in India

It easily could be assumed that there would be at best a very tenuous link between religion and morality in India, since the general impression among Westerners is that Hinduism is polytheistic and that hence, as is typical in polytheistic religions, relationships with any given God are short-term and utilitarian. But this is quite erroneous (Fowler 1997; Knipe 1993; Parrinder 1983; Smart 1984; Weightman 1984). First of all, the Hindu Gods really number only two: Vishnu and Shiva. Each of the many other apparent Gods is regarded as an additional aspect, avatar, or incarnation of one of these two. Thus, although there exist many different Hindu sects devoted to different incarnations, it is understood that each really is either Vishnu or Shiva. The terrifying Krishna is an avatar of Vishnu. Some scholars claim that, in fact, Hindus *do not worship both* Vishnu and Shiva (Fowler 1997; Weightman 1984). Following a principle known as *ishtadeva* (the chosen deity), the individual Hindu worships one or the other "exclusively as the supreme God": "[O]ne could spend a lifetime in India and never find a 'polytheist' in Western terms, because even an unlettered peasant who has just made offerings at several shrines will affirm that . . . God is one" (Weightman 1984, 212). Ninian Smart (1984, 136) suggests that Hindus do not really believe that there are two Gods, but only one, who can be worshiped either in the form of Vishnu or that of Shiva.

No matter which form a Hindu chooses to represent God, morality is central to Hindu teachings and is subject to divine sanctions, which take the form of "bad Karma." Moral living in this world is specified in the dharma sutras and the dharma *shastras,* which are essentially religious law books. And, as Simon Weightman (1984, 197) explained, right living in this world, or dharma, is "the very centre of Hinduism." Observing dharma is regarded as an end in itself, but it is crucial in terms of Karma, the doctrine that every action influences one's future incarnations. This is closely related to another central doctrine concerning the sanctity of the caste system: that anyone's position in *this* life is God-given and earned through sin or righteousness. Hence, if the lowest castes suffer hell on earth, that is regarded as simple justice in that they *are in hell,* having earned their punishment in a prior life. Thus, in terms of moral edification, for a Hindu to observe the misery of low-caste life is tantamount to an actual visit to hell. These views have declined and softened to some extent over the past century, as has the concept of hell within Christianity. But there still ought to be a strong religious component to morality.

Table 7.8 God, Temple Visits, and the Moral Order in India

	Stolen Goods	Hit/Run	Smoke Dope
Correlations with importance of God	–.25**	–.20**	–.27**
Correlations with temple visits	.02	–.05	.08

**Significant above .01. *Significant above .05.

It follows that in India, the importance given to God will be negatively correlated with tolerance for immorality. Table 7.8 confirms hypothesis 3: all three correlations in the top row are negative and significant. The correlations in the second row are quite remarkable. Had no question been asked about God, forcing the use only of temple visits as a measure of religiousness, it would have seemed that religion fails to support morality in India: all three correlations are trivial. This would have been very misleading since, in India, God matters, even if ritual participation does not. Hypotheses 3 and 4 are strongly supported.

God & Morality in Japan

The spiritual life of the Japanese takes the form of individual "religious portfolios" (Iannaccone 1995). There are many Gods, and most Japanese select a subset from whom to seek benefits, much as cautious investors distribute their funds among various options. In addition to many Gods, two major religious traditions dominate in Japan—Shinto and Buddhism—and most Japanese "belong" to both. Buddhism, like American Protestantism, is fractured into many factions and sects, but whereas most American Protestants belong to only one group, many Japanese Buddhists adhere to several. Consequently, many Japanese report multiple religious affiliations, with the result that statistics on religious membership add up to nearly 200 percent of the total population (Parrinder 1983). As Alan S. Miller (1995, 235) explained, "[p]robably the most accurate way a Japanese person can answer the question 'what religion do you belong to?' is to reply 'I am Japanese.' One does not become a Shintoist, but rather participates in some Shinto-based rituals or festivals. Similarly, one does not become a Buddhist, but rather uses Buddhist teachings as guidelines for how to care for deceased relatives or pray for spiritual assistance. And, of course, one does not stop being a Shintoist or Buddhist when one no longer needs these services." Consequently, when asked if they are Shintoists, many Japanese probably will say no, and the next day they will drive their new automobile to a Shinto Temple to have it blessed by the priest or invite the priest to a building site to quiet the spirits prior to construction (Nelson 1992). As this widespread reliance on Shinto demonstrates, there is a great deal of magic involved in Shinto practices. Moreover, the Gods of Shinto are many, small in scope, and lacking in concern for humans. Like the Greco-Roman Gods, they may provide benefits in return for proper sacrifices, but the wise supplicant seeks aid from several Gods at once and is prepared to switch her or his patronage on the basis of results (Earhart 1984, 1993; Parrinder 1983).

In all of its forms, Buddhism emphasizes morality, as expressed in the five observances recited as part of devotions. These pledge the individual not to injure others, to not steal or lie, to avoid sexual immorality, and not to use alcohol or drugs (Parrinder 1983, 272). However, these moral obligations are *not* associated with God's will, because most Buddhists reject the existence of a conscious, all-powerful, concerned God of the sort worshiped by Jews, Christians, or Muslims. Indeed, the existence of such a God has for many centuries been the basis of dispute between Buddhists and Hindus, and "Buddhists have even gone so far as to say that belief in such a God often leads to ethical degradation" (Clough 1997, 57).

However, rank-and-file Buddhists are not atheists and do embrace a whole "pantheon of spirits and minor deities" (Clough 1997, 58), and supernatural creatures abound in Shinto (Earhart 1984, 1993). Indeed, "one of the chief characteristics of Shinto is the close and intimate relationship between humans and *kami*," which are acknowledged in Japanese Buddhism as well (Earhart 1984, 16). The *kami* are supernatural entities, but of small scope, as they are subject to many of the laws of nature and have very limited power. Other deities are known as *buddhas* (not to be confused with Buddha himself). These are closely related to the *kami*, and there is a Japanese term that includes both (Earhart 1993, 1115). However, the *buddhas* are deities of substantially greater power and scope, and, like Hindu Gods, a given *buddha* takes several forms. Thus Kannon, the Goddess of mercy who is one of the most popular *buddhas*, also takes the form of Koyasu Kannon, to whom appeals are directed for an easy childbirth, as well as the form of Bato Kannon, who serves as a sort of patron saint of livestock breeders (1117). But although the various *kami* and *buddhas* may grant favors or inflict harm, issues of morality are not germane to pleasing them.

The core of Japanese religion consists of frequent rites and rituals, most of which are conducted at home. Most Japanese maintain a *kami-dana*, or Shinto home shrine, before which they make ceremonial offerings each morning and evening. In addition, nearly every household headed by a first son also has a Buddhist altar devoted to the spirits of the family dead. This altar contains scrolls listing ancestors of the family—ancestor "worship" is an important part of both Buddhism and Shinto.

Table 7.9 God, Rituals, and the Moral Order in Japan

	Stolen Goods	Hit/Run	Smoke Dope
Correlations with importance of God	−.07	−.08	.11
Correlations with temple visits	−.06	−.09	.04
Correlations with prayer or meditation	−.04	−.09	.01

**Significant above .01. *Significant above .05.

Each year, on the anniversary of each family member's death (going back for several generations or more), the family gathers at the altar to make offerings to the ancestors; sometimes a priest is engaged for the occasion. Thus, religion in the Japanese household approaches the functionalist ideal type, since it maximizes collective rituals and minimizes the significance of the Gods.

It follows from hypothesis 3 that, given their conceptions of the Gods, there should *not be* significant correlations between the importance placed on God and moral attitudes in Japan. Table 7.9 confirms the hypothesis: all three correlations are insignificant.

Nor does ritual sustain morality in Japan. The second row of correlations shows that none of the three correlations involving temple visits is significant. Since so much of the ritual of Japanese religious life occurs in the home, I have added a third row to examine the effects of the frequency of "prayer or meditation." Here, too, all three correlations are trivial.

No matter how it is measured, religion does not sustain the moral order in Japan. This is in keeping with the chapter 6 discussion concluding that unchurched religions lack moral authority.

God & Morality in China

China has four great religions: Confucianism, Taoism, Buddhism, and the ancient, vigorous, and highly magical faith known variously as "popular religion" or as "Chinese folk religion" (Shahar and Weller 1996). The first two are indigenous and originated more as elite and Godless philosophies than as religions. Just as Buddha denied the existence of a God, Confucius is believed to have advised that "[a]bsorption in the study of the supernatural is most harmful" (Giles 1993, 94). As for the Tao, the

Chinese do acknowledge it as a sort of First Cause in the creation of the world, but it is thought to be an inactive, nonconscious essence—not only a nonbeing, but a "not-being" (Eichhorn 1959, 393). As noted, Buddhism also originated as a Godless philosophy in India, but by the time it migrated to Japan about fifteen hundred years ago, it had acquired a pantheon of supernatural creatures. The same came to be true of Chinese Confucianism and Taoism too. In fact, the four religions are somewhat amalgamated: "Gods are mutually borrowed and sometimes are shared by two, three, or all four religions" (Shahar and Weller 1996, 3). But all of these Gods are of very limited power and scope and usually lacking in moral concern and even dignity (Eichhorn 1959; Lang and Ragvald 1993; Shahar and Weller 1996). Thus, Chinese who have made an offering in a temple and not received the requested boon often return to attack the image of the God who failed (Chen 1995, 1).

For these reasons, consistent with hypothesis 3, I would *not* expect a link between commitment to God and morality in China. Moreover, the militant campaign against religion that raged in China for forty years (and which intermittently recurs) also should have some effect. Indeed, antireligious propaganda and repression may be the reason that it is necessary to use a substitute "God variable" in the Chinese data. The item used in the other nations was a ten-point scale of "how important is God in your life." In the 1991 Chinese survey, this item was essentially invariant; virtually no one in China said God was important. However, the Chinese survey also included this question concerning God:

Which one of these statements comes closest to your beliefs?
There is a personal God.
There is some sort of spirit or life force.
I don't really know what to think.
I don't really think there is any sort of spirit, God, or life force.

These responses can be converted into a three-point scale of the degree of belief in God. Since only 22 Chinese expressed faith in a personal God, I combined them with the 311 (out of 1,000) who believed in some sort of spirit or life force and scored them as 3 to indicate belief. Those who didn't know what to think were scored 2. The nonbelievers were scored 1. It is precisely in keeping with my analysis of Chinese religion that 94 percent of the believers (those scored 3), clearly rejected the exis-

Exploring the Religious Life

Table 7.10 God, Prayer, and the Moral Order in China

	Stolen Goods	Hit/Run	Smoke Dope
Correlations with belief in God	–.01	.04	–.11
Correlations with prayer or meditation	.32**	.27**	.42**

**Significant above .01. *Significant above .05.

tence of God as a supernatural *being*. As in Japan, such a God has no influence on moral judgments in China (table 7.10): all three correlations are tiny and insignificant.

It was impossible to pursue the effects of temple visits in China, since no one goes to the temples—only 2 percent admitted doing so even once a year. However, 20 percent said they sometimes prayed or meditated. Scored as a four-point scale of the frequency of prayer or meditation, this variable resulted in a surprising effect, as can be seen in the second row of correlations. Each correlation is strong, highly significant, and *positive!* That is, the more often they pray or meditate, the more tolerant the Chinese are of immorality. Upon reflection, the reasons for this seem clear: "prayer" in China today is far more a magical than a religious act, mainly involving divinities of the folk religion. Viewed as magical behavior, praying is somewhat antisocial in the sense of being narrowly self-seeking (Chen 1995; Green 1988; Lang and Ragvold 1993). In any case, these correlations offer no support to the "law" concerning religion and the moral order.

Conclusion

Durkheim made a major error when he dismissed Gods as mere religious epiphenomena. Unfortunately, his error had severe, widespread, and long-lasting consequences, for it quickly became the exclusive sociological view that religion consists of rites and ritual and that these exist only because their latent function is to integrate societies and to thereby lend sacred sanctions to the norms. In retrospect, it seems remarkable that such a notion gained such rapid acceptance and went unchallenged for so long. Stripped of its functionalist jargon, the basic argument seems to have been that since "we" know there are no Gods, they can't be the real object of religion. The notion that things are real to the extent that people define them as real failed to make any headway in this area of social science.

The results presented above show that, in and of themselves, rites and rituals have little or no impact on the major effect universally attributed to religion—conformity to the moral order. Thus, it seems necessary to revise the opening line of this chapter as follows: *Images of Gods as conscious, powerful, morally concerned beings function to sustain the moral order.*

Discovering Data on Religion

All research methods textbooks devote extended attention to data collection, usually offering advice on how to do surveys, experiments, field research, and content coding. But all texts, including my own (Stark and Roberts 2002), neglect the method I have most often used in my own studies: how one *discovers* data. From some of my earliest work to my most recent, I have repeatedly found that the data most appropriate for testing a particular theory were simply there, waiting to be used. By discovering data, I do not mean using surveys from one of the fine data archives, although I often have done that. I mean seeing data in places ignored or overlooked by everyone else. Nor am I referring to crude, make-do measures; discovered data often are precise and extremely appropriate measures of the variables of interest. Of equal significance is the fact that these data usually are free or nearly so.

In this final chapter, I will illustrate the discovery of data with an extensive set of examples, in hopes that this will convey the essential strategy as well as clarify the connection between discovered data and theory-driven research. The examples also are of substantial interest to those pursuing the social scientific study of religion.

Turning Wine into Communicants

For many years a controversy has raged over the issue of secularization. The traditional view has been that once upon a time, people in Europe

A portion of this chapter appeared as "Discovering Data: A Neglected Virtue of Theory-Driven Research," *Theory and Methods: The Official Journal of the Japanese Association of Mathematical Sociology* 40 (2001): 379–92.

were ardent Christians, but, beginning several centuries ago, modernization has eroded faith. The very low current rates of church attendance are given as proof. Recently, some social scientists have argued that modernization has no negative effects on religiousness and that the European example is false because the Age of Faith never existed. The initial Christianization of northern and western Europe was never more than superficial, and church attendance in those areas was always low, probably about the same as now. Hence, there has been no decline. In demonstration of that point, I have summarized a great deal of qualitative data (Stark 1999; Stark and Iannaccone 1994; Stark and Finke 2000). Only recently did I learn that a few years ago a French sociologist had discovered very appropriate *quantitative* data on levels of attendance in France centuries ago.

For at least fifty years, Catholic sociologists in Europe, especially in France and Belgium, have devoted themselves to parish studies, to exploring the dynamics of religious life at the very local level. Eventually, some of them began to explore the history of various parishes, utilizing the elaborate records that have been kept by parish priests for many centuries. One day Jacques Toussaert (in Delumeau 1977) discovered solid data on church attendance hidden in these documents: receipts for the purchase of communion wine. Until recently, in order to remain in good standing, all Roman Catholics were required to attend a communion service at least once a year, Easter being the preferred time to do so. A communion service briefly reenacts the Last Supper, during which Jesus shared bread and wine with his disciples. During this service, groups of parishioners come to the front of the church, where the priest gives each a sip of wine and a wafer of unleavened bread.

There are many grumbles in surviving letters, documents, and official reports from late medieval and early modern times that only a small number of persons in a community met this obligation, despite the fact that "everyone" was ostensibly a Catholic. But Toussaert now had a basis for estimating the actual attendance at communion services. That is, knowing the amount of wine purchased for the occasion and having established an amount per sip, he could simply divide to obtain the *maximum* number of people who attended. Dividing this number by the number of those eligible to attend yields a rate of attendance. If we suppose that the priest drank some of the wine, or that some was left over, or that some people gulped rather than sipped, then attendance was *lower* than Toussaert's figures show. Even assuming that every drop was sipped by communicants, however, Toussaert ended up finding low levels of attendance. The Age of Faith did not exist—at least not in terms of ritual participation.

Calculations based on wine purchases seem to be at least as accurate as data based on a survey of parishes to ask about church attendance— even had such surveys been conducted back then. And Toussaert's data were free. All that he needed was the ability to *recognize* wine receipts as data on attendance. It took no great feat of imagination for Toussaert to see data in wine receipts, because he was sensitized by his concern to test a theory. It is thus appropriate for me to pause here and explain the one paramount axiom that has shaped my career: *research should be driven by theories.*

Social scientists typically are trained to prefer a single methodology; hence they commonly identify themselves as experimentalists, survey researchers, participant observers, or demographers, and they predicate their research on the basis of their methodological commitments. It is common to hear them wonder what they should do a survey on next, what experiment they could do, or what social scene they might observe.

This is backward. And it is the major reason why so much pointless research is conducted. The fact is that research questions must determine what method or methods are suitable—*how* to find out depends on *what* you want to know. When one's primary commitment is to a particular methodology, one's ability to pursue important questions is severely limited.

Over the course of my career, I have used every legitimate social scientific method of research, not because I get bored easily, but because I always have been theory-driven. I have selected research questions because of their theoretical importance and have selected methods because they were appropriate. Not only has this experience yielded a fund of cautionary tales that may usefully be shared, but it may help others see how to discover data and thereby overcome what may appear to be insurmountable barriers to research.

Studying Religious Nonconformity

The year before I began graduate school at Berkeley, I worked as a reporter for the *Oakland Tribune,* a major metropolitan newspaper. After writing a well-received feature story about a speaker at the Oakland Space Craft Club who recounted his trips to Mars and Venus as a guest on a flying saucer, I was routinely given stories concerning various occult gatherings and new religious movements. Thus did I become interested in why and how people converted to deviant religious groups. My initial efforts to find answers in the social scientific literature were unsatisfactory. For example, I found a book in the University of California library about an exotic religious movement that flourished in northern California during the late 1930s and early 1940s. The author claimed that, because the movement proposed an elaborate, state-supported pension scheme for the elderly, this movement's primary recruitment base was older people, especially elderly widows. It turned out that the *Oakland Tribune*'s morgue (a library of newspaper clippings and photos) had a voluminous file on this group. In it was a wide-angle photo of a public meeting of the group held in the ballroom of the Leamington Hotel during the late 1930s when the movement was at its height. There were 312 members in the picture, and not only were there no grey heads among them, but the crowd was overwhelmingly made up of quite young adults, with only a modest excess of women. That experience made me very skeptical of "expert judgments"; it also helped me recognize that *data* are *anything* that can be used as evidence pertinent to what one wants to know: that old photograph became data when I counted and sorted the people in it by age and sex.

Although one of my earliest published studies was based on participant observation of how a new religious movement recruited members, which showed that people are brought into these groups on the basis of social relationships (Lofland and Stark 1965), my interest in such movements soon took a more macro approach. Having also learned from studying conversion that it is the "irreligious" and unchurched who join new religions (very "religious" people do not change faiths), I formulated theories about where and when such movements would prosper or decline. More specifically, I hypothesized that such movements would be more successful in areas where the conventional religious organizations were weaker, hence, along the West Coast of the United States and in northern Europe. But how could I test these hypotheses? There were no available statistics. Appropriate data could be collected by conducting very large surveys in each of the ecological areas of interest, such as American states or cities. But that would cost millions of dollars. However, because I knew what I wanted to find out, I was able to see data in places everyone else had ignored.

Consider magazines and other periodicals. Many of them are edited to appeal to very special interests. One such specialized magazine is *Fate*. Founded in 1948, it specializes in stories and reports on a range of occult topics: ESP, psychic phenomena, reincarnation, ghosts, mystical experiences, various New Age therapies such as healing crystals, and the like. I had seen *Fate* on the newsstands since I was in high school. But it was not until William Sims Bainbridge and I wanted to test the hypotheses about where nonconforming religions would have greater success, that I saw this small magazine as *data*.

The most obvious way to use any magazine as data is its circulation figures. The basic assumption is simple; variations in circulation will reflect variations in cultural patterns: where hunting and fishing magazines are popular, the local culture will tend toward the "masculine"; where feminist magazines do best, one will find a concentration of feminists; where occult and New Age periodicals sell well, one can assume that religious nonconformity is high.

Because potential advertisers require magazines to provide their circulation data, broken down in many different ways, most will send these figures to anyone who writes and asks for them. In fact, magazines hoping to sell ads must have their circulation statistics audited by one of several firms that specialize in making sure that they are accurate, and these audit reports are made public. So Bainbridge and I obtained *Fate*'s circulation report, which showed sales of 148,000 copies a month. Next, we created rates for all fifty American states and for the larger American cities (dividing the number of copies sold in each state or city by its total population). The results very strongly confirmed our hypothesis. For the nation as a whole, there were 366 copies of *Fate* sold per million population. In the states of the Northeast (New York, Massachusetts, etc.) the figure was 297. In the Deep South it was 218. But, in the Far West (California, Oregon, Washington, Alaska, and Hawaii) it was 565 (Stark and Bainbridge 1985).

As it turned out, there was another way to turn *Fate* magazine into data. Beginning in 1960 it regularly ran two columns featuring letters sent in by readers, and nine or ten of these letters were published in each issue. Each letter included the name and address of the writer. We gained access to a complete set of back issues of the magazine and began to count and sort letter-writers by state. Counting each person only once, altogether there were 2,086 writers from 1960 to 1979. In the Northeast there were 7.5 writers per million; in the Deep South, 3.8. But in the Far West there were 24.1. Once again our hypothesis was confirmed.

A second source of data was an annual periodical named the *Spiritual Community Guide*. This publication listed New Age centers and groups across the United States, especially those having an Eastern aspect (Hindu, Zen, etc.). Again we created rates per million for each state. Again the hypothesis was confirmed. We repeated these procedures with three other publications, and the results were the same.

At that point we realized that there was another fine source of data on occultism: telephone listings. American telephone directories include a section (or in large cities a separate book) called the *Yellow Pages*. These are for commercial and organizational listings and are arranged by particular specialties. For example, restaurants have a section, and so do astrologers. Many local libraries have a collection of telephone directories. With a bit of effort, we were able to count the listings for astrologers in all the states and in the major cities. And once again, the Far West had a rate far higher than anywhere else in the nation. Thus we were able to assemble an impressive body of data in support of our hypothesis, for a total cost of less than one hundred dollars.

Next I turned my attention to Europe. I hypothesized not only that nonconforming religious groups would be more successful there than in the United States but also that such groups would do far better in those nations having low rates of church attendance (such as Scandinavia and Great Britain) than in those with higher rates (such as Italy and Spain). One source of data was the *Spiritual Community Guide*, mentioned above, since it covered western Europe as well. When I used that publication to obtain a rate of New Age centers per million population, both hypotheses were strongly confirmed. For western Europe as a whole, there were 1.8 of these centers per million, compared with 1.3 in the United States. This difference is especially striking since the *Guide* was edited and published in the United States, and its listings were likely more complete for the United States than Europe. As for the second hypothesis, Scotland had a rate of 3.2, Denmark's was 3.1, and England's was 3.0, while Italy's rate was 0.7 and Spain's was 0.6. These results were matched by data on Mormon membership (published annually in *The Church Almanac*) and data on the location of ISKON (Hare Krishna) temples taken from the back cover of the group's monthly magazine (Stark 1984). Some years later I was able to obtain far more comprehensive data on new religious movements in Europe from a directory prepared by J. Gordon Melton and his associates, and these agreed with the earlier findings in every detail (Stark 1993).

These were not trivial hypotheses. Virtually no other sociologists of religion, and none in Europe, would have expected them to be confirmed. In fact, some sociologists are still trying to deny that Europeans have any interest in nonconforming religious groups. Imagine how certain they would be, and how they would dominate the discussion, had I not discovered these data.

Documenting the Decline of Christian Science

The *Yellow Pages* also provided data for another study. As one of a series of papers testing a theory about why new religious groups succeed or fail (Stark 1996b), I did a study of Christian Science as an example of a group that had enjoyed immense early success but then had begun to fail (Stark 1998). The trouble was that this group ceased to reveal its membership statistics during the 1930s (about the time when I hypothesized it had begun its decline). The group is too small to turn up in sufficient numbers in surveys to provide an adequate basis for estimating membership. One day I was looking through the *Yellow Pages* for Los Angeles and turned to the section for churches. Looking at the subsection devoted to the Church of Christ, Scientist, I noticed many breaks in the numbers of listed congregations. I realized the significance of this at once, because I knew that Christian Science congregations are always numbered consecutively as they are opened in any community. That is, the first Christian Science church in Los Angeles (or anywhere) would have been named First Church of Christ, Scientist, the next to open would have been named Second Church of Christ, Scientist, and so on. In Los Angeles there was a Forty-fifth Church of Christ, Scientist. But there were 22 missing numbers between 1 and 45. That meant that at least 22 local Christian Science churches had been closed in Los Angeles. A trip to the library gave me access to the 1960 *Yellow Pages*. That year there were no missing numbers! So these 22 churches had closed between 1960 and 1995. Had I wished to do so, I could have looked in the *Yellow Pages* year by year to document the closings precisely. Instead, I consulted the *Yellow Pages* for other major cities and found the same pattern of many missing numbers, each revealing a closed congregation. There were the needed data, clearly documenting the decline (Stark 1998). Cost: zero. But had I not had a theoretical need for these data, I would not have seen anything in the Los Angeles *Yellow Pages* but a list of phone numbers and addresses.

In recent years I have devoted a great deal of my time to applying sociological theories and methods to historical questions. One of the first of these involved the rise of Christianity (Stark 1996a). How did it happen? How did a tiny and obscure messianic group at the far eastern edge of the Roman Empire dislodge classical paganism and become the dominant faith of Western civilization? To suggest some answers to that question, the first thing it was necessary to know was more precisely what needed to be explained. How *fast* must Christianity have grown in order to become as large as it did in the time allowed? Clearly, there were no old membership statistics lying around in the Vatican library to answer that question. So I decided to discover a plausible answer through use of what I call the "arithmetic of the possible."

Fortunately, historians provided me with a beginning and an ending point for calculating growth curves. There probably were about 1,000 Christians in the year 40. Historians agree that by the year 300 there were from 5 million to 7.5 million Christians. Moreover, everyone is agreed that growth became extremely rapid from 250 on and that by the year 350 about half of the population of the empire had become Christians, or about 30 million to 35 million people. So I began fiddling with different rates of growth to see what growth curves they produced. Almost at once I found the perfect fit. If Christianity grew at a rate of 40 percent per decade (or 3.42% per year), then the 1,000 Christians in 40 would have become 6.2 million in 300 and 33.8 million in the year 350. As with exponential curves, growth would have been very slow in early years, and the rapid increase in numbers subsequent to 250 would have taken place without any increase in the rate of growth. What made this result so particularly compelling was that it precisely matched the rate of growth achieved by the Mormons over the past century (Stark 1984). Hence, no miraculous rate of growth need be proposed: the rise of Christianity is entirely compatible with the prevailing theory of conversion.

My theoretical analysis of the rise of Christianity proposed that Jews were a far larger source of converts than had been believed. Jews made up about 10 percent of the population of the Roman Empire, so their numbers were more than sufficient to have provided the bulk of Christian converts for a long time, while at the same time sustaining substantial Jewish communities. However, this was quite contrary to the accepted wisdom, which said that relations between Judaism and early Christianity were so ruptured late in the first century that virtually no more Jewish conversion occurred after that time. Of course, the available data on Jewish conversion consisted of a variety of literary and archeological fragments. I thought they best supported me but was well aware that most historians would not be persuaded.

The same was true for my position on the considerable dispute over how the Gnostics fit into the picture. They long had been regarded as early Christian heretics and typically were referred to as the Christian Gnostics. However, during much of the twentieth century, the majority of scholars agreed that this was incorrect, that Gnosticism was a Jewish heresy and developed *parallel* to Christianity—it, too, being a Jewish heresy. The distinguished Birger Pearson (1973) was the leading proponent of this view and based his position on showing that many Gnostic ideas originated in Judaism. I concluded that the older view was correct. I was particularly skeptical of the revised version on grounds that ideas are not social movements and the origins of the two need not be the same. Gnostic writers could have been profoundly influenced by earlier Jewish writings while still being part of a social movement that had split away from Christianity.

However, so long as there were no better data available, this was a somewhat sterile argument. Then I found justification for my view as well as for my self-indulgent habit of buying historical atlases.

Historical atlases are an amazingly independent area of history. I have discovered things about various topics on maps that are absent from the other published literature on those topics, although the atlas author provided extensive and convincing documentation of the points, often citing primary sources. For a century, beginning with the extraordinary work of Adolf von Harnack (1908), historical mapmakers have been literally charting the rise of Christianity. In particular they have mapped its spread across the empire, dating its appearance in various cities. This work is a vital addition to prose histories; too many historians write as if something like the rise of Christianity occurred in a geographical vacuum. One day it occurred to me that these maps were data. So I proceeded to create a data set appropriate to testing both of the claims outlined above.

I selected cities for my units of analysis. Preliminary explorations showed that I would need to limit myself to the largest cities, so I selected the twenty-two cities in the Roman Empire with the largest populations in the year 100. These ranged from Rome with 650,000 residents and Alexandria with 400,000, down to London with 40,000, Salamis with 35,000, and Athens with 30,000 (Chandler and Fox 1974) .

Then I created a three-value variable of *Christianization:* cities having a Christian church by the year 100, those having a church by the year 200, and those not yet having a church in 200. This was based on the consensus of the five atlases that listed the most impressive sources.

Next, I consulted the most recent map of the Jewish Diaspora and coded cities as to whether or not they had a synagogue in this era: nine of them did, and thirteen did not (MacLennan and Kraabel 1986). I intended this two-value variable as a measure of the *size of the Jewish community* in each city.

A fourth variable involved the spread of *Gnosticism:* a map of Gnostic presence in Greco-Roman cities provided data on whether Gnostics were operating there by the year 200, by the year 400, or not (Layton 1987).

A fifth variable measured the distance of each city from Jerusalem and a sixth, the distance from Rome. I then turned these into a ratio to measure the degree of *Romanization* (how much closer to Rome than to Jerusalem was a city). I measured the mileage with a mechanical map gauge, following the known trade routes and using sea routes when appropriate.

Finally, I was ready to do some analysis. Everyone knows that Christianity spread from east to west. Hence, there was a huge negative correlation (−.71) between Romanization and Christianization. Of course, this also was the geography of the Jewish Diaspora: the correlation with Romanization was −.44. And there was a strong positive correlation between synagogues and Christianization (.69). When entered into a regression analysis, both variables had a strong, independent effect on Christianization and together accounted for 67.2 percent of the variance. Of course this does not show that Jewish conversion continued as late as I believe it did. But negative results would have been very damaging to that view.

The results concerning the Gnostics came closer to being definitive. When Christianization and synagogues were entered into a regression analysis having Gnosticism as the dependent variable, it turned out that despite a strong positive correlation between synagogues and Gnostics, the entire effect was produced by Christianization. That is, Christianization accounted for 34.4 percent of the variation in Gnostics, whereas synagogues accounted for none.

But I wasn't quite finished with this data set. It also offered a rather exotic basis for testing Claude S. Fischer's subcultural theory (1975) of urbanism. A central proposition in the theory is that "the more urban the place, the higher the rate of unconventionality." Fischer's thesis is that the larger the population, in absolute numbers, the easier it is to assemble the "critical mass" needed to form a deviant subculture, and he specifically included unconventional religious movements in deviant subcultures. The data showed very robust positive correlations between city size and both Christianization and Gnosticism.

Although Fischer was amused (and pleased) by the results, I believe this was the first time historians of either early Christianity or Gnosticism ever confronted regression analysis. Not all of them regarded it as progress. But the important point is that a collection of historical atlases need not be just a bunch of pretty pictures.

Finally, I wished to confirm my judgment that paganism was inherently weak in terms of levels of individual commitment and hence very vulnerable to being displaced by Christianity. In particular, I was convinced that there was a considerable lack of public reverence. This is consistent with remarks by some contemporary writers, but there are great dangers involved in making judgments about public opinion from the surviving writing by elite members of society. Indeed, it is thought to be so hard to accurately gauge public opinion in modern societies that hundreds of millions of dollars are spent each year to conduct opinion polls. So how could I possibly attempt to discover a lack of reverence in classical times? One day I ran across precisely the necessary evidence while reading an archaeological report on Pompeii for an entirely different purpose. It turns out that in this Roman city, preserved by its nearly instant burial by a volcanic eruption, the walls are covered with graffiti, much of it extremely blasphemous as well as obscene. Although I harbor no suspicion that these lurid attacks on the Gods were connected with the city's fate, they do strongly suggest the state of public attitudes. This is true not simply because some residents were prompted to write and draw these things, but because no one felt prompted to remove or cover them. One of the leading experts on inscriptions from this period noted that "we may take [the existence of similar graffiti] for granted elsewhere" (MacMullen 1981, 63). A scholar with proper command of Latin and Greek could even code the immense collections of inscriptions, including graffiti, that are preserved and published from this era to create rates for various cities to test the hypothesis that Christianity did better, sooner, in places abounding in graffiti blaspheming the pagan Gods. For my purposes it was sufficient to know that such stuff was common and seemed an adequate substitute for surveys as an insight into public opinion.

Witchcraft Burnout

Recently I wrote a long chapter on the European witch-hunts (Stark 2003). Between 1450 and 1750, approximately sixty thousand people were executed as witches, most of them convicted of having gained magical powers by giving their souls to Satan. While I was examining data on the pattern of executions in small communities (five thousand population or under) that experienced a "large" outburst of executions for witchcraft (more than twenty in one year), I noticed something very odd. Whereas many of these communities experienced long periods of low levels of executions (one or two, or sometimes three, in a year), after a large outburst they did not then return to the previous low level. Instead, following such an episode, executions ceased entirely and never began again, even though witch-hunting continued in other towns nearby. As I pondered why this might have been, I began to realize that it might have something to do with the kinds of people usually convicted of witchcraft in Europe. And this led me to consider the implications of the most basic principles of sociology.

Stripped to the essentials, all communities consist of social networks, structures of relationships among people. These relationships are based on ties of family, neighborhood, friendship, work, and the like. Social networks are the basis of all social life. They provide members with security, emotional satisfaction, and identity. They provide information, attitudes, and social resources. Moreover, networks impose conformity: certain kinds of behavior not only can cost individuals their network ties but also can cause the network to impose punishments on them. However, not everyone in any community is part of a network. Always there are isolated individuals who don't belong or fit in. These are such elementary insights that the whole of sociology rests upon them.

In small European towns during the time in question, most people had many strong ties to the local social network, but some were only weakly connected and some were virtual isolates. Some were isolated by circumstances. For example, elderly, childless, impoverished widows often were without social ties, as were wandering beggars and some elderly spinsters and bachelors. Others were lacking in social ties because of disagreeable personalities, bad habits, lack of character, or unsavory reputations—sometimes entire families were isolated for these reasons.

Much is known about the kinds of people usually accused of witchcraft. Most accusations came from the neighbors of the accused and reflected long-standing enmity: most "witches" were isolated, disliked, disagreeable, unattractive, disreputable people. Much has been written about how vulnerable these people were to being accused, but little or nothing about matters of social costs. To execute disreputable isolates puts no strain on social networks. In effect, there is no one to miss them, and perhaps many will be glad they are gone. In contrast, accusations against persons securely embedded in networks will arouse opposition from those who love, respect, or are dependent on those persons. And such accusations will arouse fears that no one is safe.

Out of these considerations, I hit upon the idea that although the isolated and disreputable part of a population could sustain a few executions each year, a large outburst of executions would rapidly exhaust the socially "inexpensive" segment of the community, whereupon the social costs of continuing to burn witches would rise rapidly to unsustainable levels. Of course, speculations like this are cheap; for real intellectual bite, I needed some quantitative support—and I discovered some.

If my explanation is correct, then it ought to be the case that there was a reasonably consistent pattern in the death tolls at the time when executions ceased. That is, the proportion of credibly and readily available victims ought to be similar in the towns where an outburst of executions was followed by an end of witch-hunting. I had data on the number executed by year in many communities. The trick was to find population statistics. In the end I found adequate data for eight towns. The data overwhelmingly supported me: in each town the witch-hunt ended after about one person in twenty had been executed! Specifically, I found these percentages: Miltenburg, 8 percent; Obermarchtal and Oppenau, 7 percent; Gengenbach, Lindheim, Mergentheim, and Rottenberg, 6 percent; and Offenburg, 4 percent.

It seems more than coincidental that this proportion is compatible with modern studies of the size of the relatively unattached and disreputable portion of a community, research in both England (Farrington 1988) and the United States (Wolfgang, Figlio, and Sellin 1972) placing the number at about 6 percent. I do not suggest that this percentage is precise, but I think it does help us see that there were natural limits on the witch-hunts and that they burned out when they began to extend to those people firmly embedded in conventional social networks.

I might add that this death toll was exceeded in some much larger communities before an outburst ended—in Strasburg, about 18 percent were executed before the witch "craze" subsided. But of course, larger communities contain proportionately more isolated and disreputable people. Such people tend to drift from villages into cities, and cities tend to produce more such persons as well (Fischer 1975).

In any event, I found all of the data involved in formulating and testing this interpretation in the secondary literature—I did no original study of primary sources. But without a theory, these were merely numbers, not data.

Governance & the Reformation

It has often been remarked that during the Reformation, places became Protestant or remained Catholic depending on the responsiveness of local governments to public sentiments. That is, other things being equal, to the extent that local governments responded to popular preferences, people turned Protestant.

A leading proponent of this view was Guy E. Swanson. Early in the 1960s, he spent a year at the Center for Advanced Study of the Behavioral Sciences, during which time he assembled a bibliography on the Reformation. He then received a grant that enabled him to hire graduate students to create a data set consisting of 41 European regimes at the time of the Protestant Reformation. Each regime was classified as to the responsiveness of its governance and whether it had become Protestant or remained Catholic. In *Religion and Regime: A Sociological Account of the Reformation* (1967) Swanson presented statistics supporting the claim that governance mattered. Of the 21 autocratic regimes, 19 remained Catholic. Of the 20 more responsive regimes, all became Protestant. However, Swanson's methods were subject to many savage attacks from historians. For one thing, his "cases" are a very mixed bag. Some of them are nations, including England, France, and Spain. Other units are regions such as the Highlands of Scotland. Still others are Italian city-states such as Florence and Venice. To this, Swanson added all 14 Swiss cantons. Clearly, severe issues of comparability arise: are Venice, France, and the Scottish Highlands sufficiently alike to support statistical analysis? Moreover, in his coding Swanson ignored matters such as the degree of external coercion, as in the instance of Italian city-states vulnerable to Spanish military control, again brushing aside issues of incomparability. An additional criticism of Swanson concerned the validity of his coding of regimes as to their responsiveness. That he placed Denmark, Sweden, and England among the more responsive regimes, while placing Poland among the most autocratic, suggests that Swanson's coding was unduly influenced by knowledge of which regimes turned Protestant—a potential danger in all such coding projects.

When I became interested in the Reformation, I had no interest whatever in retracing Swanson's steps. But as I pondered how to more convincingly test the proposition that the responsiveness of regimes to public preferences played a major role in joining the Reformation, I discovered that the needed data already existed (Stark 2003).

Discussions of the Reformation give particular emphasis to the Free Imperial Cities. Beginning in the thirteenth century, these communities evolved slowly out of the conflict between the burghers of the growing cities and their local feudal lords. By the fourteenth century, many cities, especially in the Germanic areas, gained control over their internal affairs, as even "the most obvious sovereign rights—military and judicial sovereignty—slipped slowly out of the lord's hands" (Rörig 1967, 25). They came to be called Imperial because they owed allegiance to the (Holy Roman) emperor, but they were otherwise free and sovereign. Thus, they paid taxes directly to the emperor, but they retained complete control over their own tax systems. The Free Imperial Cities enjoyed freedom in another sense as well, for not only were they not subject to local feudal autocrats, but each was governed by a city council. The councils varied in the extent of interests they represented—sometimes they included the artisan guilds and sometimes not. Even so, council members were elected (although not everyone could vote), and there was substantial turnover. As a result, these city councils had to be at least somewhat responsive to public sentiments.

Historians agree that the Free Imperial Cities were unusually likely to accept Protestantism, but there has been no appropriate statistical comparison with similarly situated non-Imperial cities. In 1500 there were about sixty-five Free Imperial Cities (Moeller 1972). Some of them can be ignored because they were so very tiny, some having no more than one thousand residents (Rörig 1967). Others were isolated far from other Imperial Cities, being surrounded by a powerful duchy or principality that imposed some degree of caution on the city council. In contrast, many of them, because they had arisen as trading communities, were clustered in the area along or near the Rhine that historians often refer to as the Borderlands. In addition, there were many cities in this area that were not Imperial Cities. This provides an opportunity to test the proposition about governance on a set of units of comparable size and similar in terms of cultural heritage and setting. Consequently, I selected all of the significant cities in this Borderlands area, ending up with a total of 43. Unlike Swanson, I was not required to assess the nature of each local regime as to its responsiveness, thereby risking some of the errors for which Swanson was pilloried. All I needed to do was compare 12 non-Imperial with 31 Free Imperial Cities, on the assumption that the latter tended to have more responsive regimes. Local histories of each city are conclusive as to whether or not a city initially turned Protestant (the fact that during the religious wars some were forced to return to Catholicism is irrelevant).

My results were definitive: nearly two-thirds of the Imperial Cities in this group became Protestant, while three-fourths of the non-Imperial Cities remained Catholic. No one can say my coding was biased, that my units were an incomparable collection, or that my coders were unreliable. The data were free and could have been assembled anytime in the past four hundred years.

Catholic Culture & Slavery

For a long time historians accepted that New World slavery was far less brutal in Catholic than in Protestant colonies (Elkins 1976; Tannenbaum [1946] 1992). The reason was that, first in the French colonies and then in those belonging to Spain, the Roman Catholic Church played a leading role in formulating and enforcing slave codes that recognized the humanity of slaves, guaranteed them various rights, and imposed limits on how they could be treated. As Eugene Genovese (1974, 179) put it, "Catholicism made a profound difference in the lives of the slaves. [It] imparted to . . . slave societies an ethos . . . of genuine spiritual power."

The French slave code—the Code Noir—was formulated during the reign of Louis XIV and promulgated in 1685. Under the direct influence of French bishops, the code expanded on the premise that a slave is "a being of God." It was in this spirit that the code required owners to baptize their slaves, provide them with religious instruction, and allow them the sacrament of holy matrimony, which, in turn, became the basis for prohibiting the selling of family members separately. Slaves also were exempted from work on Sundays and holy days (from midnight to midnight), and masters were subject to fines or even to the confiscation of their slaves for violating this provision. Other articles specified minimum amounts of food and clothing that masters must provide and ordered that the disabled and the elderly must be properly cared for, including their hospitalization. Article 39 ordered officers of justice "to proceed criminally against the masters and overseers who will have killed their slaves or mutilated them."

Spanish treatment of slaves also was greatly influenced by Catholic concerns. Guided by the Church, Spain adopted the Código Negro Español toward the end of the eighteenth century. The Código not only included most of the provisions of the French Code Noir but was far more liberal in that it guaranteed slaves the right to own property and to purchase their freedom. Specifically, slaves were enabled to petition the courts "to have themselves appraised and to purchase themselves from even unwilling masters or mistresses at their judicially appraised market value" (Schafer 1994, 2–3). This was greatly facilitated by terms of the code that gave slaves the right to work for themselves on their days off, including the eighty-seven days a year they were at liberty because of not having to work for their owners on Sundays and holy days.[1] In rural areas, slaves typically were permitted to sell the produce raised in their own gardens and keep the proceeds (Tannenbaum [1946] 1992).

As for enforcement of the Código, just as the Church had played the major role in its formulation, bishops held frequent synods to "deal with local conditions," during which they "always legislated in favor of the fullest freedom and rights [for slaves] that were permissible" under the Código. Meanwhile, "the lower clergy, especially at the parish level, effectively carried this law into practice" (Klein 1969, 145). They did this not only by maintaining close contacts with their black parishioners, but also by imposing religious definitions on many aspects of the master-slave relationship. Newborn slaves were baptized in formal church services that emphasized their "humanity," church weddings were held for slave couples, and even manumission was made into a religious ceremony held in church (Klein 1967; Meltzer 1993; Thomas 1997; Turley 2000).

The British did not baptize slaves or seek their conversion to Christianity; indeed, several colonial assemblies imposed heavy fines on Quakers for doing so (Dunn 1973). Moreover, when the British Parliament declined to formulate a slave code, it was left to the British colonies to enact their own. Since the colonies were fully under the control of a slave-owning "ruling class" (the Church of England did not even pretend to be concerned), the laws enacted were a planter's dream and a slave's nightmare.

In 1661 the plantation owners of Barbados adopted the Act for the Better Ordering of Slaves, sometimes referred to as the Code of Barbados or the Act of Barbados. This code was soon copied in other British colonies: in Jamaica in 1664, South Carolina in 1696, and Antigua in 1702 (Dunn 1973). Whatever its title, this code was at least as brutal as any formulated by the ancient Romans (Beckles 1989; Dunn 1973; Goveia 1969; Sheridan 1974; Watson 1989). It characterized black slaves as "heathenish, brutish, and an uncertaine, dangerous kinde of people" (in Dunn 1972, 239). Masters had the right to "apply unlimited force to compel labor" without penalty, even if this resulted in maiming or death (Fogel 1989, 36). Thus, although the code imposed a fine for "wantonly" killing a slave, this did not apply when slaves were punished for "cause," no matter how insignificant their offense. Consistent with the principle that slaves were private property, the fine was substantially larger if someone wantonly killed someone else's slave (Dunn 1972). The code also specified that overseers must keep slaves under very close surveillance, including searching their cabins at least twice a month for stolen goods and contraband such as clubs. Slaves were not allowed to marry, and masters were prohibited from setting a slave free, except by a special act of the legislature. This legal restriction on manumission was soon replaced with a tax so heavy as to virtually prohibit it. In the northern Leeward Islands, an owner was required to pay five hundred pounds to the public treasury in order to free a slave, which was many times the purchase price of a slave (Johnston 1910, 231). A similar tax on manumission was imposed by the legislators on St. Christopher in 1802, with the declared intent of preventing increases in the number of "free Negros," whom they regarded as a "great inconvenience" (Mathieson 1926, 38–40). The planters on Barbados were so concerned to minimize the number of free blacks that they placed an even heavier tax on the freeing of a female slave (38–40).

Slave policies in the American South initially were modeled on the British code. Moreover, "free blacks" were deemed as undesirable by southerners as they were in the British colonies. Thus, the U.S. Census of 1860 reported that in 1849, of more than 3.2 million slaves, only 1,467 had been set free during the year. Of the more than 3.9 million slaves in the nation in 1859, 3,018 were set free that year. Contrast this with the fact that in 1817 there were 114,058 free blacks in Spanish Cuba alone.

Nevertheless, in recent years it has been fashionable to dismiss the Code Noir and the Código Negro Español as unimportant pieces of paper having no impact on actual conditions. Many of these claims originated with Marxists, who agree that religion has no effects, that only "real" things such as class and modes of production *can* influence history; hence the Catholic slaves *must have* suffered as much as those owned by Protestants (Harris 1963, 1964). From a slightly different perspective, David Brion Davis condemned all claims that there were significant differences in the treatment of slaves in the various colonies as tantamount to apologies for slavery! He argued instead that "Negro bondage was a single phenomenon, or *Gestalt*, whose variations were less significant than underlying patterns of unity" (1966, 228–29). In addition, Davis concluded that for "lack of detailed statistical information" and because the subject is "too complex," it is impossible "to assume that the treatment of slaves was substantially better in Latin America than in the British colonies, taken as a whole" (243).

As it turns out, statistical information is not lacking. It simply was ignored. Statistics on free blacks in the United States, mentioned earlier, present an opportunity for a "natural experiment" to assess whether and to what extent the Code Noir and the Código Negro Español made a difference in the lives of slaves. This involves comparing Catholic Louisiana with the rest of the Protestant South (Stark 2003).

Louisiana came under the Code Noir in 1724 as the French consolidated their administration. When control of Louisiana shifted to Spain in 1769, the circumstances of slaves were greatly improved owing to the liberal provisions of the Código Negro Español concerning the right of slaves to own property and to purchase their freedom. France regained Louisiana in 1802 and sold it to the United States the next year, but by then French and Spanish norms concerning slavery and the treatment of free blacks were deeply rooted. This is evident in the fact that the U.S. Census of 1830 found that a far higher percentage of the blacks in Louisiana were free (13.2%) than in any other slave state. The contrast is especially sharp in comparison to neighboring states having similar plantation economies: Alabama (1.3%), Mississippi (0.8%), and Georgia (1.1%). Moreover, the contrast between New Orleans and other major cities of the South is even more revealing.[2] In New Orleans, more than four of ten (41.7%) black residents were free! In comparison, of other cities in the Deep South, Charleston had the largest percentage of free blacks (6.4%), followed by Savannah (4.3%), Augusta (3.6%), and so on down the list to less than one of a hundred (0.5%) in Vicksburg (Stark 2003). What could be more compelling evidence?

Can such immense differences stem from anything other than the effects of Catholic codes and attitudes toward slavery? Rather than to shed crocodile tears over the lack of "detailed statistical information" to reveal whether Catholic slave codes made a difference, David Brion Davis might better have done these simple calculations—the data have been available and free for about 170 years.

Conclusion

The points I have tried to make in this chapter are deceptively simple. Research should be theory-driven. Because theories tell us where to look and what to expect to see, they can prevent much of the aimless "fact collecting" that wastes so much of our limited time and money. Moreover, when our research is theory-driven, we usually can be spared the futile debates about the relative value of different research methods. The correct method is always the one best suited to answer the specific question we are asking. Finally, when we are sure about what we need to know, we often will discover that adequate data already are at hand.

$\mathcal{N}otes$

Chapter 1. *Religion, Magic & Science*

1. There is now an immense body of very reputable research demonstrating the preventive and curative effects of religious belief and practice (Ellison and Levin 1998).

2. It is hard to imagine that the substantial amount of praying that went on among these intellectuals was directed to nothing.

3. Some contemporary magicians do offer reasons why their techniques "work," probably in response to the modern emphasis on *why* concerning all things.

Chapter 2. *In Praise of "Idealistic Humbug"*

1. All quotations from the Bible are from the Revised Standard Version unless indicated otherwise.

2. Many Greeks and Romans acknowledged an afterlife, but it was a gray and quite unrewarding existence in a netherworld.

Chapter 3. *Upper-Class Asceticism*

1. The data were transferred to punch cards and analyzed on an early IBM counter-sorter. Of course, the actual data set disappeared long ago.

2. I mention this because I have grown very impatient with those who assure one other that I owe much of my productivity to "crews" of graduate assistants. I have rarely had a graduate assistant, and only once did I allow a graduate student to do *any* coding for me. Having had to recode those data, I have never again asked a student to code.

3. It may be unfair to report that Sorokin attributed the lack of female saints to the "fact" that men are superior to women in all areas requiring creativity, including religious creativity (1950, 94–95).

4. Some will object that many daughters of royalty were "forced" into convents. No doubt. But they were not forced to become saints once they got there.

The immense literature on immorality in medieval convents and monasteries demonstrates the more typical outcome of compulsory vows.

Chapter 4. *Faith & Gender*

1. World Values Survey data provided by the Inter-University Consortium for Political and Social Research, Ann Arbor, Michigan.

Chapter 5. *How Are Revelations Possible?*

1. Mental patients who claim to talk to God or to be Muhammad are of no interest. At issue is the mental health of people who succeed in convincing others to accept the authenticity of their revelations, not the incidence of religious imagery in the delusions of the mentally ill.

2. Robinson interprets this, I think correctly, as a sign of intimacy, not of ignorance.

3. This holy period and the custom of making a pilgrimage to Mecca preceded Islam, having been well established in Arab paganism.

4. A person in a bridge position is one who bridges or links two or more networks.

5. I thank L. W. Hurtado for bringing this study to my attention.

Chapter 6. *Spirituality & Unchurched Religions in America, Sweden & Japan*

1. This was the only year in which a follow-up question asked respondents if they belonged to a specific congregation of the religious group they had just named.

2. World Values Survey data provided by the Inter-University Consortium for Political and Social Research, Ann Arbor, Michigan.

3. The NSF study (2002) found no educational effects on belief in psychics and visiting aliens, and a very weak effect on astrology.

Chapter 7. *Gods, Rituals & the Moral Order*

1. In response to Crane Brinton's rhetorical excess "Who now reads Spencer?"—quoted with glowing approval by Talcott Parsons as the opening sentence of his now unread classic *The Structure of Social Action* (1937)—it seems fitting to note that throughout my career I have cited Spencer rather more frequently than Parsons and I cannot recall ever having cited Brinton.

2. Now distributed by Wadsworth Publishing Company.

3. World Values Survey data provided by the Inter-University Consortium for Political and Social Research, Ann Arbor, Michigan.

4. By 1994 there were 5,000!

5. From 1700 until 1917, the Russian Orthodox Church was under strict state control, a policy begun by Peter the Great.

Chapter 8. *Discovering Data on Religion*

1. Fifty-two Sundays and thirty-five holy days.

2. Data for cities are reconstructed from county data.

Bibliography

Ahlstrom, Sidney E. 1972. *A Religious History of the American People*. New Haven, Conn.: Yale University Press.

Allen, Charlotte. 1998. *The Human Christ: The Search for the Historical Jesus*. New York: Free Press.

Allen, James B., and Glen M. Leonard. 1992. *The Story of the Latter-Day Saints*. 2d ed. Salt Lake City: Deseret Book Co.

Anderson, Bonnie S., and Judith P. Zinsser. 1989. *A History of Their Own: Women in Europe from Prehistory to the Present*. Vol. 1. New York: Harper & Row.

Anderson, John. 1994. *Religion, State, and Politics in the Soviet Union and Successor States*. Cambridge: Cambridge University Press.

Anderson, Richard Lloyd. 1971. "The Impact of the First Preaching in Ohio." *Brigham Young University Studies* 11:474–96.

Argyle, Michael. 1959. *Religious Behaviour*. Glencoe, Ill.: Free Press.

Armstrong, Karen. 1993. *Muhammad: A Biography of the Prophet*. San Francisco: Harper.

Arrington, Leonard J., and Davis Bitton. 1979. *The Mormon Experience: A History of the Latter-Day Saints*. New York: Alfred A. Knopf.

Athyal, Saphir. 1998. "Agencies Work Together in Romania." *Marc Newsletter* 98 (3): 1, 6.

Attwater, Donald, and John Cumming, eds. 1994. *A New Dictionary of Saints*. Rev. ed. Collegeville, Minn.: Liturgical Press.

Attwater, Donald, and Catherine Rachel John. 1995. *The Penguin Dictionary of Saints*. 3d ed. London: Penguin Books.

Ayerst, David, and A. S. T. Fisher. 1971. *Records of Christianity*. Vol. I. Oxford: Basil Blackwell.

Azzi, Corry, and Ronald Ehrenberg. 1975. "Household Allocation of Time and Church Attendance." *Journal of Political Economy* 83:27–56.

Backman, Milton V., Jr. 1988. "Lo, Here! Lo, There! Early in the Spring of 1820." In *The Prophet Joseph: Essays on the Life and Mission of Joseph Smith*, ed.

Larry C. Porter and Susan Easton Black, 19–35. Salt Lake City: Deseret Book Co.

Bader, Christopher. 1999. "When Prophecy Passes Unnoticed: New Perspectives on Failed Prophecy." *Journal for the Scientific Study of Religion* 38:119–31.

Bailey, Edward. 1998. *Implicit Religion: An Introduction.* London: Middlesex University Press.

Bainbridge, William Sims, and Rodney Stark. 1980. "Superstitions: Old and New." *Skeptical Inquirer* 25 (4): 22–27.

———. 1979. "Cult Formation: Three Compatible Models." *Sociological Analysis* 40:283–95.

Balch, Robert. 1985. "'When the Light Goes Out, Darkness Comes': A Study of Defection from a Totalistic Cult." In *Religious Movements: Genesis, Exodus, and Numbers,* ed. Rodney Stark, 11–63. New York: Rose of Sharon Press.

———. 1982. "Bo and Peep: A Case Study of the Origins of Messianic Leadership." In *Charisma and the Millennium,* ed. Roy Wallis, 29–41. Belfast: Queen's University Press.

———. 1980. "Looking behind the Scenes in a Religious Cult: Implications for the Study of Conversion." *Sociological Analysis* 41:137–43.

Baring-Gould, Sabine. 1914. *The Lives of the Saints.* Edinburgh: J. Grant.

Barker, Eileen. 1986. "Religious Movements: Cult and Anti-Cult since Jonestown." *Annual Review of Sociology* 12:329–46.

———. 1984. *The Making of a Moonie.* Oxford: Basil Blackwood.

Barkun, Michael. 1986. *Crucible of the Millennium.* Syracuse, N.Y.: Syracuse University Press.

Barrett, David B. 1982. *World Christian Encyclopedia.* Oxford: Oxford University Press.

Barrett, David B., George T. Kurian, and Todd M. Johnson. 2001. *World Christian Encyclopedia.* 2d ed. Oxford: Oxford University Press.

Barrow, Logie. 1980. "Socialism in Eternity." *History Workshop* 9:37–69.

Barton, Ralph. 1946. "The Religion of the Ifugaos." *American Anthropologist* 40:4.

Bastide, Roger. 1978. *African Religions in Brazil.* Baltimore: Johns Hopkins University Press.

Bauckham, Richard. 1990. *Jude and the Relatives of Jesus in the Early Church.* Edinburgh: T & T Clark.

Baumgarten, Albert I. 1997. *The Flourishing of Jewish Sects in the Maccabean Era: An Interpretation.* Leiden: Brill.

Beard, Mary, John North, and Simon Price. 1998. *Religions of Rome.* Vol. 1, *A History.* Cambridge: Cambridge University Press.

Beattie, John. 1966. "Ritual and Social Change." *Man* 1:60–70.

Becker, Gary S. 1964. *Human Capital: A Theoretical and Empirical Analysis.* New York: Columbia University Press.

Beckford, James A. 1984. "Holistic Imagery and Healing in New Religious and Healing Movements." *Social Compass* 31:259–70.

Beckles, Hilary. 1989. *White Servitude and Black Slavery in Barbados, 1627–1715.* Knoxville: University of Tennessee Press.

Beit-Hallahmi, Benjamin, and Michael Argyle. 1997. *The Psychology of Religious Behaviour, Belief, and Experience.* New York: Routledge.

Bellah, Robert N. 1970. *Beyond Belief.* New York: Harper & Row.

———. 1964. "Religious Evolution." *American Sociological Review* 29:358–74.

Ben-David, Joseph. 1990. "Puritanism and Modern Science: A Study in the Continuity and Coherence of Sociological Research." In *Puritanism and the Rise of Modern Science,* ed. I. Bernard Cohen, 246–61. New Brunswick, N.J.: Rutgers University Press.

Benedict, Ruth. 1938. "Religion." In *General Anthropology,* ed. Franz Boas, 627–65. New York: C. D. Heath.

Berger, Peter. 1967. *The Sacred Canopy.* Garden City, N.Y.: Doubleday.

Berrett, Lamar C. 1988. "Joseph, a Family Man." In *The Prophet Joseph: Essays on the Life and Mission of Joseph Smith,* ed. Larry C. Porter and Susan Easton Black, 36–48. Salt Lake City: Deseret Book Co..

Beyer, Peter. 1994. *Religion and Globalization.* London: Sage.

Bienert, Wolfgang A. 1991. "The Relatives of Jesus." In *New Testament Apocrypha,* rev. ed., ed. Wilhelm Schneemelcher, trans. R. McL. Wilson, 470–88. Louisville: Westminster/John Knox Press.

Bloch, Marc. 1961. *Feudal Society.* 2 vols. Chicago: University of Chicago Press.

Bobrovnikov, Vladimir. 1996. "The Islamic Revival and the National Question in Post-Soviet Dagestan." *Religion, State, and Society* 24:233–38.

Booth, Alan, and James Dabbs Jr. 1993. "Testosterone and Men's Marriages." *Social Forces* 72:463–77.

Bowker, John, ed. 1997. *The Oxford Dictionary of World Religions.* Oxford: Oxford University Press.

Bråkenhielm, Carl Reinhold. 2001. *Världbild och mening: En empirisk studie av livsåskådningar i dagens Sverige.* Nora, Sweden: Nya Doxa.

Brodie, Fawn W. 1945. *No Man Knows My History: The Life of Joseph Smith.* New York: Alfred A. Knopf.

Brønsted, Johannes. 1965. *The Vikings.* Baltimore: Penguin Books.

Brooke, Christopher. 1971. *Medieval Church and Society.* London: Sidgwick & Jackson.

Brown, R. E. 1966. "The Gospel according to John I–XII." In *The Anchor Bible 29.* Garden City, N.Y.: Anchor Books.

Bultina, Louis. 1949. "Church Membership and Church Attendance in Madison, Wisconsin." *American Sociological Review* 14:385–88.

Bunson, Stephen, Margaret Bunson, and Matthew E. Bunson. 1998. *Our Sunday Visitor's Encyclopedia of Saints.* Huntington, Ind.: Our Sunday Visitor.

Burchinal, Lee G. 1959. "Some Social Status Criteria and Church Membership and Church Attendance." *Journal of Social Psychology* 49:53–64.

Burkert, Walter. 1987. *Ancient Mystery Cults.* Cambridge: Harvard University Press.

———. 1985. *Greek Religion.* Cambridge: Harvard University Press.

Burn, A. R. 1953. "Hic breve vivitur." *Past and Present* 4:2–31.

Bushman, Richard L. 1988. "Joseph Smith's Family Background." In *The Prophet Joseph: Essays on the Life and Mission of Joseph Smith,* ed. Larry C. Porter and Susan Easton Black, 1–18. Salt Lake City: Deseret Book Co.

——. 1984. *Joseph Smith and the Beginnings of Mormonism.* Urbana: University of Illinois Press.

Butler, Alvan. [1756–59] 1995–2000. *Lives of Saints.* 12 vols. Collegeville, Minn.: Liturgical Press.

Butler, Jon. 1990. *Awash in a Sea of Faith: Christianizing the American People.* Cambridge: Harvard University Press.

——. 1982. "Enthusiasm Described and Decried: The Great Awakenings as Interpretative Fiction." *Journal of American History* 69:305–25.

Cameron, Euan. 1984. *The Reformation of the Heretics: The Waldenses of the Alps, 1480–1580.* Oxford: Oxford University Press.

Cantril, Hadley S. 1943. "Educational and Economic Composition of Religious Groups." *American Journal of Sociology* 48:574–79.

Capps, Donald, and Michael Carroll. 1988. Interview. *Journal for the Scientific Study of Religion* 27:429–41.

Carroll, Michael P. 1987. "Praying the Rosary": The Anal-Erotic Origins of a Popular Catholic Devotion." *Journal for the Scientific Study of Religion* 26:486–98.

Chandler, Tertius, and Gerald Fox. 1974. *Three Thousand Years of Urban Growth.* New York: Academic Press.

Charles, Elizabeth. 1887. *Martyrs and Saints of the First Twelve Centuries.* New York: E. & J. B. Young & Co.

Chen, Hsinchih. 1995. "The Development of Taiwanese Folk Religion, 1683–1945." Ph.D. diss., University of Washington.

Christiansen, Karl O. 1977. "A Review of Studies of Criminality among Twins." In *Biological Bases of Criminal Behavior,* ed. Karl O. Christiansen and Sarnoff Mednick. New York: Gardner.

Clagett, Marshall. 1961. *The Science of Mechanics in the Middle Ages.* Madison: University of Wisconsin Press.

Clausen, Christopher. 2000. *Faded Mosaic: The Emergence of Post-Cultural America.* Chicago: Ivan R. Dee.

Clendenin, Daniel B., ed. 1995. *Eastern Orthodox Theology: A Contemporary Reader.* Grand Rapids, Mich.: Baker Books.

Clough, Bradley S. 1997. "Buddhism." In *God,* ed. Jacob Neusner, 56–84. Cleveland: Pilgrim Press.

Codrington, R. H. 1891. *The Melanesians.* Oxford: Oxford University Press.

Cohen, Gershon D. 1967. "Messianic Postures of Ashkenazim and Sephardim (Prior to Sabbatai Zevi)." In *Studies of the Leo Baeck Institute,* ed. Max Kreutzberger, 117–56. New York: F. Ungar.

Cohen, I. Bernard. 1985. *Revolution in Science.* Cambridge: Belknap Press.

Cohen, Shaye J. D. 1987. *From the Maccabees to the Mishnah.* Philadelphia: Westminster Press.

Cohn, Norman. 1961. *The Pursuit of the Millennium.* New York: Harper & Row.

Coleman, James S. 1956. "Social Cleavage and Religious Conflict." *Journal of Social Issues* 12:44–56.

Collins, Randall. 1998. *The Sociology of Philosophies: A Global Theory of Intellectual Change.* Cambridge: Harvard University Press.

Colquhoun, Frank. 1955. *Harringay Story: The Official Record of the Billy Graham Greater London Crusade, 1954.* London: Hodder & Stoughton.

Condran, John G., and Joseph B. Tamney. 1985. "Religious 'Nones': 1957 to 1982." *Sociological Analysis* 46:415–23.

Cornwall, Marie. 1988. "The Influence of Three Agents of Religious Socialization." In *The Religion and Family Connection,* ed. Darwin Thomas, 207–31. Provo, Utah: Brigham Young University Religious Studies Center.

Cortés, Juan B., and Florence M. Gatti. 1972. *Delinquency and Crime: A Biopsychological Approach.* New York: Seminar Press.

Costen, Michael. 1997. *The Cathars and the Albigensian Crusade.* Manchester: Manchester University Press.

Coulson, John. 1958. *The Saints: A Concise Biographical Dictionary.* New York: Hawthorn Books.

Cox, Harvey. 1983. "Interview." In *Hare Krishna, Hare Krishna,* ed. Steven J. Gelberg. New York: Grove Press.

Crawford, Patricia. 1993. *Women and Religion in England, 1500–1700.* London: Routledge.

Cross, F. L., and Elizabeth A. Livingston. 1974. *The Oxford Dictionary of the Christian Church.* Oxford: Oxford University Press.

Cross, Whitney R. 1950. *The Burned-Over District.* Ithaca, N.Y.: Cornell University Press.

Curry, Patrick. 1999. "Magic vs. Enchantment." *Journal of Contemporary Religion* 14:401–12.

Dabbs, James M., Jr. 1992. "Testosterone and Occupational Achievement." *Social Forces* 70:813–24.

Dabbs, James M., Jr., Robert L. Frady, T. S. Carr, and N. F. Besch. 1987. "Saliva Testosterone and Criminal Violence in Young Adult Prison Inmates." *Psychosomatic Medicine* 49:174–82.

Dabbs, James M., Jr., and Robert Morris. 1990. "Testosterone, Social Class, and Anti-Social Behavior in a Sample of 4,462 Men." *Psychological Science* 1:209–11.

Dabbs, James M., Jr., R. Barry Ruback, Robert L. Frady, Charles H. Hopper, and Demetrios S. Sgoutas. 1988. "Saliva Testosterone and Criminal Violence among Women." *Personality and Individual Differences* 9:269–75.

Daitzman, Reid, and Marvin Zuckerman. 1980. "Disinhibitory Sensation Seeking, Personality, and Gonadal Hormones." *Personality and Individual Differences* 1:103–10.

Darwin, Charles. 1903. *More Letters of Charles Darwin.* Ed. Francis Darwin and A. C. Seward. 2 vols. New York: Appleton.

Davie, Grace. 1994. *Religion in Britain since 1945: Believing without Belonging.* Oxford: Blackwell.

Davis, David Brion. 1966. *The Problem of Slavery in Western Culture.* Ithaca, N.Y.: Cornell University Press.

Davis, Kingsley. 1949. *Human Society.* New York: Macmillan.

Delehaye, Hippolyte. 1998. *The Legends of the Saints.* 2d ed. Dublin: Four Courts Press.

Delooz, Pierre. 1962. "Pour une étude sociologique di Canonizzazione della Controriforma," *Archives de Sociologie des Religions* 13:17–43.

Delumeau, Jean. 1977. *Catholicism between Luther and Voltaire.* London: Burns & Oats.

Demerath, Nicholas J., III. 2000. "The Varieties of Sacred Experience: Finding the Sacred in a Secular Grove." *Journal for the Scientific Study of Religion* 39:1–11.

———. 1965. *Social Class in American Protestantism.* Chicago: Rand McNally.

Demerath, Nicholas J., III, Peter Dobkin Hall, Terry Schmitt, and Rhys H. Williams, eds. 1998. *Sacred Companies: Organizational Aspects of Religion and Religious Aspects of Organizations.* New York: Oxford University Press.

Derrida, Jacques. 1972. *Marges de la philosophie.* Paris: Editions de Minuit.

de Vaus, David, and Ian McAllister. 1987. "Gender Differences in Religion: A Test of the Structural Location Theory." *American Sociological Review* 51:472–81.

Dodd, C. H. 1963. *Historical Tradition in the Fourth Gospel.* Cambridge: Cambridge University Press.

Dorn, Harold. 1991. *The Geography of Science.* Baltimore: Johns Hopkins University Press.

Douglas, Mary. 1975. *Implicit Meanings: Essays in Anthropology.* London: Routledge & Kegan Paul.

———. 1966. *Purity and Danger.* London: Routledge & Kegan Paul.

Downing, Michael. 2001. *Shoes outside the Door: Desire, Devotion, and Excess at San Francisco's Zen Center.* Washington, D.C.: Counterpoint Press.

Duby, Georges. 1977. *The Chivalrous Society.* Berkeley: University of California Press.

Duffy, Eamon. 1997. *Saints and Sinners: A History of Popes.* New Haven, Conn.: Yale University Press.

———. 1992. *The Stripping of the Altars: Traditional Religion in England, 1400–1580.* New Haven, Conn.: Yale University Press.

Dulles, Avery, S.J. 1992. *Models of Revelation.* Maryknoll, N.Y.: Orbis Books.

Dunn, Richard S. 1973. *Sugar and Slaves: The Rise of the Planter Class in the British West Indies, 1624–1713.* New York: W. W. Norton.

Durkheim, Emile. [1912] 1995. *The Elementary Forms of Religious Life.* Trans. Karen E. Fields. New York: Free Press.

———. [1897] 1951. *Suicide.* Glencoe, Ill.: Free Press.

———. [1886] 1994. "Review of Part VI of the *Principles of Sociology* by Herbert

Bibliography

Spencer. *Revue Philosophique de la France et de l'Etranger* 21:61–69. Trans. W. S. F. Pickering, in *Durkheim on Religion*, 13–23, Atlanta: Scholars Press.

———. [1894] 1982. *The Rules of Sociological Method*. London: Macmillan.

Durkin, John, Jr., and Andrew Greeley. 1991. "A Model of Religious Choice under Uncertainty: On Responding Rationally to the Nonrational." *Rationality and Society* 3:178–96.

Dynes, Russell R. 1955. "Church-Sect Typology and Socio-Economic Status." *American Sociological Review* 20:555–60.

Eades, Carla, Jerry Eades, Yuriko Nishiyama, and Hiroko Yanase. 1986. "Houses of Everlasting Bliss." In *Globalization and Social Change in Contemporary Japan*, ed. J. Eades, Tom Gill, and Harumi Befu, 159–79. Melbourne: Transpacific.

Eagleton, Terry. 1996. *The Illusions of Post Modernism*. Oxford: Blackwell.

Earhart, H. Byron. 1993. "Religions of Japan: Many Traditions, One Sacred Way." In *Religious Traditions of the World*, ed. H. Byron Earhart, 1077–187. San Francisco: HarperSanFrancisco.

———. 1984. *Religions of Japan*. San Francisco: HarperSanFrancisco.

Edbury, Peter. 1999. "Warfare in the Latin East." In *Medieval Warfare: A History*, ed. Maurice Keen, 89–112. Oxford: Oxford University Press.

Eichhorn, Werner. 1959. "Taoism." In *The Concise Encyclopaedia of Living Faiths*, ed. R. C. Zaehner, 385–401. Boston: Beacon.

Eisenman, Robert. 1997. *James the Brother of Jesus*. New York: Viking.

Ekelund, Robert B., Robert F. Hèbert, Robert D. Tollison, Gary M. Anderson, and Audrey B. Davison. 1999. *Sacred Trust: The Medieval Church as an Economic Firm*. New York: Oxford University Press.

Eleta, Paula. 1997. "The Conquest of Magic over Public Space: Discovering the Face of Popular Magic in Contemporary Society." *Journal of Contemporary Religion* 12:51–67.

Elkins, Stanley M. 1976. *Slavery: A Problem in American Institutional and Intellectual Life*. 3d ed., rev. Chicago: University of Chicago Press.

Ellison, Christopher G., and Jeffrey S. Levin. 1998. "The Religion-Health Connection: Evidence, Theory, and Future Directions." *Health Education and Behavior* 25:700–720.

Engels, Friedrich. 1894–95. "On the History of Early Christianity." *Die Neue Zeit* 1:4–13, 36–43.

Epps, P., and R. W. Parnell. 1952. "Physique and Temperament in Women Delinquents Compared with Women Undergraduates." *British Journal of Medical Psychology* 25:249–55.

Evans-Pritchard, E. E. 1965. *Theories of Primitive Religion*. Oxford: Clarendon Press.

Farah, Caesar E. 1994. *Islam: Beliefs and Observances*. 5th ed. Hauppauge, N.Y.: Barron's.

Farmer, David. 1997. *Oxford Dictionary of Saints*. 4th ed. London: Oxford University Press.

Farrington, David P. 1988. "Social, Psychological, and Biological Influences on

Juvenile Delinquency and Adult Crime." In *Explaining Criminal Behavior*, ed. Wouter Buikhuisen and Sarnoff A. Mednick, 68–89. Leiden: E. J. Brill.

Ferraro, Kenneth F., and Jessica A. Kelley-Moore. 2000. "Religious Consolation among Men and Women: Do Health Problems Spur Seeking?" *Journal for the Scientific Study of Religion* 39:220–34.

Feuerbach, Ludwig. [1841] 1957. *The Essence of Christianity*. New York: Harper Torchbooks.

Fichter, Joseph H. 1952. "The Profile of Catholic Religious Life." *American Journal of Sociology* 58:145–49.

Filatov, Sergei. 1994. "On Paradoxes of the Post-Communist Russian Orthodox Church." In *Religions sans frontières?* ed. Roberto Cipriani, 117–25. Rome: Dipartimento per L'Informazione e Editoria.

Finegan, Jack. 1992. *The Archeology of the New Testament*. Rev. ed. Princeton, N.J.: Princeton University Press.

Finke, Roger, and Rodney Stark. 1992. *The Churching of America, 1776–1990*. New Brunswick, N.J.: Rutgers University Press.

Fischer, Claude S. 1975. "Toward a Subcultural Theory of Urbanism." *American Journal of Sociology* 80:1319–41.

Fletcher, Richard. 1997. *The Barbarian Conversion: From Paganism to Christianity*. New York: Henry Holt.

Fogel, Robert William. 2000. *The Fourth Great Awakening and the Future of Egalitarianism*. Chicago: University of Chicago Press.

———. 1989. *Without Consent or Contract: The Rise and Fall of American Slavery*. New York: W. W. Norton.

Fortune, Reo F. 1935. "Manus Religion." *Memoirs of the American Philosophical Society* 3.

Fowler, Jeaneane, 1997. *Hinduism: Beliefs and Practices*. Brighton, Eng.: Sussex Academic Press.

France, John. 1997. *Victory in the East*. Cambridge: Cambridge University Press.

Francis, Leslie J. 1997. "The Psychology of Gender Differences in Religion: A Review of Empirical Research." *Religion* 27:81–96.

———. 1991. "The Personality Characteristics of Anglican Ordinands: Feminine Men and Masculine Women?" *Personality and Individual Differences* 12:1133–40.

Francis, Leslie J., S. H. Jones, C. J. Jackson, and M. Robbins. 2001. "The Feminine Personality Profiles of Male Anglican Clergy in Britain and Ireland." *Review of Religious Research* 43:14–23.

Francis, Leslie J., and C. Wilcox. 1998. "Religiosity and Femininity: Do Women Really Hold a More Positive Attitude toward Christianity?" *Journal for the Scientific Study of Religion* 37:462–69.

———. 1996. "Religion and Gender Orientation." *Personality and Individual Differences* 20:119–21.

Frazer, James G. [1922] 1950. *The Golden Bough*. New York: Macmillan.

Fregosi, Paul. 1998. *Jihad in the West*. Amherst, N.Y.: Prometheus Books.

Freud, Sigmund. [1927] 1961. *The Future of an Illusion*. Garden City, N.Y.: Doubleday.

Frisk, L. 1998. *Nyreligiositet i Sverige: Ett religionsventenskapligt perspektiv*. Falun, Sweden: Nora Nya Doxa.

Fück, J. [1936] 1981. "The Originality of the Prophet." Trans. from German in *Studies in Islam*, ed. Merlin L. Swartz, 86–98. New York: Oxford University Press.

Fukutake, Tadashi. 1981. *Japanese Society Today*. Tokyo: University of Tokyo Press.

Fuller, Robert C. 2001. *Spiritual but Not Religious*. Oxford: Oxford University Press.

Gallup International. 1984. *Human Values and Beliefs*. London.

Geertz, Clifford. 1973. *The Interpretation of Cultures*. New York: Basic Books.

Genovese, Eugene D. 1974. *Roll, Jordan, Roll: The World the Slaves Made*. New York: Pantheon Books.

Giles, Lionel. 1993. *The Sayings of Confucious*. New York: Charles E. Tuttle.

Gilliam, J. F. 1961. "The Plague under Marcus Aurelius." *American Journal of Philology* 94:243–55.

Gillingham, John. 1999. "An Age of Expansion: c. 1020–1204." In *Medieval Warfare: A History*, ed. Maurice Keen, 59–88. Oxford: Oxford University Press.

Ginzberg, Louis. [1911] 1939. *The Legends of the Jews*. Vols. 2 and 3. Philadelphia: Jewish Publication Society.

Glass, J. C., and B. B. Kilpatrick. 1998. "Gender Comparisons of Baby Boomers and Financial Preparation for Retirement." *Educational Gerontology* 24: 719–45.

Glock, Charles Y. 1964. "The Role of Deprivation in the Origin and Evolution of Religious Groups." In *Religion and Social Conflict*, ed. Robert Lee and Martin E. Marty, 24–36. New York: Oxford University Press.

——. 1959. "The Religious Revival in America." In *Religion and the Face of America*, ed. Jane Zahn, 25–42. Berkeley: University of California Press.

Glueck, Sheldon, and Eleanor Glueck. 1956. *Physique and Delinquency*. New York: Harper.

Goldenweiser, Alexander A. 1915. Review of *Les formes élémentaires de la vie religieuse, le système totémique en Australie. American Anthropologist* 17: 719–35.

Goode, William J. 1951. *Religion among the Primitives*. Glencoe, Ill.: Free Press.

Goody, Jack. 1961. "Religion and Ritual: The Definitional Problem." *British Journal of Sociology* 12:142–64.

Gordon-McCutchan, R. C. 1983. "Great Awakenings." *Sociological Analysis* 44: 83–95.

Goring, Charles. 1913. *The English Convict*. London: His Majesty's Stationery Office.

Gottfredson, Michael R., and Travis Hirschi. 1990. *A General Theory of Crime*. Stanford, Calif.: Stanford University Press.

Gove, Walter R. 1985. "The Effect of Age and Gender on Deviant Behavior: A

Biopsychosocial Perspective." In *Gender and the Life Course,* ed. Alice S. Rossi. New York: Aldine.

Goveia, Elsa V. 1969. "The West Indian Slave Laws of the Eighteenth Century." In *Slavery in the New World: A Reader in Comparative History,* ed. Laura Foner and Eugene D. Genovese, 167–88. Englewood Cliffs, N.J.: Prentice-Hall.

Granqvist, Pehr, and Berit Hagekull. 2001. "Seeking Security in the New Age: On Attachment and Emotional Compensation." *Journal for the Scientific Study of Religion* 40:527–45.

Grant, Edward. 1996. *The Foundations of Modern Science in the Middle Ages: Their Religious, Institutional, and Intellectual Contexts.* Cambridge: Cambridge University Press.

Grant, Robert M. 1977. *Early Christianity and Society: Seven Studies.* San Francisco: Harper & Row.

Greeley, Andrew M. 1975. *Sociology of the Paranormal: A Reconnaissance.* Beverly Hills, Calif.: Sage.

Green, Ronald M. 1988. *Religion and Moral Reason: A New Method for Comparative Study.* New York: Oxford University Press.

Greil, Arthur L., and Thomas Robbins, eds. 1994. *Between Sacred and Secular: Research and Theory of Quasi-Religion.* Greenwich, N.J.: JAI Press.

Guerry, André Michel. 1833. *Essai sur la statistique morale de la France.* Paris: French Royal Academy of Science.

Gustafsson, Göran. 1990. "Politicization of State Churches—A Welfare State Model." *Social Compass* 37:107–16.

Hamberg, Eva. 2001. "Kristen tro och praxis i dagens Sverige." In Bråkenhielm 2001, 33–65.

———. 1990. *Studies in the Prevalence of Religious Beliefs and Religious Practice in Contemporary Sweden.* Uppsala: Act Universitatis Upsaliensis.

Hamberg, Eva M., and Thorleif Pettersson. 1994. "The Religious Market: Denominational Competition and Religious Participation in Contemporary Sweden." *Journal for the Scientific Study of Religion* 33:205–16.

Harnack, Adolph von. 1908. *The Mission and Expansion of Christianity in the First Three Centuries.* 2 vols. Trans James Moffatt. New York: G. P. Putnam's Sons.

Harris, Marvin. 1964. *Patterns of Race in the Americas.* New York: Walker.

———. 1963. *The Nature of Cultural Things.* New York: Random House.

Harris, William V. 1989. *Ancient Literacy.* Cambridge: Harvard University Press.

Harrison, Jane E. 1912. *Themis: A Study of the Social Origins of Greek Religion.* Cambridge: Cambridge University Press.

Hegel, George Wilhelm Friedrich. [1840] 1996. *Lectures on the Philosophy of Religion.* Vol. 1, *Introduction and the Concept of Religion.* Berkeley: University of California Press.

Herbermann, Charles G., Edward A Pace, Conde B. Pallen, Thomas J. Shahan, and John J. Wynne, eds. 1913. *The Catholic Encyclopedia.* New York: Encyclopedia Press.

Bibliography

Hickey, Anne Ewing. 1987. *Women of the Roman Aristocracy as Christian Monastics.* Ann Arbor, Mich.: UMI Research Press.

Hobbes, Thomas. [1651] 1956. *Leviathan.* Vol. 1. Chicago: Henry Regnery.

Hodgson, Marshall G. S. 1974. *The Venture of Islam.* Vol. 1, *The Classical Age of Islam.* Chicago: University of Chicago Press.

Holdrege, Barbara. 2000. "What's beyond the Post?" In *A Magic Still Dwells: Comparative Religion in the Postmodern Age,* ed. Kimberly C. Patton and Benjamin C. Ray, 77–91. Berkley: University of California Press.

Höllinger, Franz, and Timothy B. Smith. 2002. "Religion and Esotericism among Students: A Cross-Cultural Comparative Study." *Journal of Contemporary Religion* 17:229–49.

Hood, Ralph W., Jr. 1985. "Mysticism." In *The Sacred in a Secular Age,* ed. Phillip E. Hammond, 285–97. Berkeley: University of California Press.

Hooten, Earnest Albert. 1939. *Crime and the Man.* Cambridge: Harvard University Press.

Horsely, Richard A. 1989. *Sociology and the Jesus Movement.* New York: Crossroad.

Horton, Robin. 1964. "Ritual Man in Africa." *Africa* 34:85–104.

———. 1962. "The Kalabari World-View: An Outline and Interpretation." *Africa* 32:197–220.

Houtman, Dick, and Peter Mascini. 2002. "Why Do Churches Become Empty, While New Age Grows? Secularization and Religious Change in the Netherlands." *Journal for the Scientific Study of Religion* 41:455–73.

Huff, Toby. 1993. *The Rise of Early Modern Science: Islam, China, and the West.* Cambridge: Cambridge University Press.

Iannaccone, Laurence R. 1995. "Risk, Rationality, and Religious Portfolios." *Economic Inquiry* 33:285–95.

———. 1994. "Why Strict Churches Are Strong." *American Journal of Sociology* 99:1180–211.

———. 1992. "Sacrifice and Stigma: Reducing Free-Rising in Cults, Communes, and Other Collectives." *Journal of Political Economy* 100 (2): 271–92.

———. 1990. "Religious Practice: A Human Capital Approach." *Journal for the Scientific Study of Religion* 29:297–314.

Ikado, Fujio. 1972. *Religion in a Secular Society* (Sezoku shakai no shukyo). Tokyo: Nihon Kikan Kyodan.

Jacobson, Steve. 1997. *Heart to God, Hands to Work: Connecting Spirituality and Work.* Bethesda, Md.: Alban Institute.

Jaki, Stanley L. 2000. *The Savior of Science.* Grand Rapids: Eerdmans.

———. 1986. *Science and Creation.* Edinburgh: Scottish Academic Press.

James, E. O. 1960. *The Ancient Gods: The History and Diffusion of Religion in the Ancient Near East and the Eastern Mediterranean.* New York: G. P. Putnam's Sons.

James, William. [1902] 1958. *The Varieties of Religious Experience.* New York: Mentor Books.

Johansen, Alf. 1983. "The Russian Orthodox Church As Reflected in Orthodox

Bibliography

and Atheist Publications in the Soviet Union." *Occasional Papers on Religion in Eastern Europe* 3 (2): 1–26.

Johnson, Paul. 1976. *A History of Christianity*. New York: Atheneum.

Johnston, Harry Hamilton. 1910. *The Negro in the New World*. London: Methuen.

Judge, E. A. 1960. *The Social Patterns of Christian Groups in the First Century*. London: Tyndale.

Julian, Teresa, and Patrick C. McKenry. 1989. "Relationship of Testosterone to Men's Family Functioning in Mid-Life. *Aggressive Behavior* 15:281–89.

Karmiris, John. 1973. "Concerning the Sacraments." In *Eastern Orthodox Theology: A Contemporary Reader,* ed. Daniel B. Clendenin, 21–31. Grand Rapids, Mich.: Baker Books.

Kaufmann, Yehezkel. 1960. *The Religion of Israel*. Chicago: University of Chicago Press.

Kelley, Dean M. 1972. *Why Conservative Churches Are Growing*. New York: Harper & Row.

Kennedy, Hugh. 2001. *The Armies of the Caliphs*. London: Routledge.

Kent, Stephen A. 2001. *From Slogans to Mantras: Social Protest and Religious Conversion in the Late Vietnam War Era*. Syracuse, N.Y.: Syracuse University Press.

Khomiakov, Aleksei. 1895. "The Church Is One." In *Russia and the English Church in the Last Fifty Years,* ed. W. J. Birbeck, 201–37. London: Rivington.

Kieckhefer, Richard. 1989. *Magic in the Middle Ages*. Cambridge: Cambridge University Press.

———. 1984. *Unquiet Souls: Fourteenth Century Saints and Their Religious Milieu*. Chicago: University of Chicago Press.

———. 1976. *European Witch Trials: Their Foundations in Popular and Learned Culture*. Berkeley: University of California Press.

King, Peter. 1999. *Western Monasticism: A History of the Monastic Movement in the Latin Church*. Kalamazoo, Mich.: Cistercian Publications.

Kisala, Robert J., and Mark R. Mullins. 2001. *Religion and Social Crisis in Japan*. New York: Palgrave.

Klein, Herbert S. 1969. "Anglicanism, Catholicism, and the Negro Slave." In *Slavery in the New World: A Reader in Comparative History,* ed. Laura Foner and Eugene D. Genovese, 138–69. Englewood Cliffs, N.J.: Prentice-Hall.

———. 1967. *Slavery in the Americas: A Comparative Study of Virginia and Cuba*. Chicago: University of Chicago Press.

Klugel, James L. 1997. *The Bible As It Was*. Cambridge: Harvard University Press.

Knipe, David M. 1993. "Hinduism: Experiments in the Sacred." In *Religious Traditions of the World,* ed. H. Byron Earhart, 713–840. San Francisco: HarperSanFrancisco.

Knowles, David. 1969. *Christian Monasticism*. New York: McGraw-Hill.

Koester, Helmut. 1982. *Introduction to the New Testament*. Vol. 2, *History and Literature of Early Christianity*. New York: Walter de Gruyter.

Kokosalakis, Nikos. 1994. "The Historical Continuity of Cultural Specificity of

Eastern Orthodox Christianity." In *Religions sans frontières?* ed. Roberto Cipriani, 126–43. Rome: Dipartimento per L'Informazione e Editoria.

Kosmin, Barry A., Sidney Goldstein, Joseph Waksberg, Nava Lerer, Ariella Keysar, and Jeffrey Scheckner. 1991. *Highlights of the CJF 1990 National Jewish Population Survey.* New York: Council of Jewish Federations.

Kuhn, Thomas S. 1962. *The Structure of Scientific Revolutions.* Chicago: University of Chicago Press.

La Barre, Weston. 1969. *They Shall Take Up Serpents.* New York: Schocken.

Ladurie, Emmanuel Le Roy. 1974. *The Peasants of Languedoc.* Urbana: University of Illinois Press.

Lambert, Frank. 1999. *Inventing the Great Awakening.* Princeton, N.J.: Princeton University Press.

———. 1990. "'Peddlar in Divinity': George Whitefield and the Great Awakening, 1737–1745." *Journal of American History* 77:812–37.

Lambert, Malcolm. 1998. *The Cathars.* Oxford: Blackwell.

———. 1992. *Medieval Heresy.* Oxford: Blackwell.

Lang, Graeme, and Lars Ragvold. 1993. *The Rise of a Refuge God: Hong Kong's Wong Tai Sin.* Oxford: Oxford University Press.

Lange, Johannes. 1931. *Crime as Destiny.* London: G. Allen & Unwin.

Latourette, Kenneth Scott. 1975. *A History of Christianity.* Vol. 2. Rev. ed. San Francisco: HarperSanFrancisco.

Lawrence, Peter. 1964. *Road Belong Cargo: A Study of the Cargo Movement in the Southern Madang District, New Guinea.* Manchester: Manchester University Press.

Layton, Bentley. 1987. *The Gnostic Scriptures,* Garden City, N.Y.: Doubleday.

Lenowitz, Harris. 1998. *The Jewish Messiahs: From Galilee to Crown Heights.* New York: Oxford University Press.

Lenski, Gerhard. 1966. *Power and Privilege: A Theory of Social Stratification.* New York: McGraw-Hill.

———. 1953. "Social Correlates of Religious Interest." *American Sociological Review* 18:533–44.

Lester, Robert C. 1993. "Buddhism: The Path to Nirvana." In *Religious Traditions of the World,* ed. H. Byron Earhart, 847–971. San Francisco: HarperSanFrancisco.

Levack, Brian P. 1995. *The Witch-Hunt in Early Modern Europe.* 2d ed. London: Longman.

Levine, Donald N. 1995. *Visions of the Sociological Tradition.* Chicago: University of Chicago Press.

Lévi-Strauss, Claude. 1966. *The Savage Mind.* London: Weidenfeld & Nicholson.

Lindberg, David C. 1992. *The Beginnings of Western Science.* Chicago: University of Chicago Press.

Lippy, Charles H. 1994. *Being Religious, American Style: A History of Popular Religiosity in the United States.* Westport, Conn.: Praeger.

Lofland, John, and Rodney Stark. 1965. "Becoming a World-Saver: A Theory of

Conversion to a Deviant Perspective." *American Sociological Review* 30: 862–75.

Lombroso-Ferrero, Gina. [1911] 1972. *Criminal Man.* Montclair, N.J.: Patterson-Smith.

Luckmann, Thomas. 1967. *The Invisible Religion.* New York: Macmillan.

Lyotard, Jean-François. 1993. "Answering the Question: What Is Postmodernism?" In *Postmodernism: A Reader,* ed. Thomas Docherty. New York: Columbia University Press.

Mack, Burton. 1996. *Who Wrote the New Testament? The Making of the Christian Myth.* San Francisco: HarperSanFrancisco.

MacKenzie, F. A. 1930. *The Russian Crucifixion: The Full Story of the Persecution of Religion under Bolshevism.* London: Jarrolds.

MacKenzie, Norman, and Jeanne MacKenzie. 1977. *The Fabians.* New York: Simon & Schuster.

MacLennan, Robert S., and A. Thomas Kraabel. 1986. "The God-Fearers—A Literary and Theological Invention." *Biblical Archaeology Review* 12 (September–October): 47–53.

MacMullen, Ramsay. 1981. *Paganism in the Roman Empire.* New Haven, Conn.: Yale University Press.

Madden, Thomas F. 1999. *A Concise History of the Crusades.* Lanham, Md.: Rowman & Littlefield.

Malinowski, Bronislaw. [1948] 1992. *Magic, Science, and Religion.* Prospect Heights, Ill.: Waveland Press.

———. 1935. *The Foundations of Faith and Morals.* Oxford: Oxford University Press.

Mandelbaum, David G. 1966. "Transcendental and Pragmatic Aspects of Religion." *American Anthropologist* 68:1174–91.

Marler, Penny Long, and C. Kirk Hadaway. 2002. "'Being Religious' or 'Being Spiritual' in America: A Zero-Sum Proposition." *Journal for the Scientific Study of Religion* 41:289–300.

Martin, David. 1967. *A Sociology of English Religion.* London: SCM Press.

Marx, Karl. [1845] 1998. *The German Ideology.* Amherst: Prometheus Books.

———. [1844] 1964. "Contribution to the Critique of Hegel's Philosophy of Right." In Marx and Engels 1964, 41–58.

Marx, Karl, and Friedrich Engels. 1964. *On Religion.* New York: Schocken Books. Reprint, Atlanta: Scholars Press, n.d.

Mathews, Shailer. 1921. *A History of New Testament Times in Palestine.* New York: Macmillan.

Mathieson, William Law. 1926. *British Slavery and Its Abolition.* London: Longmans, Green.

Mauss, Armand L. 1981. "The Fading of the Pharaoh's Curse: The Decline and Fall of the Priesthood Ban against Blacks in the Mormon Church." *Dialogue* 41:10–45.

Mauss, Marcel. 1950. *A General Theory of Magic.* London: Routledge & Kegan Paul.

Mayer, Hans Eberhard. 1972. *The Crusades.* Oxford: Oxford University Press.

Mayr-Harting, Henry. 1993. "The West: The Age of Conversion (700–1050)." In *The Oxford History of Christianity,* ed. John McManners, 101–29. Oxford: Oxford University Press.

McAdam, Doug. 1988. *Freedom Summer.* New York: Oxford University Press.

McBrien, Richard P. 2001. *Lives of the Saints.* San Francisco: HarperSanFranciso.

McBurnett, Keith, Benjamin B. Lahey, Paul J. Rathouz, and Rolf Loeber. 2000. "Low Salivary Cortisal and Persistent Aggression in Boys Referred for Disruptive Behavior." *Archives of General Psychiatry* 57:38–43.

McFarland, H. Neill. 1967. *Rush Hour of the Gods: A Study of New Religious Movements in Japan.* New York: Macmillan.

McLoughlin, William G. 1978. *Revivals, Awakenings, and Reform.* Chicago: University of Chicago Press.

McNeill, William H. 1976. *Plagues and Peoples.* Garden City, N.Y.: Doubleday.

McSheffrey, Shannon. 1995. *Gender and Heresy: Women and Men in Lollard Communities, 1420–1530.* Philadelphia: University of Pennsylvania Press.

Mednick, Sarnoff, William F. Gabrielli Jr., and Barry Hutchings. 1984. "Genetic Influences in Criminal Convictions: Evidence from an Adoption Cohort." *Science* 224:891–94.

Meeks, Wayne. 1993. *The Origins of Christian Morality: The First Two Centuries.* New Haven, Conn.: Yale University Press.

Melton, J. Gordon. 1988. "Testing Truisms about the 'Cults': Toward a New Perspective on Nonconventional Religion." Paper presented at the annual meetings of the American Academy of Religion, Chicago.

Meltzer, Milton. 1993. *Slavery: A World History.* New York: Da Capo Press.

Mendes-Flohr, Paul, and Jehuda Reinarz. 1995. *The Jew in the Modern World: A Documentary History.* New York: Oxford University Press.

Metford, J. C. J. 1983. *Dictionary of Christian Lore and Legend.* London: Thames & Hudson.

Middleton, John, ed. 1967. *Magic, Witchcraft, and Curing.* Austin: University of Texas Press.

Miller, Alan S. 2000. "Going to Hell in Asia: The Relationship between Risk and Religion in a Cross Cultural Setting." *Review of Religious Research* 42:5–18.

——. 1995. "A Rational Choice Model of Religious Behavior in Japan." *Journal for the Scientific Study of Religion* 34:234–44.

——. 1992. "Conventional Religious Behavior in Modern Japan: A Service Industry Perspective." *Journal for the Scientific Study of Religion* 31:207–14.

Miller, Alan S., and John P. Hoffmann. 1995. "Risk and Religion: An Explanation of Gender Differences in Religiosity." *Journal for the Scientific Study of Religion* 34:63–75.

Miller, Alan S., and Satoshi Kanazawa. 2000. *Order by Accident: The Origins and Consequences of Conformity in Contemporary Japan.* Boulder, Colo.: Westview Press.

Mills, J. P. 1922. *The Lhota Nagas.* London: Macmillan.

Moeller, Bernd. 1972. *Imperial Cities and the Reformation: Three Essays*. Philadelphia: Fortress Press.

Mol, Hans. 1985. *The Faith of Australians*. Sydney: George, Allen & Unwin.

Mooney, James. 1896. *The Ghost Shirt Religion and the Sioux Outbreak of 1890*. Washington, D.C.: U.S. Government Printing Office.

Moore, R. I. 1994. *The Origins of European Dissent*. Toronto: University of Toronto Press.

Moroto, Aiko. 1976. "Conditions for Accepting a New Religious Belief: A Case Study of Myochikai Members in Japan." Master's thesis, University of Washington.

Morris, Brian. 1987. *Anthropological Studies of Religion: An Introduction*. Cambridge: Cambridge University Press.

Murdock, George Peter. 1981. *Atlas of World Cultures*. Pittsburgh: University of Pittsburgh Press.

———. 1949. *Social Structures*. New York: Macmillan.

Murdock, George Peter, and Douglas R. White. 1969. "The Standard Cross-Cultural Sample." *Ethnology* 8:329–69.

Murray, Alexander. 1972. "Piety and Impiety in Thirteenth-Century Italy." *Studies in Church History* 8:83–106.

National Science Foundation (NSF). 2002. *Science and Engineering Indicators*. Washington, D.C.: U.S. Government Printing Office.

Needham, Rodney. 1985. *Exemplars*. Berkeley: University of California Press.

———. 1972. *Belief, Language, and Experience*. Chicago: University of Chicago Press.

Nelson, Geoffrey K. 1969. *Spiritualism and Society*. New York: Schocken.

Nelson, John. 1992. "Shinto Ritual: Managing Chaos in Contemporary Japan." *Ethnos* 57:77–104.

Neusner, Jacob. 1984. *Judaism in the Beginning of Christianity*. Philadelphia: Fortress Press.

———. 1975. *First Century Judaism in Crisis*. Nashville: Abingdon Press.

Nickerson, Colin. 1999. "In Iceland, Spirits Are in the Material World." *Seattle Post-Intelligencer*, December 25, A12.

Niebuhr, H. Richard. 1929. *The Social Sources of Denominationalism*. New York: Henry Holt.

O'Keefe, Daniel Lawrence. 1982. *Stolen Lightning: A Social Theory of Magic*. New York: Vintage Books.

Orenstein, Alan. 2002. "Religion and Paranormal Belief." *Journal for the Scientific Study of Religion* 41:301–11.

Pagels, Elaine. 1979. *The Gnostic Gospels*. New York: Random House.

Parrinder, Geoffrey. 1983. *World Religions*. New York: Facts on File.

———. 1976. *Mysticism in the World's Religions*. New York: Oxford University Press.

Parsons, Talcott. 1951. *The Social System*. Glencoe, Ill.: Free Press.

Pásztor, János. 1995. "The Theology of the Serving Church and the Theology of Diaconia in the Protestant Churches and Their Consequences in Hungary during the Time of Socialism." *Religion in Eastern Europe* 15 (6): 22–35.

Payne, Robert. 1984. *The Dream and the Tomb: A History of the Crusades.* New York: Stein & Day.

——. 1959. *The History of Islam.* Barnes & Noble.

Pearson, Birger A. 1973. "Friedlander Revisited: Alexandrian Judaism and Gnostic Origins." *Studia Philonica* 2:23–39.

Pelikan, Jaroslav. 1996. *Mary though the Centuries: Her Place in the History of Culture.* New Haven, Conn.: Yale University Press.

Peregrine, Peter. 1996. "The Birth of the Gods Revisited: A Partial Replication of Guy Swanson's (1960) Cross-Cultural Study of Religion." *Cross-Cultural Research* 30:84–122.

Peters, Edward. 1978. *The Magician, the Witch, and the Law.* Philadelphia: University of Pennsylvania Press.

Peters, F. E. 1994. *Muhammad and the Origins of Islam.* Albany: State University of New York.

Peyser, Joan. 1993. *The Memory of All That: The Life of George Gershwin.* New York: Simon & Schuster.

Poloma, Margaret, and George H. Gallup Jr. 1991. *Varieties of Prayer: A Survey Report.* Philadelphia: Trinity Press International.

Pope, Earl A. 1992. "The Role of Religion in the Romanian Revolution." *Occasional Papers on Religion in Eastern Europe* 12 (2): 1–18.

——. 1981. "The Romanian Orthodox Church." *Occasional Papers on Religion in Eastern Europe* 1 (3): 1–17.

Porter, Larry C. 1988. "'The Field Is White Already to Harvest': Earliest Missionary Labors and the Book of Mormon." In *The Prophet Joseph: Essays on the Life and Mission of Joseph Smith,* ed. Larry C. Porter and Susan Easton Black, 73–89. Salt Lake City: Deseret Book Co.

Pospielovsky, Dimitry V. 1997. "The 'Best Years' of Stalin's Church Policy (1942–1948) in the Light of Archival Documents." *Religion, State, and Society* 25:139–62.

——. 1988. *Soviet Antireligious Campaigns and Persecutions.* New York: St. Martin's Press.

Powell, Melanie, and David Ansic. 1997. "Gender Differences in Risk Behavior in Financial Decision-Making: An Experimental Analysis." *Journal of Economic Psychology* 18:605–28.

Price, S. R. F. 1984. *Rituals and Power: The Roman Imperial Cult in Asia Minor.* Cambridge: Cambridge University Press.

Quinn, D. Michael. 1994. *The Mormon Hierarchy: Origins of Power.* Salt Lake City: Signature Books.

Radin, Paul. 1957. *Primitive Religion.* New York: Dover Books.

Rahner, Karl. 1975. "Theology. I. Nature." in *Encyclopedia of Theology: The Concise "Sacranebtum Mundi,"* ed. Karl Rahner. New York: Seabury.

Raine, Adrian, Todd Lencz, Susan Bihrle, Lori LaCasse, and Patrick Colletti. 2000. "Reduced Prefrontal Gray Matter Volume and Reduced Autonomic Activity in Antisocial Personality Disorder." *Archives of General Psychiatry* 57:119–27.

Read, Piers Paul. 1999. *The Templars*. London: Weidenfeld & Nicholson.

Riley-Smith, Jonathan. 1997. *The First Crusaders, 1095–1131*. Cambridge: Cambridge University Press.

Robbins, Thomas. 1988. *Cults, Converts & Charisma*. Beverly Hills, Calif.: Sage.

Roberts, Keith A. 1995. *Religion in Sociological Perspective*. Belmont, Calif.: Wadsworth.

Roberts, Michael. 1968. *The Early Vasas: A History of Sweden, 1523–1611*. Cambridge: Cambridge University Press.

Robinson, John A. T. 1985. *The Priority of John*. Ed. J. F. Coakley. London: SCM Press.

Rodinson, Maxime. 1980. *Muhammad*. New York: Pantheon Books.

Roof, Wade Clark. 1999. *Spiritual Marketplace*. Princeton, N.J.: Princeton University Press.

———. 1993. *A Generation of Seekers: The Spiritual Journeys of the Baby Boom Generation*. San Francisco: HarperSanFrancisco.

Roof, Wade Clark, and William McKinney. 1987. *The American Mainline Religion: Its Changing Shape and Future*. New Brunswick, N.J.: Rutgers University Press.

Rörig, Frtiz. 1967. *The Medieval Town*. Berkeley: University of California Press.

Ross, Thomas W. 1985. "The Implicit Theology of Carl Sagan." *Pacific Theological Review* 18:24–32.

Runciman, Steven. 1951. *A History of the Crusades*. 3 vols. Cambridge: Cambridge University Press.

Russell, J. C. 1958. "Late Ancient and Medieval Population." *Transactions of the American Philosophical Society* 48, pt. 3.

Russell, Jeffrey Burton. 1965. *Dissent and Reform in the Early Middle Ages*. Berkeley: University of California Press.

Rydenfelt, Sven. 1985. "Sweden and Its Bishops." *Wall Street Journal*, August 21, A25.

Sakamoto, Yoshiyuki. 2000. *A Study of the Japanese National Character: The Tenth Nationwide Survey*. Tokyo: Institute of Statistical Mathematics.

Salahi, M. A. 1995. *Muhammad: Man and Prophet*. Shaftesbury, Eng.: Element.

Saldarini, Anthony J. 1988. *Pharisees, Scribes, and Sadducees in Palestinian Society: A Sociological Approach*. Wilmington, Del.: M. Glazier.

Schafer, Judith Kelleher. 1994. *Slavery, the Civil Law, and the Supreme Court of Louisiana*. Baton Rouge: Louisiana State University Press.

Scharfstein, Ben-Ami. 1973. *Mystical Experience*. Indianapolis: Bobbs-Merrill.

Schneiderman, Leo. 1967. "Psychological Notes on the Nature of Mystical Experience." *Journal for the Scientific Study of Religion* 6:91–100.

Scott, R. O. 2001. "Are You Religious or Are You Spiritual: A Look in the Mirror." *Spirituality and Health* (spring): 26–28.

Shahar, Meir, and Robert P. Weller, eds. 1996. *Unruly Gods: Divinity and Society in China*. Honolulu: University of Hawaii Press.

Bibliography

Sharot, Stephen. 1982. *Messianism, Mysticism, and Magic: A Sociological Analysis of Jewish Religious Movements*. Chapel Hill: University of North Carolina Press.

Sheldon, W. H. 1940. *The Varieties of Human Physique*. New York: Harpers.

Sheridan, Richard B. 1974. *Sugar and Slavery: An Economic History of the British West Indies, 1623–1775*. Aylesbury, Eng.: Ginn.

Sherkat, Darren E. 2002. "Sexuality and Religious Commitment: An Empirical Assessment." *Journal for the Scientific Study of Religion* 41:313–23.

Sherkat, Darren E., and T. Jean Blocker. 1994. "The Political Development of Sixties Activists: Identifying the Influence of Class, Gender, and Socialization on Protest Participation." *Social Forces* 72:821–42.

Simmel, Georg. [1905] 1959. *Sociology of Religion*. New York: Wisdom.

Simpson, George Eaton. 1978. *Black Religions in the New World*. New York: Columbia University Press.

Sjödin, Ulf. 2002. "The Swedes and the Paranormal." *Journal of Contemporary Religion* 17:75–85.

Smart, Ninian. 1984. *The Religious Experience of Mankind*. 3d ed. New York: Charles Scribner's.

Smith, Christian. 1998. *American Evangelicalism: Embattled and Thriving*. Chicago: University of Chicago Press.

Smith, Jonathan Z. 1978. *Map Is Not Territory: Studies in the History of Religions*. Leiden: E. J. Brill.

Smith, Lucy Mack. [1853] 1996. *History of Joseph Smith by His Mother*. Ed. Scot Facer Procter and Maurine Jensen Procter. Salt Lake City: Bookcraft.

Smith, Timothy L. 1983. "My Rejection of the Cyclical View of 'Great Awakenings' in American Religious History." *Sociological Analysis* 44:97–101.

Smith, W. Robertson. 1889. *The Religion of the Semites: Fundamental Institutions*. Edinburgh: Adam & Charles Black.

Snelling, John. 1993. *Buddhism in Russia*. New York: Harper-Collins.

Sorokin, Pitirim A. 1950. *Altruistic Love: A Study of American "Good Neighbors" and Christian Saints*. Boston: Beacon Press.

Southwold, Martin. 1978. "Buddhism and the Definition of Religion." *Man*, n.s., 13:362–79).

Spencer, Herbert. 1896. *Principles of Sociology*. Rev. ed. 2 vols. New York: D. Appleton.

Spielvogel, Jackson J. 2000. *Western Civilization*. 4th ed. Belmont, Calif.; Wadsworth.

Spiro, Melford E. 1966a. "Buddhism and Economic Action in Burma." *American Anthropologist* 68:1163–73.

———. 1966b. "Religion: Problems of Definition and Explanation." In *Anthropological Approaches to the Study of Religion*, ed. Michael Banton, 85–126. London: Tavistock.

Stark, Rodney. 2003. *For the Glory of God: How Monotheism Led to Reformations, Science, Witch-Hunting, and the End of Slavery*. Princeton, N.J.: Princeton University Press.

———. 2001. *One True God: Historical Consequences of Monotheism.* Princeton, N.J.: Princeton University Press.

———. 2000. *Sociology.* 8th ed. Belmont, Calif.: Wadsworth.

———. 1999. "Secularization, R.I.P." *Sociology of Religion* 60:249–73.

———. 1998. "The Rise and Fall of Christian Science." *Journal of Contemporary Religion* 13:189–214.

———. 1997. "A Theoretical Assessment of LDS Growth." In *Latter-day Saint Social Life: Social Research on the LDS Church and Its Members,* ed. James T. Duke, 29–70. Provo, Utah: Religious Studies Center, Brigham Young University.

———. 1996a. *The Rise of Christianity: A Sociologist Reconsiders History.* Princeton, N.J.: Princeton University Press.

———. 1996b. "Why Religious Movements Succeed or Fail: A Revised General Model. *Journal of Contemporary Religion* 11:133–46.

———. 1993. "Europe's Receptivity to New Religious Movements: Round Two." *Journal for the Scientific Study of Religion* 32:389–97.

———. 1992a. *Doing Sociology.* Belmont, Calif.: Wadsworth.

———. 1992b. "How Sane People Talk to the Gods: A Rational Theory of Revelations." In *Innovation in Religious Traditions: Essays in the Interpretation of Religious Change,* ed. Michael A. Williams, Collet Cox, and Martin S. Jaffe, 19–34. Berlin: Mouton de Gruyter.

———. 1991. "Normal Revelations: A Rational Model of 'Mystical' Experiences." In *Religion and the Social Order,* vol. 1, ed. David G. Bromley, 239–51. Greenwich, Conn.: JAI Press.

———. 1987. "How New Religions Succeed: A Theoretical Model." In *The Future of New Religious Movements,* ed. David Bromley and Phillip E. Hammond, 11–29. Macon, Ga.: Mercer University Press.

———. 1984. "The Rise of a New World Faith." *Review of Religious Research* 26:18–27.

———. 1971. "The Economics of Piety: Religion and Social Class." In *Issues in Social Inequality,* ed. Gerald W. Theilbar and Saul D. Feldman, 483–503. Boston: Little, Brown.

———. 1965a. "Social Contexts and Religious Experience." *Review of Religious Research* 7:17–28.

———. 1965b. "A Taxonomy of Religious Experience." *Journal for the Scientific Study of Religion* 5:97–116.

———. 1964. "Class, Radicalism, and Religious Involvement." *American Sociological Review* 29:698–706.

Stark, Rodney, and William Sims Bainbridge. 1997. *Religion, Deviance, and Social Control.* New York: Routledge.

———. 1985. *The Future of Religion.* Berkeley: University of California Press.

Stark, Rodney, and Roger Finke. 2000. *Acts of Faith: Explaining the Human Side of Religion.* Berkeley: University of California Press.

Stark, Rodney, and Charles Y. Glock. 1968. *American Piety.* Berkeley: University of California Press.

Stark, Rodney, and Laurence R. Iannaccone. 1997. "Why the Jehovah's Witnesses Grow So Rapidly: A Theoretical Application." *Journal of Contemporary Religion* 12:133–57.

———. 1994. "A Supply-Side Reinterpretation of the 'Secularization' of Europe." *Journal for the Scientific Study of Religion* 33:230–52.

Stark, Rodney, and Lynne Roberts. 2002. *Contemporary Social Research Methods.* 3d ed. Belmont, Calif.: Wadsworth.

———. 1982. "The Arithmetic of Social Movements: Theoretical Implications." *Sociological Analysis* 43:53–68.

Steggarda, M. 1993. "Religion and the Social Positions of Men and Women." *Social Compass* 40:65–73.

Suziedelis, Antanas, and Raymond H. Potvin. 1981. "Sex Differences in Factors Affecting Religiousness among Catholic Adolescents." *Journal for the Scientific Study of Religion* 20:38–50.

Swanson, Guy E. 1967. *Religion and Regime: A Sociological Account of the Reformation.* Ann Arbor: University of Michigan Press.

———. 1960. *The Birth of the Gods: The Origin of Primitive Beliefs.* Ann Arbor: University of Michigan Press.

Swatos, William H., Jr., and Loftur Reimar Gissurarson. 1997. *Icelandic Spiritualism: Mediumship and Modernity in Iceland.* New Brunswick, N.J.: Transaction.

Tannenbaum, Frank. [1946] 1992. *Slave and Citizen.* Boston: Beacon Press.

Taylor, Eugene. 1999. *Shadow Culture: Psychology and Spirituality in America.* Washington, D.C.: Counterpoint Press.

Thomas, George M. 1989. *Revivalism and Cultural Change.* Chicago: University of Chicago Press.

Thomas, Hugh. 1997. *The Slave Trade: The Story of the Atlantic Slave Trade, 1440–1870.* New York: Simon & Schuster.

Thomas, Keith. 1971. *Religion and the Decline of Magic.* New York: Scribner's.

Thompson, Edward H., Jr. 1991. "Beneath the Status Characteristic." *Journal for the Scientific Study of Religion* 30:381–94.

Thomsen, Harry. 1963. *The New Religions of Japan.* Rutland, Vt.: Charles E. Tuttle Co.

Thurston, Herbert, S.J., ed. 1926. *Lives of the Saints,* by Alvan Butler. London: Burns, Oates & Washbourne.

Timberlake, Charles. 1995. "Fate of the Russian Orthodox Monasteries and Convents since 1917." Donald W. Treadgold Papers, no. 103. Henry M. Jackson School of International Studies, University of Washington.

Tökés, László. 1990. "The Possible Role of Rumania's Churches: On the Social Renewal of the Country." *Occasional Papers on Religion in Eastern Europe* 10 (5): 29–32.

Tomasson, Richard E. 1980. *Iceland.* Minneapolis: University of Minnesota Press.

Tourn, Giorgio. 1989. *You Are My Witnesses: The Waldensians across 800 Years.* Cincinnati: Friendship Press.

Tracy, James D. 1999. *Europe's Reformations, 1450–1650*. Lanham, Md.: Rowman & Littlefield.

Troeltsch, Ernst. [1912] 1931. *The Social Teaching of the Christian Churches*. 2 vols. New York: Macmillan.

Troyanovsky, Igor, ed. 1991. *Religion in the Soviet Republics*. San Francisco: HarperSanFrancisco.

Turley, David. 2000. *Slavery*. Oxford: Blackwell.

Tyler, Stephen A. 1986. "Post-Modern Ethnography: From Document of the Occult to Occult Document." In *Writing Culture*, ed. James Clifford and George Marcus. Berkeley: University of California Press:

Tylor, Edward Burnett. [1871] 1958. *Religion in Primitive Culture*. New York: Harper.

Udry, J. Richard. 1988. "Biological Predispositions and Social Control in Adolescent Sexual Behavior." *American Sociological Review* 53:709–22.

Underhill, Evelyn. [1911] 1942. *Mysticism*. 14th ed. London: Methuen.

Underhill, Ralph. 1975. "Economic and Political Antecedents of Monotheism." *American Journal of Sociology* 80:841–61.

United Nations. 1995. "The Present Status of Equality Measures." In *Human Development Report*. New York: United Nations.

Van Wagoner, Richard S. 1994. *Sidney Rigdon: A Portrait of Religious Excess*. Salt Lake City: Signature Books.

Wagner, Melinda Bollar. 1983. "Spiritual Frontiers Fellowship." In *Alternatives to American Mainline Churches*, ed. Joseph H. Fichter, 45–66. New York: Rose of Sharon Press.

Waines, David. 1995. *An Introduction to Islam*. Cambridge: Cambridge University Press.

Wallace, Anthony F. C. 1966. *Religion: An Anthropological View*. New York: Random House.

Walter, Tony, and Grace Davie. 1998. "The Religiosity of Women in the Modern West." *British Journal of Sociology* 49:640–60.

Ward, Roy Bowen. 1992. "James of Jerusalem in the First Two Centuries." In *Aufstieg und Niedergana der Römichen Welt*, ed. Hildegard Temporini and Wolfgang Haase, 780–813. Berlin: De Gruyter.

Ware, Bishop Kallistos (Timothy). 1997. *The Orthodox Church*. London: Penguin Books.

———. 1979. *The Orthodox Way*. Crestwood, N.Y.: St. Vladimir's Seminary Press.

Watson, Alan. 1989. *Slave Law in the Americas*. Athens: University of Georgia Press.

Wax, Rosalie, and Murray Wax. 1963. "The Notion of Magic." *Current Anthropology* 4:495–518.

———. 1962. "The Magical World View." *Journal for the Scientific Study of Religion* 1:179–88.

Weaver, Mary Jo. 1998. *Introduction to Christianity*. 3d ed. Belmont, Calif.: Wadsworth.

Weber, Max. [1922] 1993. *The Sociology of Religion*. Boston: Beacon Press.

Weightman, Simon. 1984. "Hinduism." In *A Handbook of Living Religions*, ed. John R. Hinnells, 191–236. London: Penguin Books.

Weinstein, Donald, and Rudolph M. Bell. 1986. *Saints and Society: The Two Worlds of Western Christendom, 1000–1700*. Chicago: University of Chicago Press.

Whitefield, George. [1747] 1969. *George Whitefield's Journals*. Gainsville, Fla.: Scholars' Facsimiles and Reprints.

Whitehead, Alfred North. [1925] 1967. *Science and the Modern World*. New York: Free Press.

Wilson, Bryan. 1977. "Aspects of Kinship and the Rise of Jehovah's Witnesses in Japan." *Social Compass* 24:97–120.

———. 1975. *Magic and the Millennium*. Frogmore, Eng.: Paladin.

Winter, J. Alan. 1977. *Continuities in the Sociology of Religion*. New York: Harper & Row.

Wolfgang, Marvin E., Robert M. Figlio, and Thorsten Sellin. 1972. *Delinquency in a Birth Cohort*. Chicago: University of Chicago Press.

Wood, Gordon S. 1993. "Founding a Nation, 986–1787." In *The Almanac of American History*, ed. Arthur M. Schlesinger Jr. New York: Barnes & Noble.

Woodward, Kenneth L. 1996. *Making Saints*. New York: Simon & Schuster.

Wuthnow, Robert. 1998. *After Heaven: Spirituality in America since the 1950s*. Berkeley: University of California Press.

Yinger, J. Milton. 1957. *Religion, Society, and the Individual*. New York: Macmillan.

Zernov, Nicolas. 1959. Christianity: The Eastern Schism and the Eastern Orthodox Church." In *The Concise Encyclopaedia of Living Faiths*, ed. R. C. Zaehner, 86–107. Boston: Beacon Press.

Zinnbauer, Brian J., Kenneth I. Pargament, Brenda Cole, Mark S. Rye, Eric M. Butter, Timothy G. Belavich, Katheleen M. Hipp, Allie B. Scott, and Jill L. Kadar. 1997. "Religiousness and Spirituality: Unfuzzing the Fuzzy." *Journal for the Scientific Study of Religion* 36:549–64.

Zinsser, Hans. [1934] 1960. *Rats, Lice, and History*. New York: Bantam.

Zürcher, Eric. 1972. *The Buddhist Conquest of China*. Leiden: E. J. Brill.

Index

Numbers in *italics* denote illustrations and tables.

Bienert, Wolfgang A., 104
Bilāl, 104
Black Muslims, 75
Bloch, Marc, 7
Book of Mormon, 109; Smith's
  receiving of, 95–96, 100–102
Brahman priests, 19; and Buddhism,
  46
bridge position, 103, 184n. 4
Brinton, Crane, 184n. 1
British colonies, slavery in, 179–80
Brown, R. E., 106
buddhas, 158
Buddhism: asceticism in, 46–47; in
  China, 159, 160; Gods and Godless-
  ness in, 10–11, 158, 160; in Japan,
  129, 130, 131, 157; morality in, 158;
  sex-role socialization and risk of
  irreligiousness in, 78–79; in Soviet
  Union, 151; in West, 122
Buridan, Jean, 7, 8
Burkert, Walter, 47

capitalism, rise of, 22, 39–40
Cathars, 48, 49, 60
Catholic Church: in eastern Europe,
  151, 152; medieval, 50–51; theology
  of, 15
Catholic colonies, slavery in, 178–79,
  181–82
Catholic saints: asceticism among,
  54–57; data collection on, 51–54;
  female, 55, 55, 183nn. 3&4; medieval,
  51–57; recent, 57–59
Ceauşescu, Nicolas, 153, 154
charismatic authority, 110–12
China: Buddhist asceticism in, 46–47;
  gender effects on religiousness in,
  65, 66–67; God-morality relationship in, 159–61; religion in, 10–11,
  159–61, 183n. 2
Christianity: Eastern Orthodox, 148–
  50; initial followers of, 106–8;
  power to motivate, 36–39, 41; rise
  of, 170–74; risks of irreligiousness
  in, 75, 76; in Sweden, 126–29. See
  also early Christians; Jesus
Christian Science, 61; decline of, discovered data on, 169

Christiansen, Karl O., 81
Christian world: gender effects on
  religiousness in, 63; sex-role socialization and risk of irreligiousness
  in, 78–79
church attendance: in France, discovered data on, 164–65; and morality,
  145, 145–47, 148, 154
churched religion, 117
Church of Piety, 50–51
Church of Power, 50
circulation statistics, as data source, 167
class origins: of ascetics, 43, 45–59;
  of ascetics and saints in medieval
  Europe, 50–51, 55–57, 56; of recent
  saints, 57–58; and religiousness,
  43–45
Clausen, Christopher, 116–17
Clement of Alexandria, 105
client religions, 121–22; in Japan, 131
Code Noir, 178–79, 181
Code of Barbados, 180
Código Negro Español, 179, 181
Codrington, R. H., 12
Cohen, Gershon D., 31
Cohn, Norman, 23
Coleman, James S., 92
Colson, Charles, 75
communion wine receipts, 164–65
Comte, August, 17
confidence, need for religion to
  inspire, 116
Confucianism, 10–11, 78, 159
Confucius, 159
congregations: in churched vs.
  unchurched religions, 117, 118; in
  creedless religious groups, 122, 123;
  definition of, 116; religions lacking,
  117, 118, 133
control, desire for, 5–6
Copernicus, Nicolaus, 6–7
Cornwall, Marie, 68
Cowdery, Oliver, 95, 101–2
Cowdery, William, 101–2
Cox, Harvey, 32
creeds, 115; in churched vs.
  unchurched religions, 117, 118;
  religious groups lacking, 115, 118,
  122–23, 133

criminality: gender differences in, 73–75, 79–83; physiology and, 79–83
crises, and heresy, 97–98
Cross, Whitney R., 67
cross-cultural comparisons: debate over, 4–5; of gender effects on religiousness, 62–67, 70–73, 78–79; of God-morality relationship, 140–42, 144–45, 146–61
Crusades, 23–29, 45
culture: complexity of, and God-morality relationship, 140–42, *142;* and revelations, 87–90
Curry, Patrick, 4
Cyprian, 37

Dagestan, 150–51
Darwin, Charles, 7–8
data discovery, 163–82; on Catholic saints, 51–54; on church attendance in Europe, 163–65; on decline of Christian Science, 169; on Gnosticism, 171–73; on Reformation, 176–78; on religious nonconformity, 165–69; on rise of Christianity, 170–74; on slavery in Catholic vs. Protestant colonies, 178–82; on witch hunt cessation, 174–76
Davie, Grace, 61, 64, 114, 147
Davis, David Brion, 181, 182
Davis, Kingsley, 44
definitions, debate on need for, 4, 20
Delooz, Pierre, 51
Demerath, N. J., III, 44
Democritus, 8
denominationalism, Niebuhr's theory of, 22
deprivation thesis, 43–45, 58
dharma, 156
dharma *shastras*, 156
dharma sutras, 156
Dionysius (bishop), 35–36
Dionysus, cult of, 60
divine essences, 10, 15; and morality, 17, 139
doctrine. *See* religious doctrine, effectiveness of
Douglas, Mary, 137
Dulles, Avery, 15

Durkheim, Emile: on Buddhism, 11; on crime, 80; definition of religion, 1–2; on Gods, 42, 138–39, 161; on magic, 13–14, 19, 121–22; on magic and religion, 3, 9; on morality and religion, 136, 138–39; on religion and suicide, 22; on ritual and religion, 138–39. *See also* rites and rituals, as basis of religion and morality

early Christians: class origins of, 45; gender of, 60; Gnostic, 122, 171–73; Jews as, 170–72; response to plagues, 35–39; worldly rewards for, 41
eastern Europe: God-morality relationship in, 148–54, *153;* religious repression in, 148–49, 150–52
Eastern Orthodox Church: under Communism, 148–51; doctrine of, 148, 149–50; God/religion-morality relationship in, 148–54, *153;* image of God in, 148, 149, 150, 152; Romanian, 152–54
Eastern religions: coexistence with magic, 19; in 1960s United States, 32–33; sex-role socialization and risks of irreligiousness in, 78–79. *See also* Buddhism; Confucianism; Shintoism; Taoism
East Germany, God-morality relationship in, 152, *153*
Edbury, Peter, 28
education: atheistic, in Soviet Union, 128; and belief in unchurched supernaturalisms, 184n. 3
Eisai, 15
emotions, 16
Empedocles, 8
empirical falsification, 18–19, 41
empiricism, vs. science, 7–8
Engels, Friedrich, 21, 45, 49
entrepreneur model (of revelation), 85, 93
Epiphanius of Salamis, 104
essences, divine. *See* divine essences
Essenes, 47–48
Euclid, 8
Euripides, 47

40; cultural complexity and, 140–42, *142;* in eastern Europe, 148–54, *153;* functionalist view of, 138–39; and Gods unconcerned with morality, 137–38, 140–42; in India, 155–57, *156;* in Japan, 157–59, *159;* and moral Gods, 138, 140, *142;* in Turkey, 154–55, *155;* in United States, 142–46, *144, 145;* in western Europe, 147–48, *148;* in western hemisphere, 146, *147*
Goody, Jack, 5
Goring, Charles, 80
Gottfredson, Michael R., 74
governance, and the Reformation, 176–78
Granqvist, Pehr, 129
Great Awakenings, 29–31
Greco-Roman world: ascetic movements in, 47; Gnosticism in, 171–73; God-morality relationship in, 40, 137–38; lack of reverence in, 173–74; plagues in, Christian vs. pagan responses to, 35–39; rise of Christianity in, 170–73
Greek philosophers, 8
Greeley, Andrew, 58, 143
growth curves, example of use, 170
Gustavus I (king of Sweden), 127

Hadaway, C. Kirk, 125
Hagekull, Berit, 129
hanif movement, 88
Harnack, Adolf von, 171
Harris, Martin, 101
Harrison, Jane, 5
health, benefits of religion to, 10, 183n. 1
Heaven's Gate cult, 134–35
Hegel, G.W.F., 9
Hegesippus, 105
Helgi the Lean, 118
heresies: crises and, 97–98; development of, 109–11; persons likely to commit, 96–97; social and family support for, 98–100
hermits, 54, 55, *55*
Hinduism, 122, 158; God-morality relationship in, 155–57
Hirschi, Travis, 74

historical atlases, as data source, 171–73
Hobbes, Thomas, 21–22
Hoffmann, John P., 73, 74, 75
Holy Family(ies), 100, 112; Christian, 104–8; Jewish, 108; Mormon, 100–102; Muslim, 102–4
Hood, Ralph, 86
Hooten, Earnest, 80
Hospitalers, 28
huldufolk, 119

Iceland, 119
India: gender and religiousness in, *65,* 67; Gods and morality in, 155–57
Indians of North America, 97
insights, vs. revelations, 86
intellectual elites, and Godless religions, 10–11
irreligiousness: vs. no affiliation, 123–24; as risk-taking behavior, 74–79, 83. *See also* religiousness; secularization thesis
ishtadeva, 156
Isis, cult of, 60
Islam: God-morality relationship in, 154–55; original converts to, 103; rewards and punishment in, 41; Soviet repression of, 150–51. *See also* Muhammad, revelations of; Qur'an
Islamic world: gender and religiousness in, *66,* 67; sex-role socialization and risk of irreligiousness in, 78–79
isolates, and witch hunts, 174–76

James, William, 16
James (Jesus' brother), 104–5, 107
Japan: gender and religiousness in, *65,* 65–66; God/religion-morality relationship in, 133, 157–59; post–World War II religions in, 33–34; religion in, 129–33, *131,* 134, 157–59; unchurched religion and spirituality in, 129–33, *131,* 134
Jehovah's Witnesses, 44
Jerome, 105
Jesus, 87; amplification of revelations, 109; cultural context of, 89, 98; family of, 89–90, 104–8; family support for revelations, 100, 106–8;

Jesus *(continued)*
  role models for revelations, 89–90
Jethro, 90
Jews: American, gender differences in religiousness among, 76–78, *77, 78;* as converts to early Christianity, 170–72
John the Baptist, 89
Josephus, 22, 105
Judaism: belief in life after death in, 76, *77;* Essene ascetic movement in, 47–48; and Gnosticism, 171–72; initial followers of, 108; medieval messianic movements in, 31–32; Orthodox, 76–78; Reform, 76. *See also* Jews; Moses
Judas (Jesus' brother), 104, 105
Julian (Roman emperor), 38

Kabbalah, 32
Kahdījah (Muhammad's wife), 102, 103, 104
kami, 158
kamidana, 158
Kannon, 158
Karma, 156
Kaufmann, Yehezkel, 90
Kelley-Moore, Jessica, 61
Khomiakov, Aleksei, 149
Kieckhefer, Richard, 13
Kimball, Spencer W., receipt of revelations by, 85–86
Koester, Helmut, 107
Kokosalakis, Nikos, 149
Konkō-kyō, 34
Koyasu Kannon, 158
Krishna, 156

Lange, Johannes, 81
Lawrence, Peter, 137
Leeward Islands, slavery in, 180
Levine, Donald N., 17
life after death, belief in: among American Jews, 76, *77;* and gender effects on religiousness, 75–79; in Greco-Roman paganism, 39, 41, 183n. 2; in United States, 76, *77*
Lippy, Charles H., 126

Lombroso, Cesare, 80
Louisiana, slave policies in, 181–82

Mack, Burton, 90
magazines, as data sources, 166–69
magic: characteristics of, *15;* definition of, 3–4, 11–12, 14, 116; desire for control in, 5–6; explanation in, 13–14, 183n. 3; failures of, 18–19; and morality, 17; practitioner-client relationship in, 121–22; and religion, 9, *15,* 18–19, 20, 116; vs. science, *15,* 20; in Shinto, 157–58; "spirituality" as, 117; the supernatural in, 10–14; ultimate meaning in, 13–14; worldly rewards in, 9–10, 11–12
Malinowski, Bronislaw, 11, 13, 18, 136, 138
mana, 12
Mandelbaum, David G., 19
Marcion, 106
Marcus Aurelius (emperor), 35
Marler, Penny Long, 125
Marx, Karl, 21, 43, 59
Marxism, 21, 23, 43, 45, 49, 181. *See also* materialists, on religion as motivation
Mary, 104, 107; as role model for Jesus, 89–90; theology concerning, 15, 105–6
materialists, on religion as motivation, 21–23; historical examples, 23–24, 29–33
Mauss, Marcel, 3, 9
Mayer, Hans Eberhard, 23–24
McFarland, Neill, 34
McKinney, William, 123–24
McLoughlin, William G., 29–30
McNeill, William H., 37
McSheffrey, Shannon, 61
meaning of life. *See* ultimate meaning
medieval Europe: asceticism in, 43, 48–57; Church of Power and Church of Piety in, 50–51; Crusades from, motivations for, 23–29; folk religion in, 118–19; gender and religiousness in, 60; Jewish messianic movements in, 31–32; saints in, 51–57

meditation, 86, 161
Melton, J. Gordon, 168
men, risky behavior in: and criminality, 73–75, 79–83; and irreligiousness, 73–75; physiology and, 79–83
messianic movements, 31–32, 97
methodology, role in research, 163,
165, 182
Middleton, John, 11, 14
Miller, Alan S., 73, 74, 75, 157
Mills, J. P., 137
Miriam (Moses' sister), 90, 108
Mishnah, 15
Moon, Sun M., receipt of revelations
by, 86
morality: in Buddhism, 158; doctrinal
influence on, factors in, 39–42;
Godless religions and, 17, 139;
God's role in (see God-morality
relationship); magic and, 17; otherworldly rewards and, 16–17; religion and, debates on, 17, 136–42,
161–62; rituals as basis of, 138–39,
140, 145–48, 154, 155, 157, 159, 161–
62; science and, 17–18; unchurched
religions and, 133
Mormonism, original converts to,
100–102. See also Book of Mormon;
Smith, Joseph, Jr.
Moroni (angel), 87, 88, 100–101
Moroto, Aiko, 34
Moses, 87; cultural context of, 90, 98;
family of, 90, 108; revelations of,
108, 109
mosque attendance, in Turkey, 155, 155
motivation, religious doctrine as: in
Christian vs. pagan response to
plagues, 35–39, 41; in Crusades, 23–
29; factors in effectiveness of, 39–
42; in Great Awakenings, 29–31; in
medieval Jewish messianic movements, 31–32; in postwar Japanese
religions, 33–35; social scientific
views of, 21–23, 42
Mozart, Wolfgang A., 93
Muhammad, revelations of: amplification of, 108, 109; cultural context
and role models for, 87, 88–89, 98;

family support for, 102–4; process
of receiving, 94–95
Murdock, George Peter, 140, 141
mysticism: among medieval ascetic
saints, 54–55, 55, 57; control by religious organizations, 92, 110–11;
dogmatic vs. nondogmatic, 92;
nature of mystical experiences, 91–
92; as psychopathology, 84–85, 91.
See also revelations

National Jewish Population Survey,
76–77
National Science Foundation, 119,
184n. 3
natural religions, 42
Needham, Rodney, 23, 139
newspaper libraries, as data sources,
166
New York, revivalism in, 87
Niebuhr, H. Richard, 22–23, 45
1960s, religious movements during,
32–33
non-Western societies, gender and
religiousness in, 64–67, 65
North America, gender and religiousness in, 63

Oresme, Nicole, 7
organized religion. See religious
organizations
Origen, 106–7
Orphics, 47
Orthodox Judaism, 76–78
otherworldly rewards, 16–17

paganism (Arabic), 88, 109, 184n. 3
paganism (Greco-Roman): belief in
life after death in, 39, 41, 183n. 2;
God-morality relationship in, 40,
137–38; responses to plagues, 35–39;
weakness of commitment to, 173–74
Parsons, Talcott, 13, 184n. 1
"Pascal's Wager," 74
Paul, 104, 106, 108
Payne, Robert, 26, 93
Pearson, Birger, 171
perfecti, 48

periodicals, as data sources, 166–69
Philo of Alexandria, 94
photographs, as data sources, 166
physiology: and criminality, 79–83; and risk-taking behavior, 82–83
piety. *See* religiousness
plagues, pagan vs. early Christian responses to, 35–39
Plato, 47
plausibility, of doctrines, 41
PL Kyōdan, 34
Poland, God-morality relationship in, 152, *153*
Poloma, Margaret, 91
Pompeii, 173
the poor: and asceticism, 46, 49–50, 56, 57; as Catholic saints, 56, *56*, 57–58; and religiousness, 43–45
Pope, Earl A., 153–54
postmodernism, 4–5
prayer, 91; by Americans without religious affiliation, 124, *125*; curative effects of, 10; and morality, in China, *161*, 161
Price, S.R.F., 139
Prison Fellowship, 75
privatized religion, 121, 124
profane (term), 2
prophets: charisma of, 110, 111–12; culture and role models of, 87–90; family and social support for, 98–108, 112; process of receiving revelations, 93–96; as psychopaths, 84–85, 91, 93, 112; social scientific views of, 84–85, 86, 110. *See also* Jesus; Moses; Muhammad; revelations; Smith, Joseph, Jr.
Protestant colonies, slavery in, 178, 179–82
The Protestant Ethic and the Spirit of Capitalism (Weber), 39
Protestant Reformation, governance and, 176–78
psychopathology model (of revelations), 84–85, 91, 93, 112
public opinion, historical, 173–74
Pythagoreans, 47

Qur'ān, 93, 94–95, 154–55

Radin, Paul, 12
Rahner, Karl, 15
recluses, 54, 55, *55*
Reformation, governance and, 176–78
Reform Judaism, 76
Reiyukai Kyodan, 34
religion(s): audience, 119–20; characteristics of, *15*; churched, 117; client, 121–22, 131; collective nature of, 115–16; without congregations, 117, *118*, 133; creedless, 115, *118*, 122–23, 133; creeds in, 115; crises and, 97–98; definition of, 1–5, 14–16; desire for control and, 5–6; explanation in, 14, 16; falsification and, 18–19, 41; folk, 118–19, 159; Godless (*see* Godless religions); health benefits of, 10, 183n. 1; high- vs. low-risk, and gender effects on religiousness, 75–79; and magic, 9, *15*, 18–19, 20, 116; materialist view of, 21–23; in modern nations, 114–15; and morality, debates on, 17, 136–42, 161–62; motivational power of (*see* religious doctrine, effectiveness of); need to inspire confidence, 116; otherwordly rewards in, 16–17; privatized, 121, 124; revealed, 42, 115; ritual as basis of, 138–39, 145, 146, 157, 159, 161–62; and science, 9, *15*, 20; the supernatural in, 14, 16, 41–42; ultimate meaning in, 14, 16; unorganized (*see* unchurched religions); worldly rewards in, 9–10, 183n. 1
Religion and Regime: A Sociological Account of the Reformation (Swanson), 176–77
religiosity. *See* religiousness
religious affiliation: Americans claiming "none," beliefs and practices of, 123–26, *125*; in Japan, 157; "none," vs. irreligion, 123–24
religious doctrine, effectiveness of: in Christian vs. pagan response to plagues, 35–39, 41; in Crusades, 23–29; factors in, 39–42; in Great Awakenings, 29–31; in medieval Jewish messianic movements, 31–32; in postwar Japanese reli-

gions, 33–35; social scientific views of, 21–23, 42

religious experiences. *See* mysticism

religious freedom, 33–34

religious groups: creedless, 115, *118*, 122–23, 133; nonconformist, data sources on, 165–69. *See also* religious organizations

religiousness: of Americans with unchurched religions, 123–26; and belief in life after death, 75–79; class and, 43–45; gender and (*see* gender differences in religiousness); of Japanese, 129–33, *131*; and morality, 140; in United States, 142–46; and risk, 74–79; of Swedes, 126–29

religious nonconformity, data sources on, 165–69. *See also* spirituality; unchurched religions

religious orders, medieval, 50–51; family background of members, 55–57, *56*

religious organizations: confidence in, need to inspire, 116; control of mysticism by, 92, 110–11; creedless, 115, *118*, 122–23, 133

religious repression/suppression: in China, 160; in eastern Europe, 148–49, 150–52; in postwar world, 33, 34

research, theory- vs. methods-driven, 163, 165, 169, 182

revealed religions, 42, 115

revelations, 84–113; amplification of, 108–11; as artistic creation, 93–96; and charisma, 110–12; confirming orthodoxy, 92; crises precipitating, 97–98; cultural context and role models and, 87–90; definition of, 14–15, 86; family and social support for, 98–108, 112; genius and, 93–96; heretical, 96–100, 109–11; nature of, 91–92; persons likely to receive, 96–97; process of receiving, 93–96; as psychopathology, 84–85, 91, 93, 112; religions based on, 42, 115; social scientific models of, 84–85, 86, 110; sources of, 86, 96, 112–13

revival campaigns, 30

rewards: otherworldly, 16–17, 41; worldly, 9–10, 11–12, 41

Rhäticus, Georg Joachim, 6

Rigdon, Sidney, 95–96

Riley-Smith, Jonathan, 29

risk-taking behavior: gender differences in, 73–75, 82–83; and gender differences in religiousness, 75–79; irreligiousness as, 74–79. *See also* criminality

Risshō Kōsei-kai, 34

rites and rituals, 16; as basis of religion and morality, 138–39, 140, 145–48, 154, 155, 157, 159, 161–62; in Eastern Orthodoxy, 148, 149; in Japanese religion, 158–59. *See also* church attendance; mosque attendance, in Turkey; temple visits

Robbins, Thomas, 32

Roberts, Keith, 4

Robinson, John A. T., 89, 184n. 2

Rodinson, Maxime, 109

Roman Empire. *See* Greco-Roman world

Romania: God-morality relationship in, 152, *153*; religion in, 152–54

Roof, Wade Clark, 123–24

Runciman, Steven, 25, 28

Russia: belief in God in, 128, 151; God-morality relationship in, 152, *153*. *See also* Soviet Union

sacred (term), 2

Sagan, Carl, 14

St. Christopher (colony), 180

saints. *See* Catholic saints

Salahi, M. A., 103

Scharfstein, Ben-Ami, 84

science, 6–9; attitudes toward, in churched vs. unchurched religions, 133–34; characteristics of, *15*; definition of, 6; and desire for control, 5–6; falsification in, 18–19; limited scope of, 19–20; and magic, 3–4, *15*, 20; and morality, 17–18; and religion, 9, *15*, 20; and ultimate meaning, 14; worldly rewards in, 9–10

scope: of doctrinal demands, 40; of Gods' powers, influence on morality, 40, 139–40; of science, limitations on, 19–20

sect movements, and class, 45
secularization thesis, 114–15, 123, 126–27, 129, 130, 133, 134, 135, 163–64
Seichō no Ie, 34
self-realization, search for, 58–59
Seljuk Turks, 25–26
sex-role socialization: and religiousness, 68–73, *71, 72*, 78–79, 83; and risk-taking, 79, 83
SFF. *See* Spiritual Frontiers Fellowship (SFF)
Shakers, 61
Sharot, Stephen, 31–32
Sheldon, W. H., 80
Sherkat, Darren, 69
Shintoism, 78, 129, 130, 131, 157; Gods of, 157–58
Shiva, 155–56
Simmel, Georg, 44
Simon (Jesus' brother), 104, 107
Sjödin, Ulf, 129
slavery, in Catholic vs. Protestant societies, 178–82
Smart, Ninian, 156
Smith, Alvin, 100, 101
Smith, Emma (Joseph Jr.'s wife), 101
Smith, Jonathan Z., 4
Smith, Joseph, Jr., 112; cultural context and role models of, 87–88, 98; revelations of, 15, 87, 95–96, 100–102, 108, 109, 110
Smith, Joseph, Sr., 88, 100, 102
Smith, Lucy Mack, 100, 101, 102
Smith, W. Robertson, 136, 138
social isolates, and witch hunts, 174–76
socialization, sex-role. *See* sex-role socialization
social networks, 174
sociology, origins of, 17
Sōka Gakkai, 34, 131, 134
sorcery, 12
Sorokin, Pitirim A., 51, 55, 183n3
South America, gender and religiousness in, *64*
South Korea, 33; gender and religiousness in, *65*, 66–67
Southwold, Martin, 5
Soviet Union, 33, 128; religious repression in, 148–49, 150–51

Spanish slave code (Código Negro Español), 179, 181
Spencer, Herbert, 9, 136, 138, 140, 141, 146, 184n. 1
Spiritual Community Guide, 168
Spiritual Frontiers Fellowship (SFF), 122
Spiritualism, 58, 61, 125–26
spirituality, 116–17; in Japan, 129–33, *132;* in Sweden, 129; in United States, 123–26. *See also* unchurched religions
state churches, 33; Swedish, 127–29
Stone, Barton, 30
subcultural-evolution model (of revelation), 85, 110
the supernatural, 10–13; compulsion of, in magic, 12–13, 14; definition of, 10; impersonality of, and morality, 17; in religion, 14, 16, 41–42; in revealed vs. natural religions, 42; in spirituality, 116
Swanson, Guy E., 42, 140–41, 176–77
Sweden: God-morality relationship in, 147, *148;* unchurched religion in, 126–29, 134
Swedenborgians, 61

Taiwan, 33; gender and religiousness in, *65,* 66
Taoism, 10–11, 139, 159–60
Templars, 28
temple visits: in China, 161; in India, *156,* 157; in Japan, 159, *159*
Tertullian, 38, 105–6, 106
testosterone, and crime, 81–82
theology, 14–16
theorizing, in science, 6, 7–8
theory-driven research, 163, 165, 169, 182
Theosophy, 61
therapeutic spirituality centers, 58–59
Thompson, Edward H., Jr., 68
Thomsen, Harry, 34
Thucydides, 36
Toussaert, Jacques, 164–65
"transvaluation of values," 44
Troeltsch, Ernst, 45, 92
Turkey: gender and religiousness in,

66, 67; God-morality relationship in, 154–55, *155*
Turks, 25–26
twin studies, of criminality, 81
Tyler, Stephen, 4, 9
Tylor, Edward Burnett, 1, 136–37, 138, 140, 141, 146

Ubaydallah ibn Jahsh, 88
UFO-oriented religious groups, 122–23
ultimate meaning, 2; in magic, 13–14; in religion, 14, 16; and science, 14
unchurched religions, 115, 117–35; audience, 119–20; authority in, 133–34; client, 121–22; creedless groups, 115, *118*, 122–23, 133; definition of, 117; folk, 118–19; in Japan, 129–33, *131*, 134; and moral order, 133; privatized, 121; and science, 133–34; social implications of, 134–35; in Sweden, 126–29, 134; types of, 117–23, *118*; in United States, 119–20, 123–26. *See also* religious nonconformity, data sources on
Underhill, Evelyn, 92, 94, 96
Underhill, Ralph, 42
United States: belief in life after death in, 76, *77;* gender effects on religiousness in, 61, *63*, 68, 69–70, *70, 71*, 76–78, *77;* God-morality relationship in, 142–46, *144, 145;* Great Awakenings in, 29–31; images of God in, 143–44, *144;* Jews in, gender effects on religiousness among, 76–78, *78;* 1960s religious movements in, 32–33; nonconforming religious groups in, 165–68; persons with no religious affiliation in, beliefs and practices of, 123–26, *125;* slave policies in South, 180–82; unchurched religions and spirituality in, 119–20, 123–26
upper-class asceticism, 43, 45–59; and choice, 46; current analogues to, 58–59; historical examples of, 46–50; of medieval European saints, 55–57

Urban II (pope), speech at Clermont, 26–28
urbanism, subcultural theory of, 173

Valdes. *See* Waldo
Vedanta Society, 61
Vishnu, 155–56
visions. *See* revelations

Wagner, Melinda Bollar, 122
Waldensians, 48–49, 60
Waldo, 49
Wallace, Anthony F. C., 97, 114, 126
Walter, Tony, 61, 64
Waraqa ibn Naufal, 88, 102–3, 108
Ware, Kallistos (Timothy, bishop), 149
Watt, W. Montgomery, 95, 99, 112–13
Wax, Murray, 4–5
Wax, Rosalie, 4–5
Weber, Max, 13, 22, 39; on charismatic authority, 110, 111
Weightman, Simon, 156
Weinstein, Donald, 51
western Europe: God-morality relationship in, 147–48, *148;* nonconforming religion in, 168–69. *See also* Europe; medieval Europe
Western Hemisphere, God-morality relationship in, 146, *147*
West Germany, God-morality relationship in, 152, *153*
Whitefield, George, 30–31
Whitmer, David, 102
Whitmer, Elizabeth Ann, 102
Wilson, Bryan, 97
wine receipts, as data source, 164–65
witch hunts, 19; cessation patterns of, 174–76
women: religiousness of, 60–73; as saints in medieval Europe, 55, *55*, 183nn. 3&4
world, gender effects on religiousness in, 70–73, *71, 72*
worldly rewards: in magic, 9–10, 11–12; in religion, 9–10, 41, 183n. 1
World Values Survey, 62, 70, 126, 144, 146
World Vision, 154

Index